OECD Green Growth Studies

Green Growth in Bandung, Indonesia

OECD
BETTER POLICIES FOR BETTER LIVES

Please cite this publication as:
OECD (2016), *Green Growth in Bandung, Indonesia*, OECD Green Growth Studies, OECD Publishing, Paris.
http://dx.doi.org/10.1787/9789264264113-en

ISBN 978-92-64-26213-3 (print)
ISBN 978-92-64-26411-3 (PDF)

Series: OECD Green Growth Studies
ISSN 2222-9515 (print)
ISSN 2222-9523 (online)

Foreword

This report presents the results of a study on urban green growth in the Bandung Metropolitan Area, Indonesia, and is the third case study in the OECD project on Urban Green Growth in Dynamic Asia. It analyses the economic and environmental performance of Bandung, assesses its policies and governance practices that can promote green growth, and provides recommendations to enhance its green growth potential.

The report identifies certain urban challenges holding back the economic and environmental performance of the city, including traffic congestion, air pollution, limited access to piped water, underground water depletion, inefficient municipal waste management, increasing greenhouse gas (GHG) emissions and exposure to disaster risk, such as flooding and seismic activity. The report identifies both internal and external opportunities the city might consider to overcome these challenges and increase its economic growth in the long term.

The Urban Green Growth in Dynamic Asia project explores how to promote green growth in cities in Asia, examining policies and governance practices that encourage greening and competitiveness in a rapidly expanding economy. The project contributes both to the OECD Green Growth Strategy and to the OECD Strategy on Development, as well as to ongoing discussions on the role of cities in tackling the urgent challenges of climate change. Five case studies have been conducted, in Bangkok (Thailand), Hai Phong (Viet Nam), Bandung, Iskandar Malaysia (Malaysia) and Cebu (Philippines). They were chosen on the basis of criteria such as population size, speed of growth, economic structure, and the centrality of the city in the national and regional economy. The results of the case studies will culminate in a synthesis report on Urban Green Growth in Dynamic Asia.

The project is part of the OECD Green Cities Programme, launched in 2010, which has conducted four metropolitan case studies (Paris, Chicago, Stockholm and Kitakyushu), two national case studies (China and Korea) and produced a synthesis report, *Green Growth in Cities* (2013).

The analysis is based on a "focused comparison" strategy of case study research. This entails asking the same questions in the different case study cities, to discern similarities and draw general lessons. Although the analysis focuses on Asian cities, the lessons for promoting green growth are relevant for other OECD member countries and cities.

The report was prepared by the Directorate for Public Governance and Territorial Development. The directorate's mission is to help governments at all levels design and implement strategic, evidence-based and innovative policies to strengthen public governance, respond effectively to diverse and disruptive economic, social and environmental challenges, and to deliver on governments' commitments to citizens.

The publication benefited from guidance by the OECD Regional Development Policy Committee and its Working Party on Urban Policy, as well as the support of the local team co-ordinated by the City of Bandung. It draws on data provided by the local team and the OECD Metropolitan Database. The analytical approach draws on *Urban Green Growth in Dynamic Asia: A Conceptual Framework* (2014). The expertise and experience of OECD member countries provided relevant international benchmarks and policy examples.

Acknowledgements

This publication was prepared by Tadashi Matsumoto (Project Manager, Urban Green Growth/Knowledge Sharing), Loïc Daudey (Consultant, Green Growth/Knowledge Sharing in Southeast Asia) and Martin Abbott (Consultant, Green Growth in Southeast Asia) under the direction of Joaquim Oliveira Martins (Head of the Regional Development Policy Division). It benefited from comments and input from numerous colleagues: Karen Maguire, William Tompson, Olaf Merk, and Kwame Boye Frimpong. Ulrike Chaplar, Pilar Philip and Victoria Elliott prepared the manuscript for publication.

Our thanks go to the local team that provided support throughout the study, including the preparation of the background report and organisation of the OECD study missions to Bandung. The OECD Secretariat would like to thank in particular: M. Ridwan Kamil (Mayor of Bandung), Kamalia Purbani (Head of Local Development Planning Board), Hery Antasari (Secretary, Local Development Planning Board), Anton Sunarwibowo (Head of Spatial and Infrastructure Planning Division), Ayu Sukenjah (Head of Division for Environment Rehabilitation), Nunun Yanuati (Head of Infrastructure Planning Sub Division) Lisa Surya (Highway and Irrigation Agency), Tamni Lasmini (Head, Spatial Planning Division), Enjang Mulyana (Secretary, Transport Agency), Yunita Caroline (Informatics and Communication Department), Sofyan Pranaja(Environment Management Agency), Endar Desri Kumala Dewi (Local Development Planning Board), Sulistiyo Feti Dahlia (Health Agency), Aswin Sulaeman (Asset and Finance Management Agency), Evrilina (Settlement and Spatial Agency).

We also thank the members of the Indonesian government who participated in the OECD study missions and provided comments on the report including Adi Cahyadi, Bara Ampera, Mahpud Sujai (Fiscal Policy Agency, Ministry of Finance), Zaenal Arifin (Ministry of National Development Planning). In addition, Siti Fatimah (Bandung Institute of Governance Studies), Ilham Cendekia Srimarga (Senior Researcher, Sinergantara) and Suhono H. Supangkat (Institut Teknologi Bandung) provided valuable comments. Representatives from relevant organisations, including the *Agence Française de Développement* (AFD), the *Deutsche Gesellschaft für Internationale Zusammenarbeit* (GIZ) GmbH, Global Initiative Disaster Risk Management (GIDRM), the Asian Development Bank (ADB), United Cities and Local Governments Asia Pacific (UCLG-ASPAC), *Asosiasi Pemerintah Kota Seluruh Indonesia* (APEKSI), the C40 Cities Climate Leadership Group, Japan International Co-operation Agency (JICA), the United States Agency for International Development (USAID), Cities Alliance and the United Nations Human Settlements Programme (UN-Habitat) also provided helpful insights.

The publication has benefited from input from the Knowledge-Sharing Platform on Urban Green Growth in Dynamic Asia and the participants of the Bandung Knowledge-Sharing Workshop on Urban Green Growth in Dynamic Asia (6-7 May 2015). The workshop was supported by the OECD Knowledge-Sharing Alliance. Akira Ogihara, the case study's international peer reviewer from Kawasaki, Japan, joined the OECD study mission to Bandung (May 2015) and provided invaluable reports. Richard Carlos Worden (international environmental consultant) provided inputs on urban resilience and disaster risk management. Wahyu Mulyana (Urban and Regional Development Institute) provided support on local data collection and policy assessment. The OECD Secretariat would gratefully like to acknowledge the financial support of the City of Bandung, the government of Japan, AFD and the *Deutsche Gesellschaft für Internationale Zusammenarbeit* (GIZ) GmbH.

Table of contents

Tables

Figures

Boxes

Acronyms and abbreviations

3Rs	Reduce, reuse and recycle
AFD	French Development Agency
ASEAN	Association of Southeast Asian Nations
BMA	Bandung Metropolitan Area
BOD	Biochemical oxygen demand
BRT	Bus rapid transit
CO_2	Carbon dioxide
CTF	Clean Technology Fund
DEWATS	Decentralised wastewater treatment systems
DPI	Department of Planning and Investment
DWT	Deadweight tonnage
EE	Energy efficiency
FDI	Foreign direct investment
GCAs	Government contracting agencies
GDP	Gross domestic product
GEF	Global Environment Facility
GHG	Greenhouse gas
GIS	Geographic Information System
GRP	Gross regional product
GW	Gigawatts
ICT	Information and communications technology
IDR	Indonesian Rupiah
JMA	Jakarta Metropolitan Area
KPI	Key performance indicator
kW	Kilowatt
LFPR	Labour- force participation rate
LGUs	Local government units

LRT	Light-rail transit
MEMR	Ministry of Energy and Mineral Resources
MLD	Million litres daily
MOF	Ministry of Finance
MOT	Ministry of Transport
MRT	Mass rapid transport
MSW	Municipal solid waste
NAAQS	National Ambient Air Quality Standards United
NGO	Non-governmental organisation
NRW	Non-revenue water
ODA	Official development assistance
OOF	Other official flows
PM	Particulate matter
PPP	Public-private partnership / Purchasing power parity
RE	Renewable energy
SME	Small and medium-sized enterprise
TOD	Transit-oriented development
VRA	Vulnerability and risk assessment
WHO	World Health Organization

Executive summary

Urban green growth policies encourage economic development while reducing either negative environmental externalities (for example, air pollution and carbon dioxide emissions) or the consumption of natural resources and environmental assets, including water, energy and undeveloped land.

Bandung Metropolitan Area (BMA) has a population of 8.6 million people and is the most populous Indonesian metropolitan area after Jakarta. The BMA has benefited from strong economic growth. Between 2002 and 2012, its gross regional product (GRP) doubled in size (6.6% annual growth), underpinned by a burgeoning tertiary sector supported by strong local demand. Higher education levels in Bandung City have accompanied this strong tertiary sector growth. While Bandung continues to attract people and firms, the rapid growth has also created a number of greening challenges for the city, including traffic congestion, air pollution, municipal solid waste and water access and management. The BMA also faces several acute disaster risks, primarily related to flooding and seismic activity. Bandung will need to address these greening challenges to continue to benefit from its environmental assets.

Opportunities for action

Rapid urban expansion in flood-prone areas in the BMA is increasing the city's exposure to flooding. BMA-wide vulnerability and risk assessment and zoning regulations to restrict land use in inappropriate locations should be urgently considered to enhance urban resilience. The BMA should also draw up a metropolitan spatial land-use plan that integrates transit-oriented development with other key sectoral policies to tackle traffic congestion. It also needs to accelerate investment in public transport across the metropolitan area by strengthening collaboration with the private sector. Meanwhile, more efficient use of existing transit modes, such as minibuses, and improved service quality, could increase connectivity. Since most air pollution and CO_2 emissions in the BMA derive from the transport sector, Bandung should also consider increasing the monitoring of air pollution from transport and promoting low-emission vehicles.

Water supply, wastewater treatment and solid waste management could still use improvement. The lack of wastewater treatment has resulted in highly polluted waterways, and the unsustainable extraction of ground water has had negative effects, such as land subsidence. In addition to focused investment in wastewater treatment facilities, demand-side policies to curb water usage (e.g. applying a more progressive water tariff structure) should be considered. The same could be applied to municipal solid waste services, to better reflect the true cost of the service provided.

Indonesia is largely dependent on fossil fuels, which represented 94.5% of final energy consumption in 2013, higher than in neighbouring countries such as Thailand (76.2%). Although a new national target seeks to increase the share of renewable energy (RE) to 23% of the primary national energy mix by 2025, sub-national governments do not appear to be actively working toward this target. Bandung could take a leading role in introducing RE in its operations. Solar and waste-to-energy seem particularly promising and practical.

The housing and building sectors also present opportunities for green growth, given the increasing energy consumption in buildings. The proposed green building certificate, linked with a mandatory building permit, could help guide eco-friendly building plans and should be expanded to the entire BMA. Upgrading informal settlements requires a comprehensive approach, especially since many are in flood-prone areas.

With 78 higher education establishments, the education sector clearly offers an opportunity for the city to enlist co-operation on green growth objectives. Universities and research institutes can support the local government in producing, collecting and analysing data. The BMA should also support its existing innovation assets, such as the Institute for Innovation and Entrepreneurship Development and the Bandung Creative City Forum (BCCF).

Becoming a "smart city" with green growth

Bandung aims to become a "smart city," and the digital technologies acquired or developed thus far indicate that it could become a model for smart cities in Indonesia and the developing world. The intent is to use information communication technology and innovation to manage the city's development. The Bandung Command Centre, the flagship smart city project, collects data on traffic and violations, emergency needs and the location of public utility vehicles. Collecting input from citizens on a range of issues through social media helps identify problems and react to them more rapidly. The city should continue its efforts and tailor its smart city vision and projects to urban green growth performance, for example in the energy, water, flood resilience and solid waste systems. Social inclusion should also be an objective, as Bandung has more than 120 000 slum dwellers, and 8% of its population lives below the poverty line.

Governance for urban green growth

Indonesia's decentralisation reforms since the late 1990s have empowered sub-national governments but at the same time resulted in fragmented development at the local level that, in the BMA, has led to uncoordinated management of transport, solid waste and floods. The establishment of a BMA co-ordinating body (currently in progress) will help address these issues, if it is granted sufficient authority and support from the national and provincial governments.

Financing is critical for implementing urban green growth. The City of Bandung's budget has significantly increased over the past six years, thanks to increasing local own revenues, but resource is not yet sufficient. Indonesia needs fiscal mechanisms that can both increase local revenue and promote green growth, such as parking fees. Foreign direct investment inflows in Indonesia are lower than in other Southeast Asian countries, due to cumbersome restrictions, but Indonesia has been a pioneer in the region in fostering green investment banking, for instance by creating sustainability ratings in markets. The local government's strategy of relying on public-private partnerships (PPPs) must also be supported by the national government, at all stages of PPP project development.

The BMA could take advantage of its young population by enlisting them in efforts to green the city. Community participation is crucial, and a first step is to identify the needs and interests of different community groups in areas related to green growth and organise support for it.

Chapter 1

The economic and environmental performance of Bandung

Chapter 1 examines Bandung's economic, social and environmental performance. It first presents how the city's population has evolved over the last decade as well as provides an assessment of the city's socioeconomic growth. Environmental trends and green growth challenges are then discussed. This chapter is structured into the following four sections:

1) demographic characteristics of the Bandung Metropolitan Area

2) the BMA's socio-economic structure

3) environmental trends and challenges for green growth

4) Bandung's institutional landscape

Key findings

- The Bandung Metropolitan Area (BMA) is located in the central-west interior of Java, 140 kilometres southeast of the Indonesian capital, Jakarta. **The BMA's population is 8.6 million**, the most populous Indonesian metropolitan area after Jakarta. It has been growing faster than comparable Indonesian cities, 1.9% annually between 2000 and 2010. Recent population growth has primarily been concentrated in outlying districts. The BMA's population is expected to reach 9.1 million people by 2020, when the population of the Jakarta-Bandung urban corridor is projected to be 40 million.
- **The BMA and particularly Bandung City have benefited from robust economic growth more rapid than the Indonesian average and commensurate with that of other Indonesian metropolitan areas.** Between 2002 and 2012, the BMA's gross regional product (GRP) doubled in size, averaging 6.6% annual growth. However, the BMA's per capita GRP of USD 7 490 is less than one-quarter of that of the Jakarta Metropolitan Area (USD 32 013) and is only marginally higher than Indonesia's per capita GDP (USD 7 475).
- **The BMA's economic growth is underpinned by a burgeoning tertiary sector** and is supported by strong local demand for services, even though the manufacturing industry remains the largest employer. Bandung's urban environment and high quality of life lie at the heart of its economic competitiveness relative to other large Indonesian cities such as Jakarta, where air quality and traffic conditions are relatively poorer.
- Although the BMA has enjoyed strong economic growth in the last decade, **not all residents have benefited to the same extent. Inequality has risen sharply.** This is demonstrated by a rising Gini co-efficient and overall numbers of people living in poverty, as well as enduring and high unemployment.
- **Changing land-use patterns and a growing population have severely strained local infrastructure and the provision of basic urban services, such as transport, water management and municipal solid waste (MSW).** Vehicle numbers increased by more than 400% between 2004 and 2014, contributing to severe traffic congestion and high air pollution. Limited sanitation and water service coverage has resulted in negative environmental externalities, such as decreasing ground water levels, land subsidence and high levels of pollution in the local rivers that meet the city's water needs. Less than half of the BMA's households have access to piped water services. The volume of MSW produced has almost doubled to 56 909 cubic metres daily in 2014.
- **The BMA faces several acute disaster risks, primarily related to flooding and seismic activity.** Flooding, in particular, has been exacerbated, because the footprint of Bandung's built environment has doubled in size and reduced surface water absorption rates.

1.1. Demographic characteristics of the Bandung Metropolitan Area

Bandung is located in the central-west interior of the island of Java, about 140 kilometres south-east of the Indonesian capital, Jakarta. The Bandung Metropolitan Area (*Cekungan Bandung*, as it is widely known) covers a mountainous and elevated area of 3 488 square kilometres. Bandung City, located at the centre of this metropolitan area, is the capital of West Java Province.

Bandung's economic activities extend beyond the administrative borders of Bandung City and encompass a much larger urban agglomeration. Given the lack of commuting data, the OECD's methodology for defining the functional urban area of the BMA has not been applied in this analysis. Instead, the Bandung Metropolitan Area (BMA) boundary identified in the West Java Province Spatial Plan is the principal analytical unit of this report. On some occasions where data for the metropolitan area is not available, the analysis only takes Bandung City into account.

The Bandung Metropolitan Area (BMA) was first designated a National Strategic Area (PKN) by the National Spatial Plan (RTRWN), government regulation No. 26 of 2008. It includes two city (*Kota*) and two regency (*Kabupaten*) municipalities; i) Bandung City (*Kota Bandung*), ii) Cimahi City (*Kota Cimahi*), iii) Bandung Regency (*Kabupaten Bandung*) and iv) West Bandung Regency (*Kabupaten Bandung Barat*), as well as a part of Sumedang Regency (*Kabupaten Sumedang*), which incorporates five neighbouring sub-districts; i) Jatinangor, ii) Cimanggung, iii) Tanjungsari, iv) Sukasari and v) Pamulihan (Figure 1.1).

Figure 1.1. **The Bandung Metropolitan Area**

Source: Bandung City (2016), "Answers to the OECD case study questionnaire", internal document, unpublished.

The population of the BMA continues to expand steadily. As of 2015, its population was 8.6 million (Table 1.1). The BMA expanded rapidly between 1980 and 1990, by 2.48% per year, and is still growing steadily, at an average of 1.94% annually from 2000-10 (Table 1.1). This makes it the most populous metropolitan area in Indonesia after the Jakarta Metropolitan Area (JMA), or *Jabodetabekpunjur*, whose population is 29.5 million people[1]. The BMA's population is projected to reach 9.1 million by 2020 (Figure 1.2). The BMA's recent population growth has been concentrated primarily in outlying districts (Syabri et al., 2013). Bandung City grew 0.37% per year between 1990 and 2000 and 1.16% between 2000 and 2010. By contrast, the population of Bandung Regency grew by 2.62% per year from 1990-2000, and by 2.57% between 2000 and 2010 (Table 1.1).

The demographic structure of the BMA is young. The percentage of its population under 15 years is 29%, similar to that of Cebu City (29%) and more than double that of Tokyo (11%). The working-age population (15-64 years) is also high, at 67% (Figure 1.3). Within the BMA, the share of working-age population varies across the five districts. In Bandung City, it is 71%, compared to 64% in West Bandung Regency. Notably, 60% of Bandung City's population is under 40 (City of Bandung, 2015a).

Table 1.1. **The Bandung Metropolitan Area**

Municipal area	2015 population*	Annual population growth (%) (1990-2000)	Annual population growth (%) (2000–10)	Area (km^2)	2014 density (people/ km^2)	Sub-districts (*Kecamatan*)
Bandung City	2 481 469	0.37	1.16	167.7	14 797	30
Cimahi City	586 580	-	2.06	39.3	14 926	3
Bandung Regency	3 534 114	-2.56	2.57	1 768.0	1 999	31
West Bandung Regency	1 629 423	-	1.97	1 305.8	1 248	16
Sumedang Regency**	371 938	2.79	1.23	207.6	1 792	5
Bandung Metropolitan Area	8 603 524	1.85*	1.94	3 488.0	2 467	85

Note: *This is a projected figure. **This excludes the sub-districts outside the BMA. Although there are 26 sub-districts in Sumedang Regency, only five form part of the BMA. These five sub-districts are located along the regency's south western edge, bordering Bandung Regency. Data was not available for Cimahi City and West Bandung in 1990.

Source: Statistics West Java (2015a), Jawa Barat *Dalam Angka/West Java in Figures*, http://jabar.bps.go.id/new/website/pdf_publikasi/Jawa-Barat-Dalam-Angka-2015.pdf (accessed 20 June 2016); Statistics Sumedang (2015), *Kabupaten Sumedang Dalam Angka, Sumedang Regency in Figures,* http://sumedangkab.bps.go.id/new/website/pdf_publikasi/Kabupaten-Sumedang-Dalam-Angka-Tahun-2015.pdf (accessed 20 June 2016).

Figure 1.2. **Population of Indonesia's major metropolitan areas**

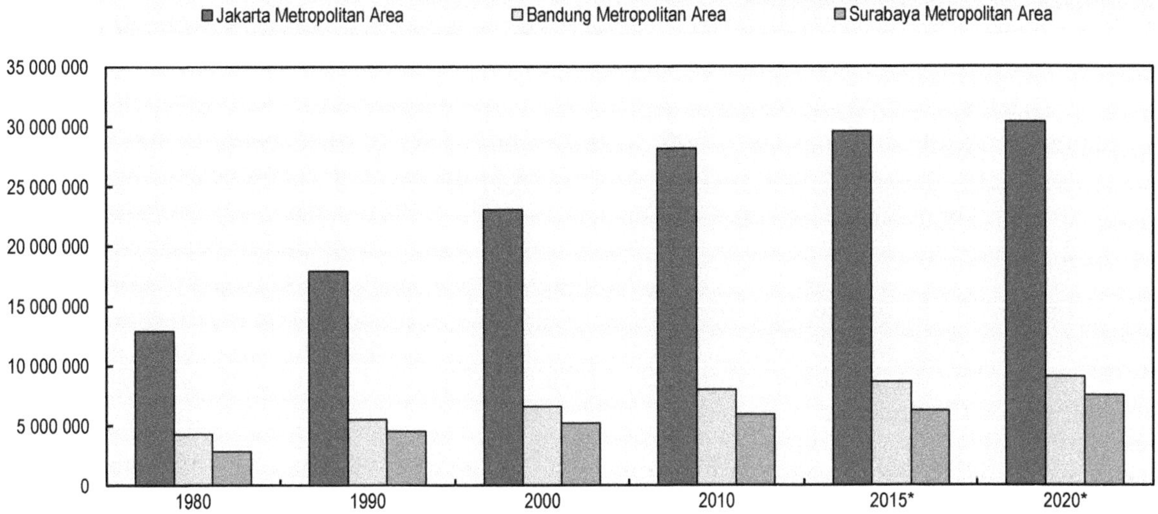

Note: *This is a projected figure.

Source: Calculations based on statistical data from: Statistics Indonesia, Statistics East Java, Statistics Jakarta and Statistics West Java.

Figure 1.3. **Age structures in selected Asian cities**

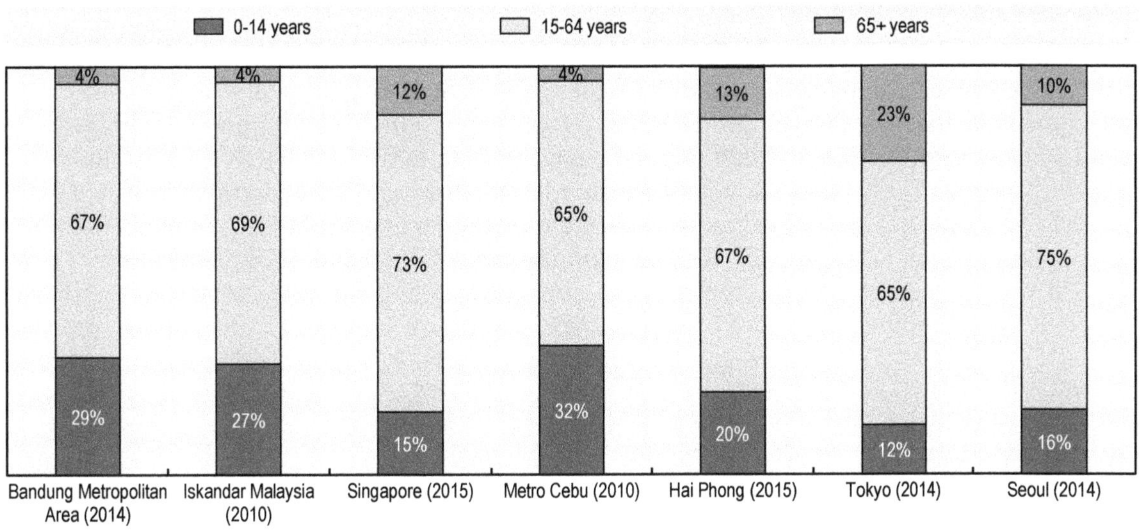

Source: City of Hai Phong (2015), "Answers to the OECD case study questionnaire", internal document, unpublished; Department of Statistics Malaysia (2011), *Population Distribution and Basic Demographic Characteristics; Population and Housing Census of Malaysia;* OECD (2016), "Metropolitan areas", *OECD Regional Statistics* (database). http://dx.doi.org/10.1787/data-00531-en (accessed 20 June 2016); Philippines Statistics Authority (2014), *Statistical Tables on Sample Variables from the results of 2010 Census of Population and Housing Cebu,* https://psa.gov.ph/content/statistical-tables-sample-variables-results-2010-census-population-and-housing-%C3%83%C2%A2%C3%A2%E2%80%9A%C2%AC%C3%A2%E2%82%AC%C5%93-cebu (accessed 20 June 2016); Statistics West Java (2015a), *Jawa Barat Dalam Angka/West Java in Figures,* http://jabar.bps.go.id/new/website/pdf_publikasi/Jawa-Barat-Dalam-Angka-2015.pdf (accessed 20 June 2016); *West Java in Figures 2015;* Statistics Singapore (2015), *Population Trends 2015: Statistical Appendices,* www.singstat.gov.sg/docs/default-source/default-document-library/publications/publications_and_papers/population_and_population_structure/population2015-table.xls (accessed 20 June 2016).

1.2. The BMA's socioeconomic structure

Strong but uneven economic growth

The BMA's GRP,[2] in terms of purchasing power parity (PPP), grew on average by 6.6% annually in constant 2000 prices, from USD 28.85 billion (Indonesian Rupiah [IDR] 41.19 trillion) in 2002, to USD 54.81 billion (IDR 78.25 trillion) in 2012. This accounts for 21.5% of West Java's GRP and 3.1% of Indonesia's GDP (Statistics Indonesia, 2007; *Bappeda Provinsi Jawa Barat*, 2013). The growth rate is substantially higher than the provincial (5.7%) and national (5.4%) average rate of growth during the period (Statistics Indonesia, 2006; Statistics Indonesia, 2015b). In comparison with other Indonesian cities, the BMA's GRP grew faster than the Jakarta Metropolitan Area's (5.9%), while the Surabaya Metropolitan Area's (SMA) grew even faster (6.8%) during this period (Figure 1.4).

The BMA's strong GRP growth is chiefly buoyed by Bandung City, which was the source of 38.1% of the BMA's GRP in 2002 and 44.5% in 2012. Economic growth within the BMA's five districts varied significantly during this period. Bandung City's GRP (PPP) grew on average by 8.1% annually in constant 2000 prices, and increased from USD 12.07 billion (IDR 17.23 trillion) in 2002 to USD 26.31 billion (IDR 37.56 trillion) in 2012 (Statistics Indonesia, 2007; *Bappeda Provinsi Jawa Barat*, 2013). Bandung Regency's GRP, on the other hand, only expanded by 2.3% during the period. Cimahi City's GRP grew on average by 4.8% annually in 2012, while West Bandung Regency grew by 5.7% (Figure 1.4).

Per capita GRP growth has been slower in the BMA and remains below the per capita GRP of other comparable Indonesian cities, although it is marginally higher than the equivalent Indonesian average. The BMA's per capita GRP (PPP) grew on average by 4.5% annually in constant 2000 prices, increasing from USD 4 826 (IDR 6.89 million) in 2002 to USD 7 490 (IDR 10.69 million) in 2012 (Figure 1.5). This contrasts sharply with the JMA's per capita GRP which increased during the same period by an average of 4.0% per year, from USD 10 562 (IDR 14.7 million) to USD 15 696 (IDR 25 million). The SMA's per capita GRP increased by an average of 5.5% per year, from USD 10 302 (IDR 14.71 million) to USD 17 534 (IDR 25.32 million). Indonesia's overall per capita GDP averaged 4.11% annual growth, rising from USD 4 998 (IDR 7.14 million) in 2002 to USD 7 475 (IDR 10.67 million) in 2012. Thus, the BMA's per capita GRP remains less than one-third of Jakarta's and less than half that of the SMA's equivalent (Figure 1.5). Contemporaneously, per capita GRP varies widely across the BMA's four local government areas (LGA). Between 2002 and 2012, the per capita GRP of Bandung City averaged 7% annual growth, reaching USD 10 686 (IDR 15.26 million), higher than the national equivalent. In Bandung Regency, on the other hand, per capita GRP grew by an average of 5.2% during this period, to USD 5 176 (IDR 7.39 million).

Figure 1.4. **Average annual GRP growth 2002-12 (PPP)**

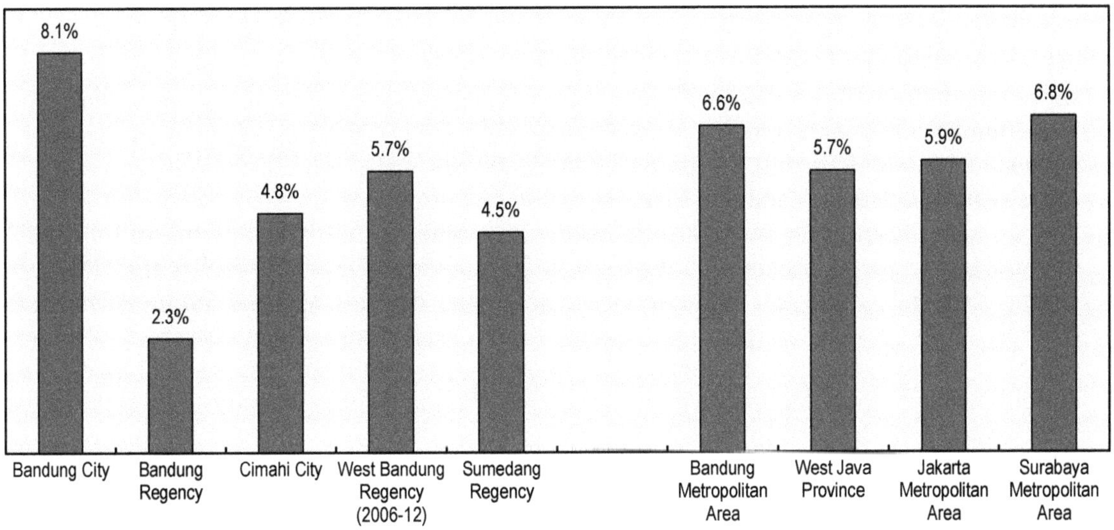

Note: Because Bandung Regency was split into two regencies in 2006, with the creation of West Bandung Regency, the analysis only considers the period from 2006 to 2012.

Source: Calculations based on data from Statistics Indonesia, Statistics West Java, Statistics East Java, Statistics Jakarta.

Figure 1.5. **Per capita GRP (2000 constant prices) 2002-12 (PPP)**

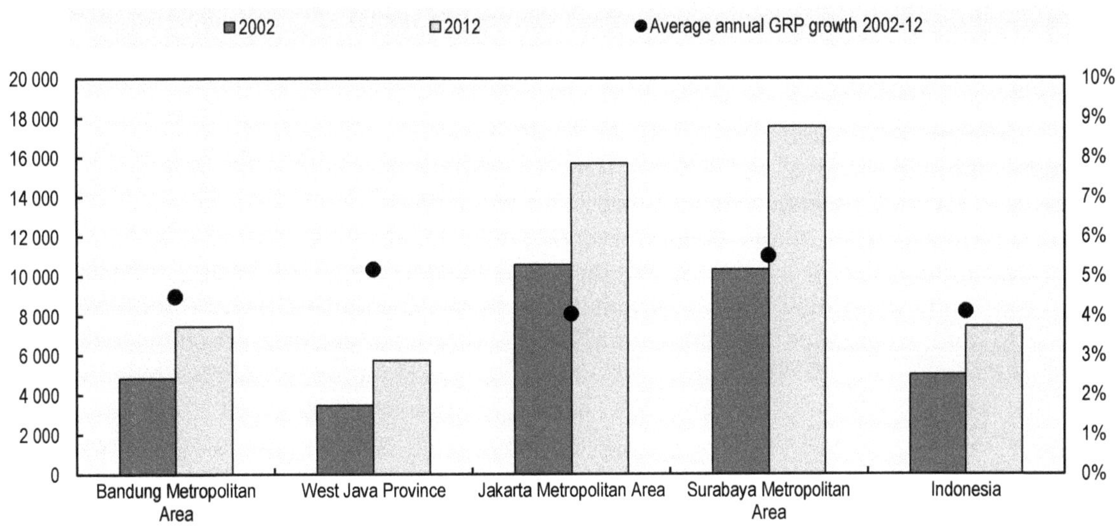

Source: Calculations based on data from Statistics Indonesia, Statistics West Java, Statistics East Java, Statistics Jakarta.

An emerging service-based urban economy, with a strong manufacturing sector

The BMA's sectorial employment structure is changing rapidly. The number of people employed has increased across all employment sectors, particularly in the manufacturing and service industries. In 2014, a total of 3 416 573 people were employed, an increase of 2 152 968 jobs since 2009. During this time, employment in the BMA has shifted rapidly away from agriculture towards an urban economy dominated by the secondary and tertiary sectors. Between 2009 and 2014, 859 837 new jobs were created in the manufacturing sector, an increase of 946%, reaching a total of 950 701. More than half (57%) of these new jobs were located in Bandung Regency, more than the total number of people employed in Cimahi City (311 476). Employment in services expanded by 577% during the period, adding 494 094 new jobs. Forty-two percent of these were located in Bandung City, the primary location of service sector jobs in the BMA. As a result, the overall proportion of people in the BMA employed in the manufacturing sector almost quadrupled (increasing from 7.2% to 27.8%), the BMA's largest sectorial employer, while services more than doubled (from 6.8% to 17%). In contrast, jobs growth in the agricultural sector was comparatively modest, adding 32 256 jobs, an increase of 8.6%. The overall proportion of people employed in agriculture and trade declined sharply, from 29.7% and 34.9% in 2009 to 11.95% and 24% respectively in 2014 (Figure 1.6).

Labour-force participation has increased significantly. In 2004, the BMA's labour-force participation rate (LFPR) was 53.2%, whereas by 2014, it had increased substantially, to 62.9%. LFPRs vary widely across the four LGUs and are highest in Bandung Regency (66.2%) and lowest in West Bandung Regency (55.7%). The growing number of people in formal employment is mirrored in West Java Province's LFPRs, which increased from 52.7% to 62.8%. However, key sectors are heavily reliant on informal workforce participation. Informal employment in Bandung often involves urban transport, such as the *ojek* motorcycle services and solid waste collection. This essential urban service is largely carried out by informal waste crews who transfer rubbish from households to neighbourhood depots (Damanhuri and Padmi, 2014). The informal sector could play a key role improving urban services (Chapter 2), as demonstrated by Surabaya's accommodation of informal waste pickers in its municipal solid waste management system.

Although the manufacturing industry still employs a greater number of people overall, the expansion of the BMA's tertiary sector shows a marked shift towards a service-based metropolitan economy. The share of the BMA's GRP grew by 10% in 2012 and contributed 49% of the BMA's overall GRP (Figure 1.7). The concentration of service-based economic activities in Bandung City includes notable growth in the tourism and retail industry, which alone contributed one-third (33%) of the BMA's overall GRP in 2012 and represented two-thirds (68%) of the tertiary sector's economic activity (Statistics Indonesia, 2014). Trade, hotel and restaurants compose the largest share (30%) of the sector, which grew by 10% in 2012. Services (8%) and transport and communications (8%) were the next largest contributors, and recorded strong growth of 7% and 10% respectively (Figure 1.7). Bandung attracted 3.9 million tourists in 2014, making it one of Indonesia's key domestic holiday destinations, although only 4.4% of these (170 982) were international visitors (Statistics Bandung City, 2015).

The share of the secondary sector's GRP was 47% in 2012, a decline of two percentage points since 2010 (Figure 1.8). This decline can be attributed to a rate of growth half (5%) that of the tertiary sector in the last two years. Manufacturing dominates the secondary sector and represents (40%) of the BMA's overall GRP. Almost half (47%) of this economic activity is located in outlying eastern city districts in Bandung Regency. The textile industry and clothing manufacturers make up the bulk of secondary sector output. In 2005, the government of Indonesia estimated that about 65% of Indonesia's textile industries were located in Bandung or surrounding areas (Mu'minah, 2011). Other notable contributors include the construction industry (4%), which grew by 11% in 2012 (Statistics Indonesia, 2014). While the overall contribution of the secondary sector is falling in the BMA, it also varies widely between the five districts. In Bandung City, the secondary sector represented less than one-third (31%) of the district's overall economic activity in 2012, whereas in Cimahi City it contributed slightly more than two-thirds (68%) of the city district's GRP (Figure 1.8). In Sumedang Regency, the secondary sector accounts for 31%, while in West Bandung it is 53%.

The BMA's primary sector, in contrast, which incorporates important agricultural and natural resource industries, remains stable. The sector expanded by 5%, and its relative economic contribution stood at 4% in 2012 (Figures 1.7 and 1.8).

Overall, the economy of the BMA is increasingly led by the burgeoning tertiary sector supported by strong local demand for services from across the BMA. It is the product of local economic policy that has prioritised service industries, such as tourism, commerce and education, since the late 1990s, due to environmental concerns (Abidin et al, 2007). The increasing value added by the tertiary sector to GRP is a trend evident in other large Southeast Asian cities. However, by contrast with Jakarta and Bangkok, where 74% and 70% of the GRP is derived from the tertiary sector, the BMA's is significantly smaller (Figure 1.8). This suggests that the BMA's economic structure, while still largely based on manufacturing, has the potential to shift towards a service-based urban economy.

Figure 1.6. **Number of people employed by industry**

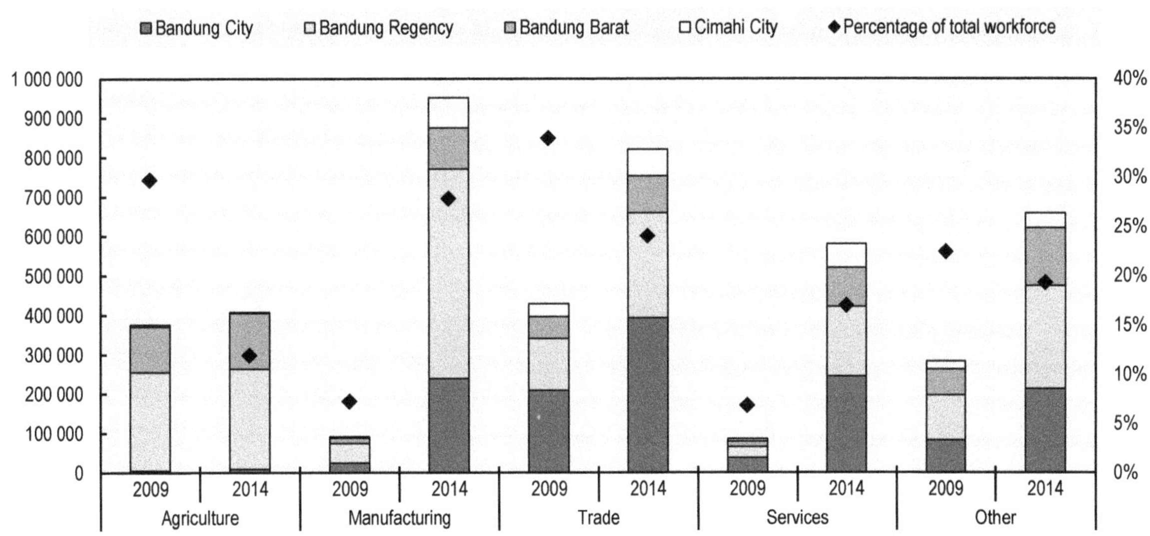

Source: Statistics West Java (2010), *Jawa Barat Dalam Angka/West Java in Figures*, www.jabarprov.go.id/root/dalamangka/JabalDalamAngka2010.pdf (accessed 20 June 2016); Statistics West Java (2015a), Jawa Barat *Dalam Angka/West Java in Figures*, http://jabar.bps.go.id/new/website/pdf_publikasi/Jawa-Barat-Dalam-Angka-2015.pdf (accessed 20 June 2016).

Figure 1.7. **The BMA economy by sector, 2012**

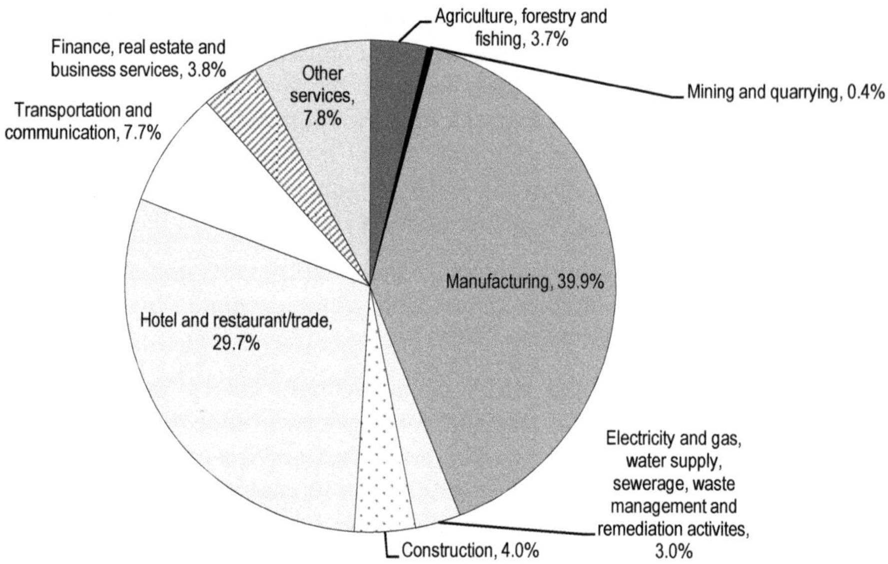

Source: Statistics Indonesia (2014), Gross regional domestic product of regencies/municipalities in Indonesia 2009-13.

Figure 1.8. **Comparative metropolitan economic structures**

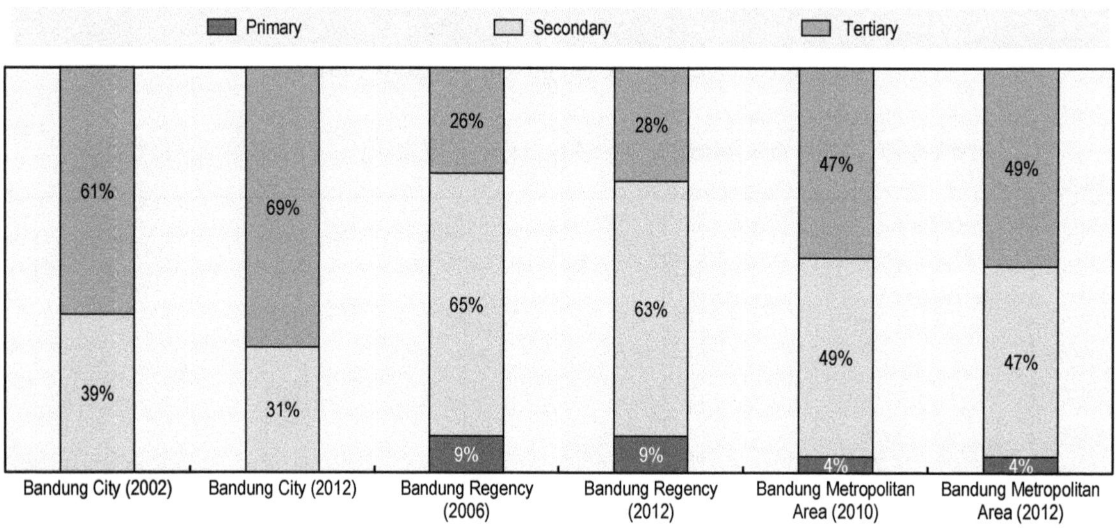

Source: Statistics Bandung City (2003), *Bandung Dalam Angka 2003/Bandung City in Figures* 2003; Statistics Bandung Regency (2008), *Produk Domestik Regional Bruto Semesteran Kabupaten Bandung 2008* [Gross Regional Product of Bandung Regency 2008]; Statistics West Java (2013), *Kompilasi dan Analisis PDRB Kabupaten/Kota di Jawa Barat 2011-2012*, http://pusdalisbang.jabarprov.go.id/pusdalisbang/downlot.php?file=872Kompilasi%20PDRB%202011-2012.pdf&direktori=produkanalisa (accessed 21 June 2016).

Higher education levels in Bandung City are linked with its high per capita GRP

Educational attainment is high in the BMA. More than 50% of men and 40% of women have graduated from high school or a higher education institution (Figure 1.9). Notably, the numbers of men and women with a post-secondary qualification indicate a high level of equal opportunity. Bandung City is home to 78 colleges and universities, including some of the most prestigious in Indonesia (Bandung City, 2016). Of several large public universities in West Java Province, at least three are in Bandung City, including the Bandung Institute of Technology (ITB), Padjadjaran University (UNPAD) and Indonesia Education University (UPI). Another education centre is located in Jatinangor sub-district in Sumedang Regency.

An important gap is observed in the level of educational attainment between Bandung City and other parts of the BMA and West Java Province (Figure 1.9). Bandung City's higher level of educational attainment is linked with its high per capita GRP. 30.5% of the BMA's public and military jobs and 53.5% of service industry jobs are concentrated in central and eastern districts of the city (Syabri, Pradono and Soegijanto 2013). In contrast, the economy of West Java in general is dominated by the secondary sector and lower per capita GRP.

Figure 1.9. **Highest achieved education level**

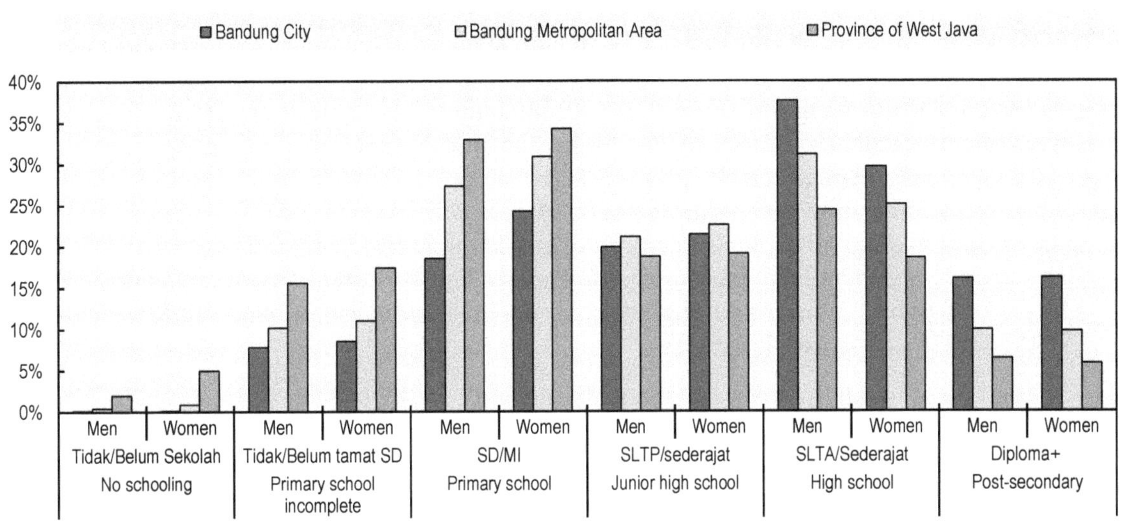

Source: Statistics West Java (2015a), Jawa Barat *Dalam Angka/West Java in Figures*, http://jabar.bps.go.id/new/website/pdf_publikasi/Jawa-Barat-Dalam-Angka-2015.pdf (accessed 20 June 2016).

Challenges to inclusive urban growth

Despite the strong economic growth in the last decade, not all residents have benefited to the same extent, and inequality has risen sharply. This is demonstrated by a rising Gini co-efficient and overall numbers of people living in poverty, as well as enduring and high unemployment.

Poverty levels in the BMA are in decline, and lower in proportional terms compared to the Surabaya Metropolitan Area and Indonesia as a whole, even though they are higher than in Jakarta (Figure 1.10). In the last 30 years, urban poverty levels have declined nationally from 29% in 1980 to 10.7% in 2009 (Statistics Indonesia, 2010). More recent data attests that this reduction has continued, with urban poverty decreasing from 11.91 million (10.7%) in 2009 to 10.65 million (8.8%) in 2012. Rural poverty also slightly decreased, from 20.6 million (17.4%) to 18.5 million (15.1%) in the period (Government of Indonesia, 2013). The overall number and the proportional share of people living below the poverty line in the BMA[3] dropped from 685 500 in 2005 (9.7% of the BMA population) to 638 500 (8% of the BMA population) in 2012 (Statistics Indonesia, 2007b; Statistics Indonesia, 2013). A notable exception to this positive development is Bandung City, where both the number and the proportion of people living in poverty has increased. In 2005, 84 600 people, about 3.7% of the population, lived below the poverty line (Statistics Indonesia, 2007b; Statistics Indonesia, 2013). By 2012, this had increased to 111 400 people, or 4.6% of the population. Bandung City's poverty level is significantly lower than provincial and national levels, but the upward trend is masked by the substantial reduction in numbers elsewhere in the metropolitan area.

Increasing income inequality is a serious policy issue. The BMA's Gini co-efficient, a widely used indicator that represents the income distribution and income inequality across a population, increased from 0.30 in 2008 to 0.40 in 2014 (Figure 1.11). The Gini co-efficient of the Province of West Java increased from 0.35 to 0.41 in the period, while rising nationally from 0.35 to 0.41. By comparison with other Indonesian cities, the BMA's Gini co-efficient rose faster than in Jakarta, Yogyakarta and Surabaya. This increase was not uniformly distributed. In 2014, the Gini co-efficient was higher in Bandung City (0.48) and Cimahi City (0.39) and rose at a greater rate than in Bandung Regency (0.37) and West Bandung Regency (0.33).

Bandung City's slum settlements also require attention. Bandung is the second largest city in Indonesia after Jakarta in terms of the total population living in slum areas, with at least 26 000 dwelling units and 120 000 inhabitants (Tarigan et al., 2016). The 2013 slum settlement database of the city shows that they cover a total of 2.53 square kilometres in 29 locations. The settlements are scattered across industrial zones, service centres, riverbanks, airport, railways, military areas and new development areas. The rapid outflow of poor rural folks to urban areas in search of employment and economic opportunity in the BMA may help explain why slums persist, despite efforts to curtail their development. The Ministry of Public Works and Housing has updated Indonesia's slum settlement data for 2014 to 384.31 square kilometres.

The rate of unemployment has markedly declined in the last ten years, from 16.1% in 2004 to 8.4% in 2014.[4] It nevertheless remains higher than the national rate of unemployment (Figure 1.12). In the BMA, the rate is lowest in Bandung City (8%) and highest in Cimahi City (9.6%). Unemployment among women is higher than the average for men. This may be the result of the greater proportion of women in the informal domestic workforce (7 in 10 unpaid jobs are performed by women) (ADB, 2011).

Figure 1.10. **Percentage of the population living below the poverty line**

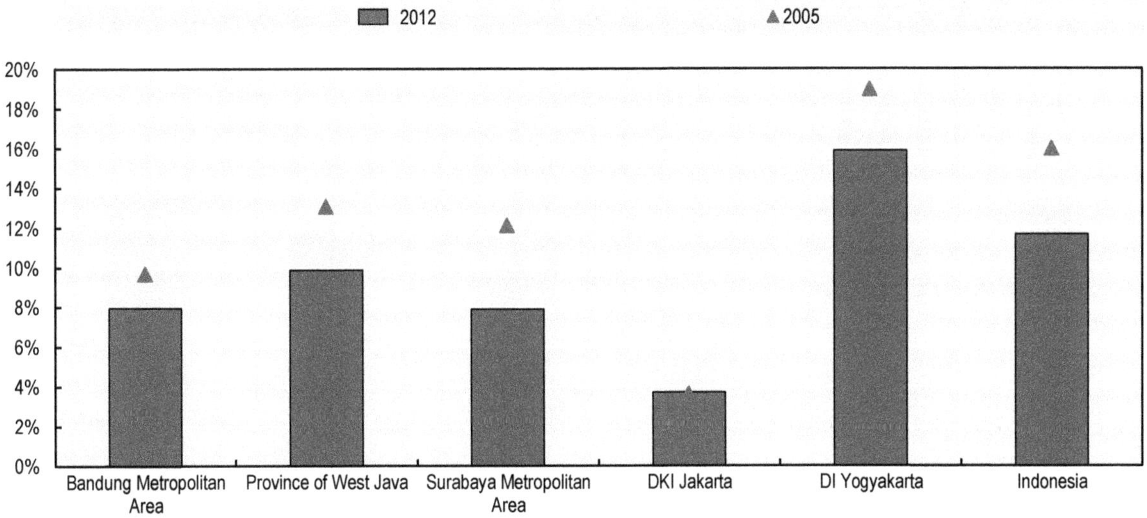

Source: Statistics Indonesia (2014b), *Data dan Informasi Kemiskinan* 2005-2006 Katalog BPS 2331, Buku 2 Kabupaten, www.bps.go.id/website/pdf_publikasi/Data-dan-Informasi-Kemiskinan-2005-2006-Kabupaten.pdf; Statistics Indonesia (2014c), *Data Dan Informasi Kemiskinan Kabupaten/Kota/ Poverty Data and Information by Regency and City*, www.bps.go.id/website/pdf_publikasi/watermark_3205014_Data%20dan%20Informasi%20Kemiskinan%20Kabupaten%20Kota%202014.pdf.

Figure 1.11. **Gini co-efficient in selected cities**

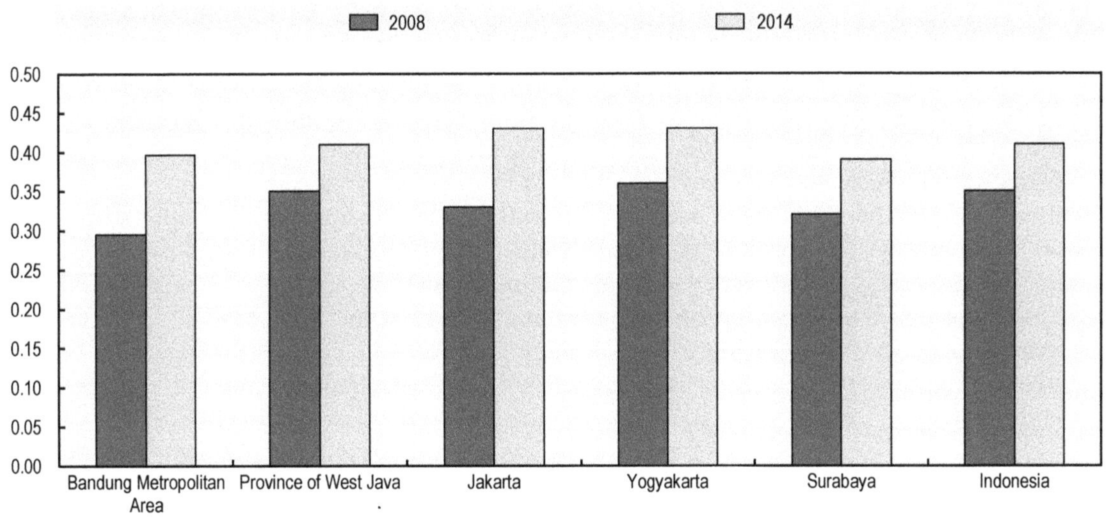

Note: Jakarta and Surabaya are cities and not representative of the JMA or SMA.

Source: Statistics Indonesia (2016), *Gini Ratio by Province 1996, 1999, 2002, 2005, 2007-2015*, www.bps.go.id/linkTableDinamis/view/id/1116 (accessed 21 June 2016); Statistics Jawa Barat (2016), *Gini Ratio Menurut Kabupaten/Kota Tahun 2008-2014/ Gini Ratio by Regency/City 2008-2014*, http://jabar.bps.go.id/index.php/linkTabelStatis/91 (accessed 21 June 2016); Statistics East Java (2016), *Gini Ratio by Regency/City 2008-2014*, http://jatim.bps.go.id/linkTabelStatis/view/id/326 (accessed 21 June 2016).

Figure 1.12. **Unemployment rates, 2004-14**

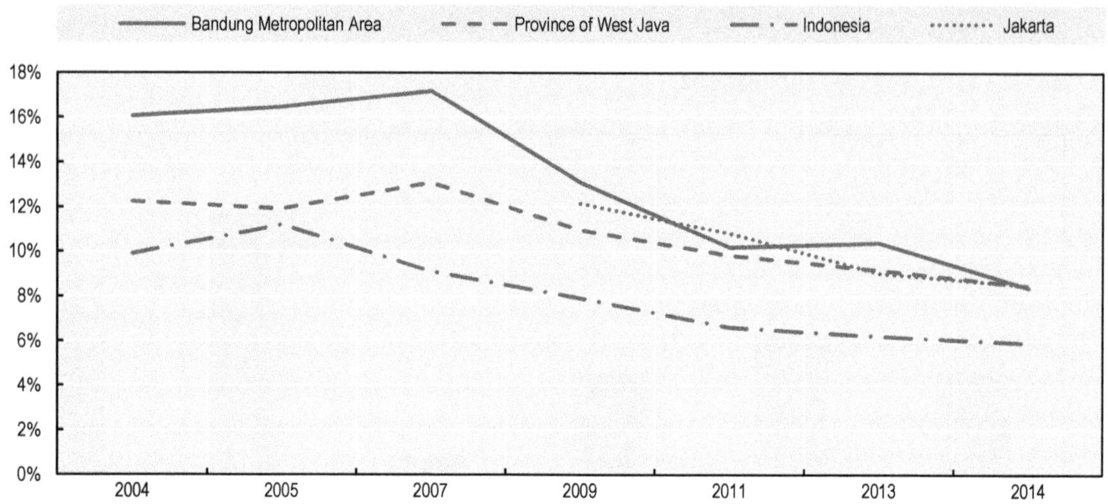

Note: In 2009, the definition of working age was increased from 10 years of age to 15 years and older.

Source: Statistics West Java (2004-05), *Jawa Barat Dalam Angka/West Java in Figures*, www.jabarprov.go.id/index.php/pages/id/1212 (accessed 22 June 2016); Statistics West Java (2006), *Jawa Barat Dalam Angka/West Java in Figures*, www.jabarprov.go.id/index.php/pages/id/1212 (accessed 22 June 2016); Statistics West Java (2008a), *Jawa Barat Dalam Angka/West Java in Figures*, www.jabarprov.go.id/root/dalamangka/dda2008.pdf (accessed 22 June 2016); Statistics West Java (2010), *Jawa Barat Dalam Angka/West Java in Figures*, www.jabarprov.go.id/root/dalamangka/JabalDalamAngka2010.pdf (accessed 22 June 2016); Statistics West Java (2012), *Jawa Barat Dalam Angka/West Java in Figures*, www.jabarprov.go.id/root/dalamangka/dda2012.pdf (accessed 22 June 2016); Statistics West Java (2014a), *Jawa Barat Dalam Angka/West Java in Figures*, http://jabar.bps.go.id/new/website/pdf_publikasi/Jawa-Barat-Dalam-Angka-2014.pdf (accessed 22 June 2016); Statistics West Java (2015a), Jawa Barat *Dalam Angka/West Java in Figures*, http://jabar.bps.go.id/new/website/pdf_publikasi/Jawa-Barat-Dalam-Angka-2015.pdf (accessed 20 June 2016).

1.3. Environmental trends and challenges for green growth

Its mountainous geography and mild climate distinguish Bandung from other major cities in Southeast Asia. On the one hand, Bandung's elevated position, on a plateau 768 metres above sea level, allows it to benefit from cooler year-round temperatures than other cities in the Indonesian archipelago and broader region. Jakarta, approximately 140 kilometres to the north west, is subjected to the full extent of a tropical monsoon climate. Bandung's comfortable mountain climate was the catalyst for a proposal to remake the city as the capital of Indonesia at the turn of the 20th century. This urban environment and quality of life explain Bandung's economic competitiveness with other large Indonesian cities, such as Jakarta, with its relatively poorer air quality and traffic conditions.

However, changing land-use patterns and a growing population have severely strained local infrastructure and the provision of urban services, such as transport, solid waste and potable water. The increasing city size and population have also led to negative environmental externalities, and Bandung faces major obstacles to green growth in any future business-as-usual scenario.[5]

Rapid urban expansion is changing land-use patterns

The footprint of Bandung's built environment doubled between 1990 and 2000, increasing from 61 square kilometres to 122 square kilometres (Table 1.2). The rate of expansion of the built environment across the broader BMA is not known, and no definitive study or spatial plan exists.

The rapid expansion of Bandung City's footprint has had a direct impact on the area's hydrology. The area now at risk of flooding increased from 8 square kilometres in 1990 to 15 square kilometres in 2010 (Table 1.2). Land that is at risk of inundation places the local population at great risk. The greater percentage of hard surfaces reduces rainfall/surface water absorption. It also reduces the rate the declining local aquifers are recharged. A study shows that 77% of new urban environment in the city of Bandung has been built on farmland, or open space in the form of non-contiguous development (UN Habitat, 2013).

Table 1.2. **Changing land-use patterns in Bandung City**

Urban parameters	1970	1980	1990	2000	2010
Built-up area (km^2)	40.4	48.54	61.25	122.28	142.32
Non-built-up area (km^2)	23.52	44.66	41.01	45.39	25.35
Total (km^2)	63.92	93.2	102.26	167.61	167.67
Estimated runoff coefficient (C) for the whole area of the city	0.48	0.45	0.48	0.51	0.55
Estimated relative urban drainage capacity (1970=100%)	1.00	0.78	0.56	0.51	0.30
Recorded flood area in the city and periphery (km^2)	2.5	3.5	8	9	15

Note: This only covers Bandung City and not the whole BMA.

Source: Permana, A.S. et al. (2015), "Three sustainability advantages of urban densification in a concentric urban form: Evidence from Bandung City, Indonesia", in *International Journal of Built Environment and Sustainability*, Vol. 2/3, http://ijbes.utm.my/index.php/ijbes/article/view/77 (accessed 22 June 2016).

Private motor vehicles dominate transport options

Total motor vehicle numbers in the BMA are increasing rapidly. From 670 941 units in 2004, total vehicle numbers had increased to 3 130 358 in 2014 (Figure 1.13). This equates to an average annual increase of 16.7%, considerably higher than in Jakarta, where vehicle numbers increased by 10.6% annually during the period. In 2014, the vast majority (80%) of the BMA's vehicle fleet were motorcycles, and only 16% were passenger vehicles (West Java Statistics, 2015a). Motorcycles lack catalytic converters, which has contributed to the BMA's poor air quality (Santosa et al, 2008).

Car ownership levels in the BMA rose to 61 vehicles per 1 000 people in 2014, and 370 if motorcycles are included, but are still low in comparison to other Southeast Asian cities. Rates in Jakarta (324 vehicles per 1 000 people), Iskandar Malaysia (548 vehicles per 1000 inhabitants) and Singapore (548 vehicles per 1 000 inhabitants) are significantly higher. However, BMA car ownership rates are double those of West Java Province, with 32 vehicles per 1 000 inhabitants.

Figure 1.13. **Total number of motor vehicles**

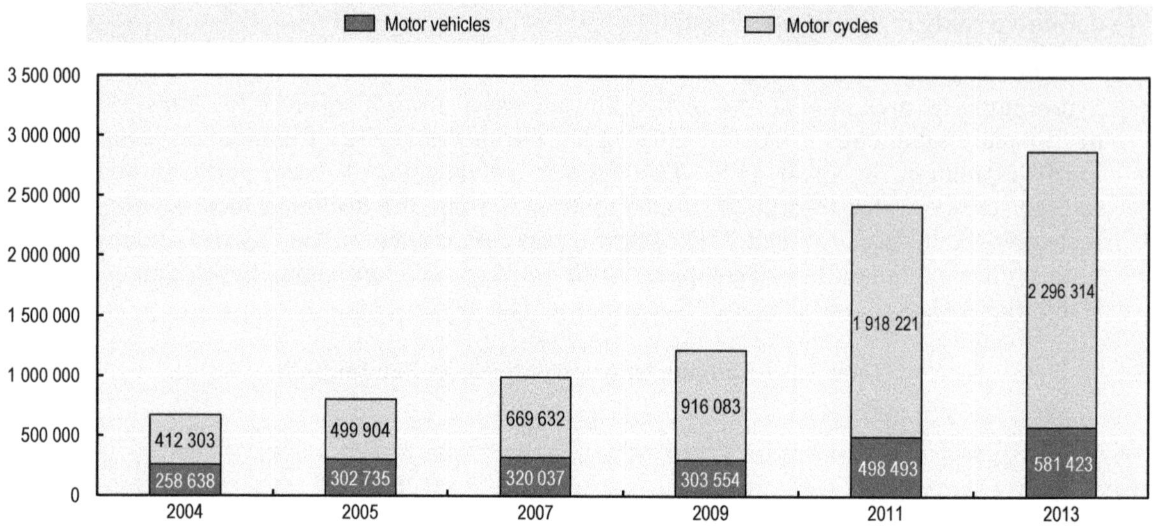

Source: Statistics West Java (2004-05), *Jawa Barat Dalam Angka/West Java in Figures*, www.jabarprov.go.id/index.php/pages/id/1212 (accessed 22 June 2016); Statistics West Java (2006), *Jawa Barat Dalam Angka/West Java in Figures*, www.jabarprov.go.id/index.php/pages/id/1212 (accessed 22 June 2016); Statistics West Java (2008a), *Jawa Barat Dalam Angka/West Java in Figures*, www.jabarprov.go.id/root/dalamangka/dda2008.pdf (accessed 22 June 2016); Statistics West Java (2010), *Jawa Barat Dalam Angka/West Java in Figures*, www.jabarprov.go.id/root/dalamangka/JabalDalamAngka2010.pdf (accessed 22 June 2016); Statistics West Java (2012), *Jawa Barat Dalam Angka/West Java in Figures*, www.jabarprov.go.id/root/dalamangka/dda2012.pdf (accessed 22 June 2016); Statistics West Java (2014a), *Jawa Barat Dalam Angka/West Java in Figures*, http://jabar.bps.go.id/new/website/pdf_publikasi/Jawa-Barat-Dalam-Angka-2014.pdf (accessed 22 June 2016); Statistics West Java (2015a), Jawa Barat *Dalam Angka/West Java in Figures*, http://jabar.bps.go.id/new/website/pdf_publikasi/Jawa-Barat-Dalam-Angka-2015.pdf (accessed June 2016).

Air pollution and greenhouse gas emissions

Air quality in Bandung ranks among the worst in Southeast Asia. PM_{10} levels have improved; in 2001, the annual average level of PM_{10} was 60 µg/m^3 in Bandung, falling by 2008, to 51 µg/m^3 (Figure 1.14). However, other pollutants, such as sulphur dioxide and ozone, have not shown improvement. Jakarta's annual average PM_{10} levels have declined more quickly than in Bandung, from 64 µg/m^3 in 2001 to 48 µg/m^3 in 2010, while in Singapore, annual average PM_{10} levels are generally below 30 µg/m^3. The transport sector and industry are the main sources of air pollution in Bandung and account for 42% and 15% respectively of all air pollution in the city (Sukenjah, 2014). Passenger cars were the main contributors to PM_{10}, CO and NO_2 emissions. This indicates a need for enhanced regulation of Bandung's transport sector to reduce air pollution (Chapter 2). Bandung's poor air quality is exacerbated by its mountainous geography which prevents the gradual dissipation of pollutants into the upper atmosphere (Sukenjah, 2014), trapping toxins in the local atmosphere. Air pollution levels are most acute in summer and autumn and fluctuate throughout the year, according to government statistics on suspended particulate matter (Statistics Indonesia, 2015a).

The BMA's CO_2 emissions are rising. In Bandung City, the transport sector is a major source of GHG emissions and accounted for 60% of emissions in the district

(Figure 1.15). This comes mainly from land-based transport, which is dominated by fossil fuels. Domestic energy use was the secondary cause, since Indonesia's electricity sector is still dominated by fossil fuels.

Figure 1.14. **Annual average ambient PM_{10} levels**

($\mu g/m^3$)

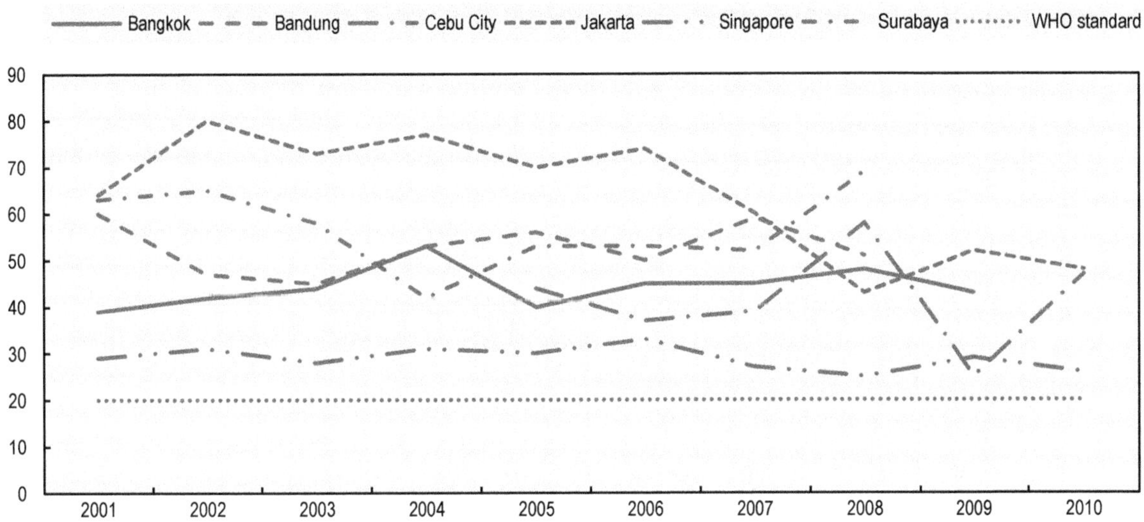

Note: PM_{10} implies particulate matter with a diameter of less than or equal to 10 micrometres.

Source: Clean Air Asia- Cities ACT (2016), *Country and City database*, http://citiesact.org/data/countries-and-cities/# (accessed 16 October 2015).

Figure 1.15. **Greenhouse gas emissions by sector in Bandung City, 2013**

Annual CO_2 equivalent gigatonnes

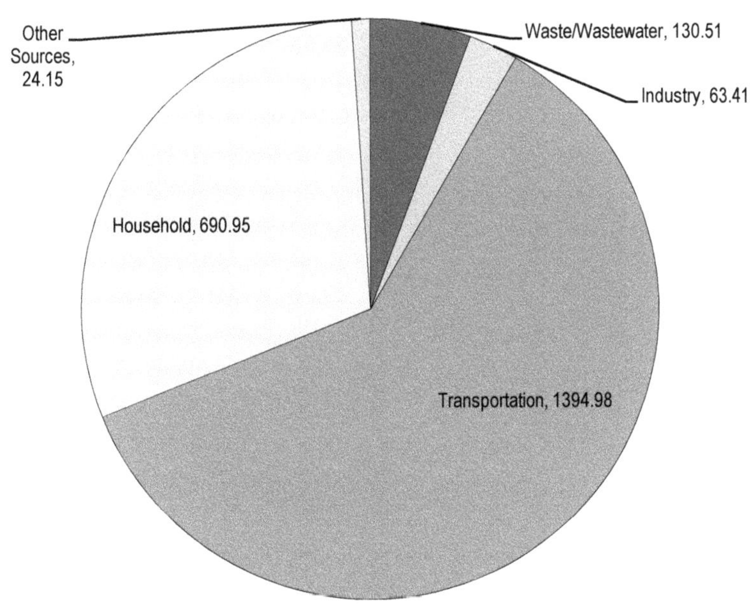

Source: Bandung City Environmental Management Agency (2013), "*Pendataan gas rumah KACA Kota Bandung Tahun* 2013" [Kota Bandung greenhouse gas inventory 2013], Bandung City Government, Bandung.

Energy production and consumption

Energy production in Indonesia is largely dependent on fossil fuels (coal, natural gas and petroleum). Combined, they accounted for 94.5% of final energy consumption (FEC) in 2013 (965.7 million barrels of oil equivalent) (National Energy Council of Indonesia, 2016). The comparative FEC rate in Thailand in 2013 was 76.2% (OECD, 2015). Petroleum (47%) represented the largest share, while natural gas (21%) and coal (16%) were the other major contributors. Alternative and renewable energy (RE) sources accounted for 4% of the national energy mix. This is less than half the rate in Thailand, where RE accounted for 10.9% of FEC and less than one-third the rate of the EU-28 member states, which was 15% in 2013 (OECD, 2015). Electricity generation in Indonesia is also largely dependent on fossil fuels. An abundance of coal has meant that half (51%) of the nation's power was generated using this non-renewable resource in 2013, in addition to 24% from natural gas and 13% using oil. The remainder came from renewable sources, such as hydroelectric (8%) and other renewables (4%), mostly geothermal (Figure 1.16). In contrast, Malaysia produces 92% of its energy using fossil fuels, while the combined OECD nations generated 21% of their power from renewable sources (IEA, 2015). Indonesia's coal and electricity use is expected to grow five- to sevenfold over 2012 prices (ADB, 2011).

Indonesia's transport sector is the primary source of rising petroleum consumption, which is predicted to double between 2010 and 2035, unless subsidies are reduced (ADB, 2011).

Electricity consumption in the BMA is rising sharply. In 2014, the State Electricity Company (*Perusahaan Listrik Negara*) West Java sold 6 667 gigawatt hours (GWh) in the BMA, in contrast to the 4 733 GWh in 2006, a 41% increase (Statistics West Java, 2006; Statistics West Java, 2015).

Figure 1.16. **Power generation in Indonesia by source, 2013**

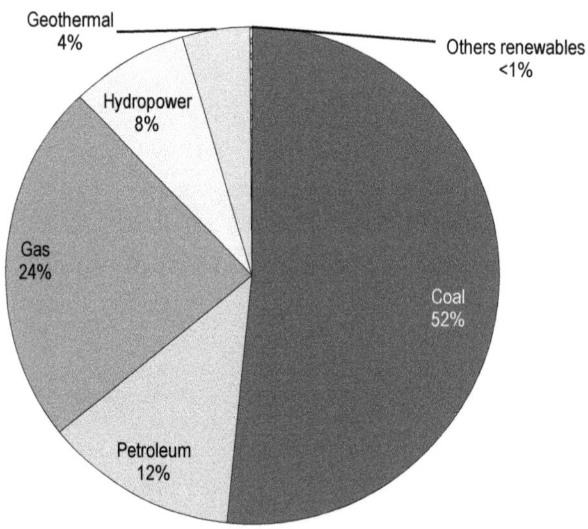

Source: National Energy Council of Indonesia (2016), "Key Energy Indicators", http://statistik.den.go.id/ (accessed 8 April 2016).

Water management challenges

The BMA does not have sufficient supplies of water, which is crucial for ensuring public health and local economic productivity. In Bandung Regency, only 8.3% of households had running water in 2010 (Table 1.3). Households that are connected to the network experience frequent interruptions and unstable water pressure (Tarigan et al., 2016). For households that are not served by the piped network, individual, private or informal water sources haphazardly make up this shortfall. Access to clean water is inconsistent across the BMA. Whereas 88% of Bandung City's residents enjoy access to clean water, the equivalent figure in West Bandung Regency was 51% (Table 1.5). Equally important are the very high non-revenue water (NRW) levels (50%) in Bandung City (Moersidik et al., 2015). This can be attributed to water leaks from the outdated pipe network, which is in need of repair and replacement, exacerbated by inadequate metering devices. Water larceny is also an issue (Tarigan et al., 2016). No further NRW data has been found concerning other districts in the BMA.

Water demand is significantly greater than the present supply. The BMA produced 267.06 million litres of clean drinking water daily, according to the 2014 water supply statistics of West Java, a slight increase of 1% on 2010, when it produced 264.04 million litres daily (MLD) (Statistics West Java, 2015). In the same period, the BMA's water production capacity increased more rapidly, from 320.46 MLD to 331.52 MLD (3.5%), with a decrease of the clean water production rate dropped from 82% to 81%. In 2014, 331.52 MLD were supplied to customers (Table 1.4). However, water demand was already equivalent to 440.64 MLD in 2010, and is anticipated to rise to 794.88 MLD by 2018, given the city's growing population (ADB, 2011).

Surface water meets 92% of Bandung City's raw water supply, which is for example, sourced from local rivers (PDAM Tirtawening, 2014). However, tributaries of the Citarum River, which is another important water source and the lifeblood of Bandung, is badly polluted (ADB, 2012). In particular, a significant proportion is pumped from local aquifers in northern Bandung (which are in decline due to unsustainable extraction rates). An additional 220 businesses in the BMA have surface-water drawing rights equal to 10 973 million litres (daily). Of these licences, 60% have been allocated to businesses in Bandung Regency, while the manufacturing sector uses 90% of the extracted surface water. The volume of water extracted from aquifers in the BMA exceeds recharge rates (ADB, 2011). As a result, in some areas, the water table has dropped by 1 metre or more on an annual basis and has led to acute water stress and depletion of aquifers. Over-extraction of water is resulting in land subsidence sometimes of up to 2 metres (Gumilar et al., 2013).

Bandung is one of 12 Indonesian cities with a centralised wastewater treatment system, although it does not cover the entire urban population (Prihandrijanti and Firdayati, 2011). Bandung City's IPAL Bojongsoang plant has a daily capacity of 89 000 cubic metres and treats wastewater only for the eastern half of the city, around 35% of Bandung City's population. However, its effective capacity of 40 000 cubic metres is lower, due to operational and maintenance problems. Several additional issues affect the BMA, such as illegal extraction of wastewater for irrigational purposes from open sewer channels and ponds. Limited coverage also means that households must install on-site septic tank systems to treat black water, while greywater is discharged untreated into these open channels and eventually flows into local rivers. Only 38% of the toilets in the City of Bandung are equipped with septic tanks (Table 1.5).

Table 1.3. **Bandung Regency water source**

	Number of households	Percentage
Bottled water	190 492	22.9
Running water	69 227	8.3
Pump (individual wells and community wells)	103 019	12.4
Well (individual wells and community wells)	328 118	39.4
Other sources	141 132	17.0
Total	831 988	100.0

Source: Komarulzaman, A. (2013), "Global Development Network Report: Increasing access to water services in Bandung Regency: A policy simulation exercise", http://gdn.int/admin/uploads/editor/files/GDN_PEM_report_cbps_bandung.pdf (accessed 12 October 2016).

Table 1.4. **Water consumption in the BMA (MLD)**

	Potential capacity production of water supply		Effective capacity production of water supply establishment		Effective clean water produced		Licence allocation	Surface water extracted (m^3)
	2010	2014	2010	2014	2010	2014	2014	2014
Bandung City	2937	2792	2426	2244	83%	80%	25	12500
Bandung Regency			No data available				132	10 231 942
West Bandung Regency			No data available				40	702 256
Cimahi City	772	1045	630	847	82%	81%	23	26411
BMA	320.46	331.52	264.04	267.06	82%	81%	220	10 973 109

Note: The West Java municipality and regency boundaries that usually apply in the BMA are not applicable to water services. For example, data is only available for Bandung City and Cimahi City, and not to Bandung Regency and West Bandung Regency.

Source: Statistics West Java (2015b), *Water Supply Statistics West Java Province 2014*, http://jabar.bps.go.id/new/website/pdf_publikasi/Statistik-Air-Bersih-Provinsi-Jawa-Barat-2014.pdf (accessed 13 May 2016); Statistics West Java (2015a), Jawa Barat *Dalam Angka/West Java in Figures*, http://jabar.bps.go.id/new/website/pdf_publikasi/Jawa-Barat-Dalam-Angka-2015.pdf (accessed 20 June 2016).

Table 1.5. **BMA sanitation profile (2014)**

	Clean water access (%)	Toilets with septic tank (%)
Bandung City	88.4	38.4
Bandung Regency	73.3	51.4
West Bandung Regency	50.5	59.0
Cimahi City	83.4	53.2
Sumedang Regency*	64.2	38.0
Province of West Java	65.6	56.6

Source: Statistics West Java (2015c), *Indicators of Social Welfare in West Java 2014,* http://jabar.bps.go.id/new/website/pdf_publikasi/Indikator-Kesejahteraan-Rakyat-Provinsi-Jawa-Barat-2013.pdf (accessed 13 May 2016).

The challenges of municipal solid waste management

Municipal solid waste (MSW) is increasing sharply. In 2014, the BMA produced 56 909 cubic metres of MSW daily, which is 92% more than the 29 689 cubic metres generated in 2006 (Table 1.6). This is the result primarily of three factors; the BMA's expanding population; increased service coverage, and the increasing per capita waste production rates, as the city has grown more prosperous. Given that Bandung Regency has the largest population share in the BMA, it also produces the largest share of MSW (24 293 cubic metres daily), while the smallest producer is Cimahi City (4 053 cubic metres daily).

The level of MSW service coverage in the BMA dramatically improved between 2006 and 2014, rising from 36% to 68% overall. Much of this improvement can be attributed to changes between 2013 and 2014 in Bandung Regency, where MSW service coverage jumped from 26% to 60%, according to Statistics West Java (2015). Nonetheless, this indicates that a significant proportion of the BMA still does not benefit from any kind of MSW service, and some uncertainty remains as to how much waste is actually produced in the BMA, because of the shortfall.

Table 1.6. **Municipal solid waste management in the BMA**

	Solid Waste per capita (L/person/day)		Quantity (m3)		Waste treatment vehicles		
	2006	2014	2006	2014	Carts	Motor tricycle	Dump trucks
Bandung City	2.64	7.00019	6 179 247	17 296 083	-	60	70
Bandung Regency	5.03	7.00017	22 127 614	24 293 341	190	60	111
Bandung Barat	-	6.99973	-	11 266 149	3	5	17
Cimahi City	2.73	7.00024	1 382 063	4 053 244	30	30	11
Bandung Metropolitan Area	4.10	7.00009	29 689	56 909	223	155	209

Source: Statistics West Java (2008a), *Jawa Barat Dalam Angka/West Java in Figures,* www.jabarprov.go.id/root/dalamangka/dda2008.pdf (accessed 22 June 2016); Statistics West Java (2015a), Jawa Barat *Dalam Angka/West Java in Figures,* http://jabar.bps.go.id/new/website/pdf_publikasi/Jawa-Barat-Dalam-Angka-2015.pdf (accessed 20 June 2016).

Risk and resilience in the BMA

Bandung's location on the valley floor close to the Citarum River, surrounded by volcanic peaks of up to 2 000 metres and with significant variation in rainfall between the wet and dry seasons, pose manifold water-induced challenges in the BMA, especially in south Bandung. This risk is exacerbated by the huge sprawl of urban development in the north of Bandung. Between 1990 and 2008, residential and commercial construction has expanded to cover 50%, and the northern part of Bandung catchment area, the location of many aquifers supplying water to Bandung City, has declined to less than 60% of its original extent (Tarigan et al., 2016). During the high volume and intense rainfall in the rainy season from December to March, surface water flows from the north, where the topography is elevated, down to lower-lying areas in the south. Mandalajati, Arcamanik and Astana Anyar districts are among the most at risk of flooding. Inadequate municipal solid waste management practices encourage the dumping of household waste in drains and local water courses, which clogs the drainage system and exacerbates localised flooding.

Bandung is exposed to several other acute environmental risks, including fires and seismic events (Bandung City, 2015b). Bandung is located in an active earthquake zone and experienced over two dozen earthquakes in the past year alone[6]. The most recent major earthquake in 2009 (magnitude 7.0 on the Richter scale) killed 79 people, injured hundreds of others and damaged many buildings in Bandung (Earthquake Track, 2016). The active Tangkuban Perahu volcano is one of 17 volcanoes monitored by Indonesia's National Agency for Disaster Management (BNBP) in West Java. According to the "Lloyd's City Risk Index 2015-2025" the threat posed to Bandung by an earthquake is identified as the greatest risk facing the city (Lloyds, 2015). The economic cost of such an event could amount to USD 2.28 billion. The second-largest economic risk Lloyds identifies is a volcanic event. Combined with an earthquake, these two factors could account for more than half (57%) of the direct potential economic fallout if such an event were to strike Bandung.

1.4. Bandung's institutional landscape

The BMA lies at the centre of the island of Java, by far the most urbanised and densely populated island in Indonesia. Java, with an area of 129 438 square kilometres, or only 7% of the country's total land area, has a population of 143.58 million but accounts for as much as 57% of Indonesia's population. The island has six of the country's largest and most densely populated provinces: the Special Capital Region of Jakarta (*DKI Jakarta*), West Java (*Jawa Barat*), Central Java (*Jawa Tengah*), the Special Region of Yogyakarta (*DI Yogyakarta*), East Java (*Jawa Timur*) and Banten. West Java is the most urbanised province, after Jakarta and Riau (Sumatra).

As noted, the Bandung Metropolitan Area (BMA) consists of: i) Bandung City (*Kota Bandung*), ii) Cimahi City (*Kota Cimahi*), iii) Bandung Regency (*Kabupaten Bandung*) and iv) West Bandung Regency (*Kabupaten Bandung Barat*), as well as a part of Sumedang Regency (*Kabupaten Sumedang*), which incorporates five neighbouring districts; i) Jatinangor, ii) Cimanggung, iii) Tanjungsari, iv) Sukasari and v) Pamulihan. Since the turn of the millennium, two new LGAs have emerged in the BMA: Cimahi City (2004) and West Bandung Regency (2007) (Firman, 2009). The jurisdiction of the BMA's five local government authorities extends over 85 administrative districts (*kecamatan*) and many hundreds more administrative villages (*kelurahan*) (Table 1.1).

The BMA was first designated one of seven National Strategic Areas (KSNs) by the National Spatial Plan (RTRWN), under government regulation No. 26 of 2008. KSNs play a significant role for central and provincial government in managing the BMA's urban development (Box 1.1). There is no commensurate level of metropolitan governance presiding over the entirety of the BMA.

Box 1.1. **Indonesia's national strategic areas**

The Indonesian National Spatial Plan (RTWN) identifies National Strategic Areas (KSN) as priority spatial planning regions, because of their significant influence on Indonesia's economy, culture and environment. Seven metropolitan areas were identified as strategic areas in the spatial plan:

- **Jakarta Metropolitan Area**: Jabodetabek-Punjur (presidential regulation No. 54, 2008)
- **Medan Metropolitan Area**: Mebidangro (presidential regulation No. 62, 2011)
- **Bandung Metropolitan Area**: Cekungan Bandung (West Java spatial plan – local regulation)
- **Semarang Metropolitan Area**: Kedung Sepur (technical study on Kedung Sepur, 2013)
- **Surabaya Metropolitan Area:** Gerbangkertasusila (Kawasan Perkotaan Gresik-Bangkalan-Mojokerto-Surabaya-Sidoarjo-Lamongan)
- **Denpasar Metropolitan Area**: Sarbagita (presidential regulation No. 45, 2011)
- **Makasar Metropolitan Area**: Maminasata (presidential regulation No. 45, 2011).

The Government of Indonesia has the authority to formulate spatial planning for national strategic areas, which are implemented by presidential decree. To date, four presidential regulations have been promulgated for Mebidanggro, Jabodetabek-Punjur, Sarbagita and Maminasata. The Bandung Metropolitan Area's (Cekungan Bandung) draft presidential decree to concretise the city's status as a KSN is currently under way. In the meantime, the area referred to in the West Java Spatial Plan will continue to be regulated by local and provincial regulations.

Source:.Republic of Indonesia (2008) *Rencana Tata Ruang Wilayah Nasional.* http://pelayanan.jakarta.go.id/download/regulasi/peraturan-pemerintah-nomor-26-tahun-2008-tentang-rencana-tata-ruang-wilayah-nasional.pdf (Accessed 11 October, 2016)

Notes

1. It is larger than the Surabaya Metropolitan Area (SMA), or *Gerbangkertasusila*, whose population is 6.2 million.

2. For the purposes of Section 1.2, Sumedang Regency has been excluded from all calculations referring to the BMA. A lack of data makes it impossible to disaggregate the five Sumedang Regency sub-districts in the BMA from the regency's remaining 21 sub-districts. In addition, the 5 sub-districts located in Sumedang Regency represent less than 5% of the BMA's total population. Nonetheless, Sumedang Regency is referred to where data is available, to provide the reader with a better overview of the BMA's five districts.

3. It is equivalent to USD 26.70 per capita monthly (IDR 279 358) in 2012. The poverty line varies across the BMA and is substantially higher in Bandung City (IDR 341 721) than in Cimahi City (IDR 318 871), Bandung Regency (IDR 241 947) and West Bandung Regency (IDR 241 892). In 2013, USD 1 = IDR 10 461.24, http://data.worldbank.org/indicator/PA.NUS.FCRF (accessed 22 October 2015).

4. This decline may partly be explained by the methodological change to the measurement of the working-age population from 10 < to 15 < years of age.

5. For the purposes of Section 1.3, Sumedang Regency has been excluded from calculations referring to the BMA, for reasons outlined in Section 1.2. However, it is referred to where data is available, to provide the reader with a more complete overview of the BMA's five districts.

6. Past year refers to 2015-16 as presented on Earthquake Track (http://earthquaketrack.com/id-30-bandung/recent) (accessed 2 September 2016).

Bibliography

Abidin, H. Z., Andreas, H., Gamal, M., Sadarviana, V., Darmawan, D., Surono, Hendrasto, M. and Suganda, O. K. (2007), "Studying landslide displacements in the ciloto area (Indonesia) using GPS surveys" in *Journal of spatial science*, 52(1), 55-63.

Agence Française du Développement (AFD) (2014), "Finding urban transport solutions: The challenges of financing and integration of networks", www.codatu.org/wp-content/uploads/DVDH_Fnancement-des-transports-urbains_version_EN2.pdf (accessed 15 March 2016).

Asian Development Bank (ADB) (2013), "Energy Outlook for Asia and the Pacific", http://adb.org/sites/default/files/pub/2013/energy-outlook.pdf (accessed 15 February 2016).

ADB (2012), "Indonesia: Water Supply and Sanitation Sector Assessment, Strategy, and Road Map", www.adb.org/sites/default/files/institutional-document/33808/files/indonesia-water-supply-sector-assessment.pdf (accessed 22 June 2016).

ADB (2011), "Republic of Indonesia: Preparing the Integrated Citarum Water Resources Management Investment Program Periodic Financing Request 2", www.adb.org/sites/default/files/project-document/74867/37049-062-ino-tar.pdf (accessed 15 March 2016).

ADB (2010), "The Informal Sector and Informal Employment in Indonesia", http://wiego.org/sites/wiego.org/files/publications/files/Asian-Devt-Bank-informal-sector-indonesia.pdf (accessed 15 February 2016).

Asia-Pacific Network for Global Change Research (APN) (2016), Bandung, Indonesia, http://apngw.ait.asia/bandung-indonesia/ (accessed 22 June 2016).

Bandung City (2016), "Answers to the OECD case study questionnaire", internal document, unpublished.

Bandung City (2015a), "Smart bdg City", a presentation by Mayor of Bandung at the fourth *OECD Knowledge Sharing Workshop*, May 2015, Bandung, Indonesia.

Bandung City (2015b), *Bandung City Disaster Resilience Score Card Report*.

Bandung City Environmental Management Agency (2013), "*Pendataan gas rumah KACA Kota Bandung Tahun* 2013" [Kota Bandung greenhouse gas inventory 2013], Bandung City Government, Bandung. Bappeda Provinsi Jawa Barat (2013), "*Kompilasi dan Analysis: PDRB Kabupaten/Kota di Jawa Barat 2011-2012*", http://pusdalisbang.jabarprov.go.id/pusdalisbang/downlot.php?file=872Kompilasi%20PDRB%202011-2012.pdf&direktori=produkanalisa (accessed 30 October 2015).

CAI-Asia (2009), *Indonesia Country Profile: Focus on Smaller Cities*, www.citiesforcleanair.org/documents/FINAL%20DRAFT%20Indonesia%20GTZ%20Country%20Profile%205Oct09.pdf (accessed 8 December 2015).

City of Hai Phong (2015), "Answers to the OECD case study questionnaire", internal document, unpublished.

Clean Air Asia- Cities ACT (2016), *Country and City database*, http://citiesact.org/data/countries-and-cities/# (accessed 16 October 2015).

Damanhuri, E. et al. (2009), "Evaluation of municipal solid waste flow in the Bandung metropolitan area, Indonesia" in *Journal of Material Cycles and Waste Management*, Vol. 11(3), pp. 270-276.

Damanhuri, E., W. Handoko and T. Padmi (2014), "Municipal solid waste management in Indonesia", A. Pariatamby and M. Tanaka (2014), *Municipal Solid Waste Management in Asia and the Pacific Islands*, Springer, Singapore, pp. 139-155.

Department of Statistics Malaysia (2011), *Population Distribution and Basic Demographic Characteristics; Population and Housing Census of Malaysia*, Government of Malaysia, Petaling Jaya.

Dorodjatoen, A.M.H. (2009), "The emergence of Jakarta-Bandung Mega-Urban Region and its future challenges", in *Jurnal Perencanaan Wilayah dan Kota*, Vol. 20(1), pp. 15-33.

Earthquake Track (2016), "Recent Earthquakes Near Bandung, West Java, Indonesia", http://earthquaketrack.com/id-30-bandung/recent (accessed 15 March 2016).

Firman, T. (2009), "Decentralization reform and local-government proliferation in Indonesia: towards a fragmentation of regional development", in *Review of Urban and Regional Development Studies*, Vol. 21(2-3), pp. 143-157.

Government of Indonesia (2013), *Data dan Informasi Kinerja Pembangunan 2004-2012* [Data and Information on Development Performance], www.bappenas.go.id/files/6613/7890/Buku_Datin_Kinerja_Pembangunan_2004-2012.pdf (accessed 28 June 2016).

Gumilar, I. et al. (2013), "Land subsidence in Bandung Basin and its possible caused factors", in *Procedia Earth and Planetary Science*, Vol. 12, pp. 47-62.

Hudalah, D., H. Winarso and J. Woltjer (2010), "Planning by opportunity: an analysis of periurban environmental conflicts in Indonesia", in *Environment and Planning*, Vol. 42(9), pp. 2 254-2 269.

IGES and City of Kawasaki (2015), *Feasibility Study on FY2014 Large-Scale JCM Project for Realizing Low-Carbon Development in Asia – Developing a Low-Carbon Society Under Collaboration between Bandung City and Kawasaki City*, www.env.go.jp/earth/coop/lowcarbon-asia/english/project/data/EN_IDN_2014_03.pdf

Komarulzaman, A. (2013), *Global Development Network Report: Increasing access to water services in Bandung Regency: A policy simulation exercise*, http://gdn.int/admin/uploads/editor/files/GDN_PEM_report_cbps_bandung.pdf (accessed 15 March 2016).

Lestari, P. (2012), "Integrated air quality management to reduce traffic emission in Bandung City", N. Oanh (ed.), in *Integrated Air Quality Management: Asian Case Studies*, CRC Press, Boca Raton, Florida.

Lloyds (2015), *Lloyds City Risk Index 2015-2025*, www.lloyds.com/cityriskindex/locations/city/bandung (accessed 15 March 2016).

Maryati, S. and A.N.S. Humaira (2015), "Extending public water supply in peri-urban areas: technical, engineering, economic, and environmental considerations", the fifth *International Conference of Euro Asia Civil Engineering Forum* (EACEF-5), http://dx.doi.org/10.1016/j.proeng.2015.11.035.

Munawar, E. and J. Fellner (2013), *Injury time for Indonesia's landfills,* waste-management-world.com/a/injury-time-for-indonesian-landfills (accessed 15 February).

Mu'minah, I. (2011), *Problems, challenges and potential developments on cluster of textile industries in Indonesia*, http://repository.widyatama.ac.id/xmlui/handle/123456789/2187(accessed 1 April 2016).

National Energy Council of Indonesia (2016), *Key Energy Indicators*, http://statistik.den.go.id/ (accessed 8 April 2016).

OECD (2016), "Metropolitan areas", *OECD Regional Statistics* (database). http://dx.doi.org/10.1787/data-00531-en (accessed 20 June 2016).

OECD. (2015), *Green Growth in Bangkok, Thailand, OECD Green Growth Studies*, OECD Publishing, Paris, http://dx.doi.org/10.1787/9789264237087-en.

OECD (2012), *Redefining Urban: A New Way to Measure Metropolitan Areas*, OECD Publishing, Paris, http://dx.doi.org/10.1787/9789264174108-en.

PDAM Tirtawening (2014), *Kapasitas produksi dari sumber air baku yang diolah oleh pdam tirtawening Kota Bandung* [The production capacity of raw water sources processed by PDAM Bandung Tirtawening], www.pambdg.co.id/new/index.php?option=com_content&view=article&id=54&Itemid=60 (accessed 29 June 2016).

Permana, A.S. et al. (2015), "Three sustainability advantages of urban densification in a concentric urban form: Evidence from Bandung City, Indonesia", in *International Journal of Built Environment and Sustainability*, Vol. 2/3, http://ijbes.utm.my/index.php/ijbes/article/view/77 (accessed 22 June 2016).

Philippines Statistics Authority (2014), *Statistical Tables on Sample Variables from the results of 2010 Census of Population and Housing Cebu*, https://psa.gov.ph/content/statistical-tables-sample-variables-results-2010-census-population-and-housing-%C3%83%C2%A2%C3%A2%E2%80%9A%C2%AC%C3%A2%E2%82%AC%C5%93-cebu (accessed 20 June 2016).

Prihandrijanti, M. and M. Firdayati (2011), "Current situation and considerations of domestic wastewater treatment systems for big cities in Indonesia" (Case study: Surabaya and Bandung), in *Journal of Water Sustainability*, Vol. 1(2), pp. 97-104.

IEA (2015), *Southeast Asia Energy Outlook 2015*. https://www.iea.org/publications/freepublications/publication/weo2015_southeastasia.pdf (accessed 11 October 2016).

Santosa, S. J., Okuda, T., & Tanaka, S. (2008), "Air pollution and urban air quality management in Indonesia", *in CLEAN–Soil, Air, Water*, 36(5-6), 466-475.

Statistics Bandung City (2015), *Bandung in Figures Year, 2015*, Bandung, Indonesia.

Statistics Bandung City (2005), *Bandung in Figures, Year 2004/2005*, Bandung, Indonesia.

Statistics Bandung City (2003), *Bandung Dalam Angka 2003/Bandung City in Figures* 2003, Bandung Indonesia.

Statistics Bandung Regency (2008), *Produk Domestik Regional Bruto Semesteran Kabupaten Bandung 2008* [Gross Regional Product of Bandung Regency 2008].

Statistics East Java (2016), *Gini Ratio by Regency/City 2008-2014,* http://jatim.bps.go.id/linkTabelStatis/view/id/326 (accessed 21 June 2016).

Statistics East Java (2015), *East Java in Figures*. BPS – Statistics of Jawa Timur Province. Publication Number : 35000.1501

Statistics Indonesia (2016), *Gini Ratio by Province 1996, 1999, 2002, 2005, 2007-2015,* www.bps.go.id/linkTableDinamis/view/id/1116 (accessed 21 June 2016).

Statistics Indonesia (2015a), *Statistical Yearbook of Indonesia 2015.*

Statistics Indonesia (2015b), *Gross Regional Product, Regencies/Municipalities in Indonesia 2002-2006.*

Statistics Indonesia (2014a), *Gross regional domestic product of regencies/municipalities in Indonesia 2009-2013.*

Statistics Indonesia (2014b), *Data dan Informasi Kemiskinan* 2005-2006 Katalog BPS 2331, Buku 2 Kabupaten, www.bps.go.id/website/pdf_publikasi/Data-dan-Informasi-Kemiskinan-2005-2006-Kabupaten.pdf (accessed 21 June 2016).

Statistics Indonesia (2014c), *Data Dan Informasi Kemiskinan Kabupaten/Kota/ Poverty Data and Information by Regency and City,* www.bps.go.id/website/pdf_publikasi/watermark_3205014_Data%20dan%20Informasi%20Kemiskinan%20Kabupaten%20Kota%202014.pdf (accessed 21 June 2016).

Statistics Indonesia (2014d), *Tinjauan Regional Berdasarkan PDRB Kabupaten/Kota 2010-2013 Pulau Jawa-Bali Buku 2.*

Statistics Indonesia (2010), *Statistical Yearbook of Indonesia*, BPS. Jakarta, Indonesia.

Statistics Indonesia (2013), *Poverty Data and Information District/City*, 2013.

Statistics Indonesia (2007), *Gross Regional Domestic Product Regencies/Municipalities in Indonesia*, Jakarta, Indonesia.

Statistics Indonesia (2007b), *Data and Information on Poverty 2005/2006.*

Statistics Indonesia (2006), *Statistical Year Book of Indonesia 2005/2006.*

Statistics Jawa Barat (2016), *Gini Ratio Menurut Kabupaten/Kota Tahun 2008-2014/ Gini Ratio by Regency/City 2008-2014,* http://jabar.bps.go.id/index.php/linkTabelStatis/91 (accessed 21 June 2016).

Statistics Singapore (2015), *Population Trends 2015: Statistical Appendices,* www.singstat.gov.sg/docs/default-source/default-document-library/publications/public ations_and_papers/population_and_population_structure/population2015-table.xls (accessed 20 June 2016).

Statistics Sumedang (2015), *Kabupaten Sumedang Dalam Angka, Sumedang Regency in Figures*, http://sumedangkab.bps.go.id/new/website/pdf_publikasi/Kabupaten-Sumedang-Dalam-Angka-Tahun-2015.pdf (accessed 20 June 2016).

Statistics West Java (2015a), Jawa Barat *Dalam Angka/West Java in Figures*, Government of Jawa Barat Province, Bandung.

http://jabar.bps.go.id/new/website/pdf_publikasi/Jawa-Barat-Dalam-Angka-2015.pdf (accessed 20 June 2016).

Statistics West Java (2015b), *Water Supply Statistics West Java Province 2014*, http://jabar.bps.go.id/new/website/pdf_publikasi/Statistik-Air-Bersih-Provinsi-Jawa-Barat-2014.pdf (accessed 13 May 2016).

Statistics West Java (2015c), *Indicators of Social Welfare in West Java 2014,* http://jabar.bps.go.id/new/website/pdf_publikasi/Indikator-Kesejahteraan-Rakyat-Provinsi-Jawa-Barat-2013.pdf (accessed 13 May 2016).

Statistics West Java (2014a), *Jawa Barat Dalam Angka/West Java in Figures*, http://jabar.bps.go.id/new/website/pdf_publikasi/Jawa-Barat-Dalam-Angka-2014.pdf (accessed 22 June 2016).

Statistics West Java (2014b), *Indikator Kesejahteraan raakyatilable*, www.jabarprov.go.id/assets/data/menu/Data_Sosial_Ekonomi_Provinsi_Jawa_Barat_Tahun_2008.pdf.

Statistics West Java (2013), *Kompilasi dan Analisis PDRB Kabupaten/Kota di Jawa Barat 2011-2012*, http://pusdalisbang.jabarprov.go.id/pusdalisbang/downlot.php?file=872Kompilasi%20PDRB%202011-2012.pdf&direktori=produkanalisa (accessed 21 June 2016).

Statistics West Java (2012), *Jawa Barat Dalam* Angka/*West Java in Figures*, www.jabarprov.go.id/root/dalamangka/dda2012.pdf (accessed 22 June 2016).

Statistics West Java (2011), *West Java in Figures 2012,* http://jabar.bps.go.id (accessed 19 October 2015).

Statistics West Java (2010), *Jawa Barat Dalam Angka/West Java in Figures,* www.jabarprov.go.id/root/dalamangka/JabalDalamAngka2010.pdf (accessed 20 June 2016).

Statistics West Java (2008a), *Jawa Barat Dalam Angka/West Java in Figures*, www.jabarprov.go.id/root/dalamangka/dda2008.pdf (accessed 22 June 2016).

Statistics West Java (2008b), *Penyusunan data sosial ekonomi daerah provinsi jawa barat tahun 2008*, www.jabarprov.go.id/assets/data/menu/Data_Sosial_Ekonomi_Provinsi_Jawa_Barat_Tahun_2008.pdf.

Statistics West Java (2006), *Jawa Barat Dalam Angka/West Java in Figures*, www.jabarprov.go.id/index.php/pages/id/1212 (accessed 22 June 2016).

Statistics West Java (2004-05), *Jawa Barat Dalam Angka/West Java in Figures*, www.jabarprov.go.id/index.php/pages/id/1212 (accessed 22 June 2016).

Sukenjah, A. (2014), *Air Pollution and Transportation Management in Bandung City, Indonesia*, Bandung City Environmental Management Board, http://hls-esc.org/documents/5hlsesc/Bandung.pdf .

Syabri, I., Pradono and B.T. Soegijanto (2013), *Embracing Paratransit in Bandung Metropolitan Area, West Java, Indonesia: Case study prepared for Global Report on Human Settlements 2013*, http://unhabitat.org/wp-content/uploads/2013/06/GRHS.2013.Case_.Study_.Bandung.Indonesia.pdf (accessed 23 June 2016).

Tarigan, A.K.M. et al. (2016), "Bandung City Indonesia", in *Cities*, Vol. 50, pp. 100-110.

UN-HABITAT (2013), *Global Report on Human Settlements: Planning and Design for Sustainable Urban Mobility*, Nairobi, UN-HABITAT.

Yachiyo Engineering (2012), *Feasibility Study for Promotion of International Infrastructure Projects in FY2011: Study on the High Speed Railway Project (Jakarta-Bandung Section)*, Republic of Indonesia, www.jetro.go.jp/ext_images/jetro/activities/contribution/oda/model_study/infra_system/pdf/h23_result03_en.pdf.

Chapter 2

Bandung's emerging green growth opportunities

Chapter 2 aims to identify green growth opportunities and analyse policies to promote green growth in the Bandung Metropolitan Area (BMA) pertaining to the following six areas: land use and transport; water resource management; solid waste management; energy; housing and buildings; and green goods and services. The analysis focuses on the following:

1) developing BMA-wide land use and public transport strategies

2) accelerating investment in water and solid waste as essential urban services

3) investing in renewable energy and increasing energy efficiency

4) promoting green buildings and combatting urban slums

Key findings

- Given the continued urban development pressure, a strong **BMA-wide land-use policy** is required to enhance urban resilience. The rapid urban expansion in the BMA is increasing the city's exposure to flooding, as people settle and build in flood-prone areas. Vulnerability and risk assessment (VRA) and zoning regulations to restrict land use in inappropriate locations should be urgently considered. The BMA should also envision a metropolitan spatial land-use plan that leverages policy synergies between transit-oriented development and other key sectoral policies.
- Bandung needs to speed up investment in **public transport systems**, including the proposed light-rail transit (LRT). At the same time, more efficient use of existing transit modes with improved service quality (reliability and safety in particular) could be pursued. The majority of air pollution and CO2 emissions in the BMA come from the transport sector. Bandung must strengthen **air pollution monitoring mechanisms** and increase transparency by making data available to the public. In addition, Bandung should consider more extensive measures to promote **low-emission vehicles**.
- **Water supply, wastewater treatment and solid waste management** in the BMA need improvement. Accelerating investment in these essential urban services would ensure that the BMA continues towards a more inclusive, resilient and sustainable city. Wastewater treatment capacity is still not sufficient, and local waterways are considered among the most polluted globally. No effective policy instruments have been devised to reduce unsustainable extraction of ground water and/or reduce the consumption of water by the industrial sector. This has led to many negative urban environmental externalities, such as land subsidence. **Demand-side policies** to curb water usage (applying a more progressive water tariff structure) should be considered. The same recommendations should be applied to municipal solid waste services, to reflect the true cost of the service provided.
- **Bandung could take a leading role in achieving Indonesia's new national target to increase the share of renewable energy (RE).** Indonesia is largely dependent on fossil fuels, which represented 94.5% of final energy consumption in 2013, higher than in neighbouring countries such as Thailand (76.2%). Among different options, solar and waste-to-energy represent promising and practical ways of achieving such a goal.
- **Housing and building** present key opportunities for green growth, given the increasing resource consumption in the sectors. The proposed green building certificate, linked with a mandatory building permit, could be a good solution for guiding eco-friendly building plans and should be expanded to the whole BMA. Upgrading informal settlements in Bandung remains a challenge requiring a comprehensive approach for enhancing urban resilience.

2.1. Developing BMA-wide land use and public transport strategies

Spatial land-use planning is an organising principle linking urban systems into an integrated whole. This tool can anchor other sectoral urban policies. How well such a tool is utilised may determine residents' access to public services and employment opportunities, energy demands and energy efficiency of the transport sector, and a city's capacity to adapt to climate change. It directly affects public finances through the demands placed on maintaining existing infrastructure or the construction of new infrastructure, such as roads, water treatment plants or drainage systems. Spatial land-use planning decisions that will be made over the next 15 years (the time frame over which it is anticipated that more than two-thirds of the infrastructure for public services will be built in Southeast Asian cities), will lock in the spatial growth of these urban areas, their energy use patterns and their greenhouse gas (GHG) emissions trajectory for decades, if not centuries, to come (Global Commission on the Economy and Climate, 2014). This section deals with land use and transport together, because many of the challenges Bandung and other Southeast Asian cities face, as well as many of the suggested approaches or measures required for resolving them, are pertinent to each other and interconnected.

A strong BMA-wide land-use policy could enhance urban resilience

Bandung is exposed to several natural hazards, due both to its topographic features and to its location in a tectonically active zone. In recent years, the BMA's population has grown in outlying urban districts in the north, especially outside the limits of Bandung City (Figure 2.1). The BMA's built-up are increased from 34282.49 square kilometres in 1991 to 65812.86 square kilometres in 2012 (Ardiwijaya et al, 2014). The rapid urban expansion has increased the city's exposure to flooding, as people are settling and building in flood-prone areas (Tarigan et al., 2016). The northern half of Bandung, encompassing territory in four of the BMA's five local government units (LGUs), has been the focus of intense and uncoordinated development pressure (ibid). The impact of these new population centres in undesirable geographical locations in the north may increase the risk of flooding in southern parts of the city. Indonesia's Ministry of Public Works (2008) estimates that in excess of 25 million people live in vulnerable situations across Java.

Given the continued urban development pressure, a **strong land-use policy** is required to enhance urban resilience in the BMA. Bandung's vulnerability to floods and other natural disasters is partially attributed to poorly enforced zoning regulations and land-use control, which is exacerbated by the concentration of poorly prepared urban populations in highly exposed parts of the city. Zoning tools in the BMA must be implemented and regulated effectively to restrict land use in unsuitable locations. Land-use policy must be applied across the entire BMA, as risks are also incurred by a lack of inter-governmental co-ordination on hazard mitigation planning. Although a general master plan for the BMA has been prepared by the provincial government, no effective land-use plan has been set up. The delivery of building permits in different local government areas in north of Bandung, for example, is at cross purposes with hazard reduction efforts at a metropolitan scale (Hudalah et al., 2010). The BMA should draw up a metropolitan spatial land use plan binding the local governments. The formation of the metropolitan institution will be a good opportunity to advance this idea (see Chapter 4).

Vulnerability and risk assessment (VRA) and asset inventory is another important component that must be integrated. Up to now, the BMA has not prepared and disclosed natural hazard maps, implying that the BMA is by and large underprepared. Preparation is critical to anticipate the intensity, frequency and extent of environmental hazards, as well as to identify vulnerable urban population groups, assets and infrastructure. A VRA and asset inventory would provide such information and provide a basis to manage and limit damage, while also considering the cost and time required to recover from a natural disaster, among other factors. Bandung's approach to hazard assessment could expand upon that of other Southeast Asian cities such as Cebu (Box 2.1).

Figure 2.1. **The Bandung Metropolitan Area and its expanding urban environment**

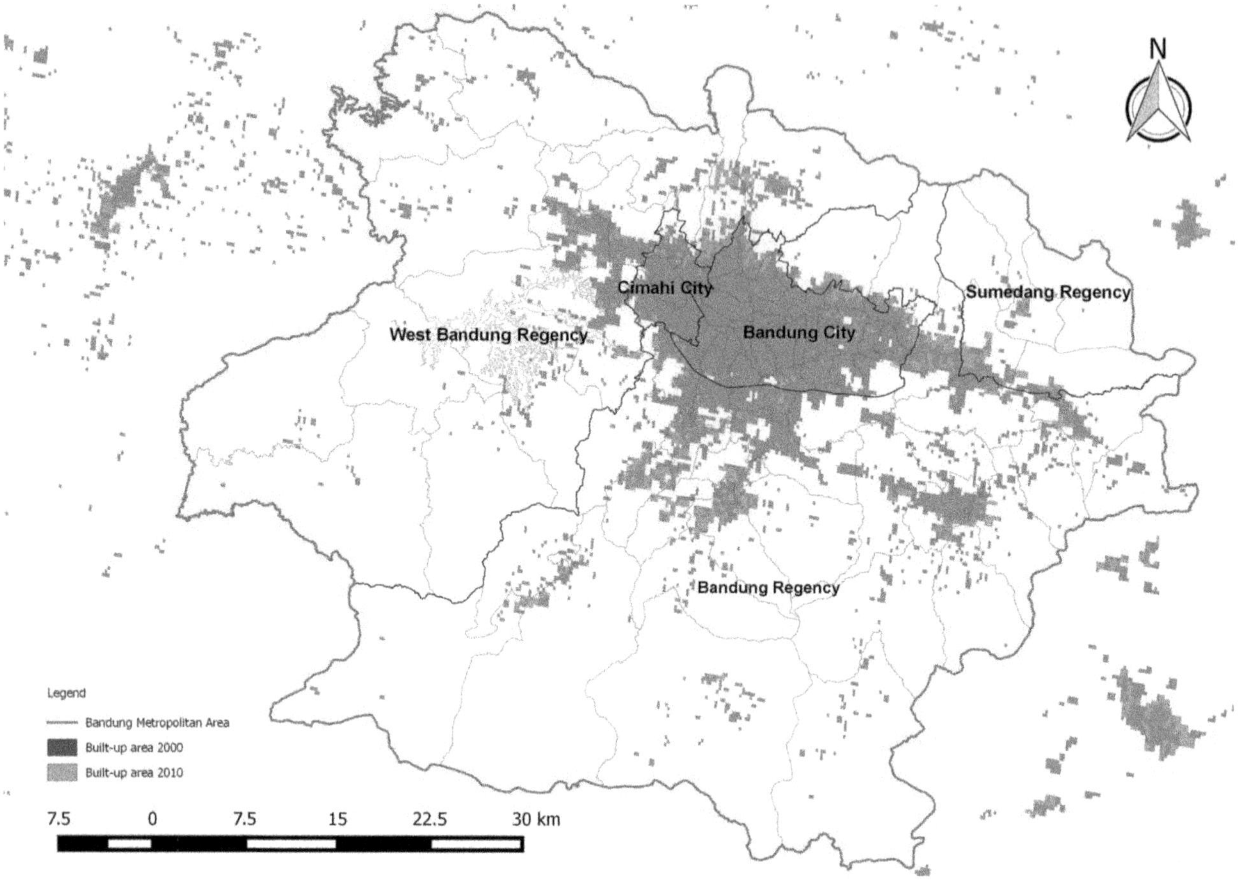

Source: Bandung City (2016), "Answers to the OECD case study questionnaire", internal document, unpublished; Schneider, A. et al. (2015), "A new urban landscape in east-Southeast Asia, 2000-2010", *Environmental Research Letters*, Vol. 10(3), http://dx.doi.org/10.1088/1748-9326/10/3/034002.

Box 2.1. **Hazard assessment in Metro Cebu, Philippines**

Cebu is the regional capital of the Central Visayas province, located on the central-eastern flank of Cebu Island in the centre of the Philippine archipelago. The Metropolitan Area of Cebu (Metro Cebu) extends along a narrow coastal strip of territory that is sandwiched between rugged mountain ranges that traverse the island's north-south spine and the Strait of Cebu. It is exposed to environmental risks posed by intense climate and geological hazards, such as floods and earthquakes. Metro Cebu consists of seven city and six municipal local government units (LGUs). Before the formation of the Metro Cebu Development and Coordinating Board (MCDCB) in 2011, no formal basis for metropolitan planning and development was in place.

Adopting the Philippine government's Disaster Risk Reduction Management Act (No. 10121) under Cebu City Executive Order No. 12-6, Cebu City is mandated to establish Cebu City Disaster Risk Reduction Management Council which undertakes detailed studies to identify physical and environmental features that make it vulnerable to natural hazards and pose a risk to the metropolitan population. This hazard risk assessment has resulted in thematic maps as well as disaster-risk reduction management (DRRM) plans in all 13 local government areas of the Cebu metropolitan area. Legislation is also in place to provide for sufficient financial resources to be allotted to local DRRM programmes. However, more work needs to be done to link the identification of these hazardous areas with the location of the populations at risk, critical infrastructure and community assets, to build a more sophisticated and long-term VRA.

Source: OECD (forthcoming) *Urban Green Growth in Cebu, Philippines.*

Green space and urban agriculture can create policy complementarities

Green space (urban parks, forests, farmland, etc.) can offer cities long-term, multi-faceted benefits, including enhancing urban resilience and amenities for citizens and avoiding urban heat island effects. Increasing green areas is also a key factor to increasing atmospheric oxygen and promoting carbon sequestration. The Ministry of Public Works of Indonesia has proposed a **mandatory green space target** (Spatial Planning Law No. 26/2007). This aims to ensure that every city or regency allocates sufficient open space, with a target of 20% public open space and 10% private open space. To support such targets, the ministry also initiated the Green Cities Initiative which encourages local efforts in eight attributes including green planning and design and green open space. It has been implemented in 112 cities/regencies in Indonesia.

Bandung City is already pursuing more ambitious targets, guided by the **green city master plan** (25% of land to be used for public space; 15% of land for green open space). The city is also actively promoting **urban farming**. Although urbanisation is increasingly making urban land more competitive with other purposes, urban farming can demonstrate multi-faceted benefits for urban residents such as providing local food, creating jobs for urban poor and reducing their food expenditure, promoting better use of underutilised land in cites, enhancing retention of rainwater and thus contributing to enhance resilience to floods, and providing amenities in cities. Mayor of Bandung is an active advocate of urban farming and encourages urban farming in Bandung in more than 1 500 spots in Bandung to be used for urban farming activities. Training was given at no cost to participants by the city council in collaboration with *Bandung Berkebun*, a community-based initiative promoting the use of urban spaces for farming.[1]

Given that urban agglomeration is encompassed beyond the border of Bandung City to the entire BMA, such initiatives would be more effective if the BMA's four other local government units could work with Bandung City with co-ordinated targets and policy instruments.

Investing pro-actively in urban transport infrastructure

Bandung's population growth and strong economic development continue to increase the need for pro-active infrastructure investment. As the BMA's population has grown, traffic volumes have expanded by 10% to 15% annually (Sukenjah, 2014), increasing average weekday commutes from 30 to 65 minutes between 2000 and 2009, and more than an hour on weekends (Syabri, Pradono and Soegijanto, 2013). Only an estimated 20% of Bandung's residents use public transport (AFD, 2014). The modal share of urban public transport in Indonesia was only 23% in 2014, although it is anticipated this will increase to 32% by 2019 (KPPN, 2014). As the BMA's urban footprint has expanded without appropriate mass transit options, congestion has become a major issue, and central areas of Bandung City are clogged and polluted, diminishing the quality of life. As daily trip numbers increase, the city's transport infrastructure will be under more strain, with even longer travel times under a business-as-usual scenario (Lubis, Isnaeni and Nurjaya, 2003). This will necessitate enhanced public transport policy and investment.

Although until recently transport infrastructure in the BMA has largely favoured the development of roads (Tarigan, 2016), Bandung City has recently been working on plans to construct new public transport infrastructure. **"Better Urban Mobility 2031"** is its integrated and comprehensive urban mobility plan. The implementation of this vision incorporates four main strategies: i) an integrated and compact city (live-work-play) concept, through a combination of land-use and traffic-demand management (TDM) measures; ii) strengthening the road network; iii) improving the role of public transport by developing a mass rapid transport (MRT) system, as the backbone of an integrated transport system supported by a feeder system; iv) using technology to influence behaviour by focusing on three critical aspects: traffic management, green transport and smart transport. Bandung City's high population density (14 687 people per square kilometre in 2014) provides a good basis for viable public transport. This density is almost twice that of Surabaya City's 8 562 people per square kilometre (Statistics East Java, 2015).

The centrepiece of the vision is a new seven-line **light rail transit (LRT)** system. This will require significant investment and infrastructure planning and serve the BMA's contiguous urban area and LGUs. The first LRT line will connect a newly proposed high-speed rail station in Teknopolis, the new planned urban development located in the east of the city, to Bandung's current urban centre (Box 2.2). While the LRT is intended to be operational for the opening of the new HSR, the connection between the existing city centre and the new station is likely to pose the greatest challenge for the HSR project, and it is thus important to integrate the two. The central, provincial and local governments will need to co-ordinate the investment necessary. The provincial government has an important role to play in developing the LRT, because the governor of West Java Province issues the recommendation for the city to implement the project.

Bandung should introduce a mechanism to guide urban development along the seven transit corridors well before the LRT is built. It is possible that government functions of West Java Province will move to one of the new towns to be built along the high-speed rail line (HSR) west of Bandung. This underscores the importance of public transport and transit-oriented development (TOD) to reduce dependence on private cars. Four concrete proposals that could be considered include:

- Secure extra land around the proposed LRT stations for public use, to ensure sufficient space for pedestrians, bikers and feeder transport systems. Surabaya has developed an integrated transport plan that incorporates feeder services, pedestrian infrastructure and park-and-ride facilities incorporating commercial spaces as part of its proposed LRT network.
- Quality connections between LRT stops and adjacent commercial and residential areas should be carefully designed. A mechanism could be created encouraging private developers to cover some of these costs.
- Use floor area ratio (FAR) regulations in combination with incentives and disincentives to encourage high-density development around the stations (for example, FAR bonuses should be granted to development that offers public space, and fees imposed on development under the desired density.
- Introduce station-area master plans to guide development, especially in relation to the first and second points.

Compact-city policies from Japan and Korea could be used as a starting point to develop such a mechanism (OECD, 2012a).

Eight more programmes will be implemented during the local medium-term development plan 2014-2019 for urban mobility in Bandung City. Projects that have already been implemented include: bike sharing, free school bus services, car sharing and car emissions testing, which also feeds into the clean emission parking areas initiative. Most of these projects are public-private partnerships (PPP). To accelerate such large-scale investments in urban transport, Bandung should consider strengthening financial arrangements for infrastructure investment. See chapter Chapter 4 for further elaboration on this.

Box 2.2. **An emerging Jakarta-Bandung urban corridor**

Recognition is emerging in the literature of a mega-urban region stretching from coastal Jakarta to Bandung (Firman, 2009; Dorodjatoen, 2009). This area, including Greater Jakarta (*Jabodetabek*: that is, Jakarta, Bogor, Depok, Tangerang and Bekasi) and the BMA had a population of 38.1 million in 2015. At this point however, little official government recognition has been devoted to this urban agglomeration.

Regional links were strengthened with the construction of the new Cipularang toll road in 2005. Average daily traffic flows along the new highway between Bandung and Jakarta have increased annually by 100% in the last ten years (Dorodjatoen, 2009). The region will benefit further from a new high-speed rail link. The proposed USD 5.5 billion Jakarta-Bandung high-speed railway will sharply reduce travel times along the 150-kilometre route, to 40 minutes from the present four-hour journey. The railway is scheduled to open in 2020, and it is estimated that 57 000 passengers will use the line daily, tripling to 171 000 by 2050 (Yachiyo Engineering, 2012). The high-speed line will be part of a much grander 750-kilometre railway traversing the densely populated island of Java, from Jakarta in the west to Surabaya in the east via Bandung, Cirebon and Semarang. It is anticipated that four stations will be located along the Jakarta-Bandung route, in i) Jakarta Halim Perdanakusuma (with a rail connection to the Jakarta airport), ii) Karawang Tegalluar, iii) Bandung Walini station and iv) Bandung Gedebage station. A consortium of Chinese and Indonesian state-owned companies was appointed to oversee the new line's development in 2015, when the Indonesian government agreed to use Chinese high-speed rail technology. Construction of the new line began in January 2016.

The new line is part of the government's policy for Indonesia's economic development. Investment in Java's rail infrastructure will revolutionise mobility on an island with a population of more than 140 million, driving economic development for years to come. This will be particularly beneficial for a city like Bandung, given its growing number of service-based industries, such as its tourism and hotel sector. The railway also has the potential to reduce the number of vehicles arriving in Bandung from Jakarta on weekends. It seems plausible that workers in Jakarta may relocate to Bandung, to benefit from the city's milder climate and higher quality of life, while continuing to commute to the capital daily on the train. This could transform the perception of Jakarta and Bandung as two separate cities, since in some cases, it might take longer to commute from suburban Jakarta than from Bandung on the high-speed train. This should provide the impetus for investment in transport infrastructure. In addition to the substantial investment and new jobs the HSR project will create in the short term, the competitive economic advantages for Bandung should also have agglomeration effects attracting new investment to the city.

Source: Yachiyo Engineering (2012), "Feasibility Study for Promotion of International Infrastructure Projects in FY2011: Study on the High Speed Railway Project (Jakarta-Bandung Section), Republic of Indonesia", www.jetro.go.jp/ext_images/jetro/activities/contribution/oda/model_study/infra_system/pdf/h23_result03_en.pdf (accessed 14 March 2016); Dorodjatoen, A.M.H. (2009), "The emergence of Jakarta-Bandung Mega-Urban Region and Its future challenges", *Jurnal Perencanaan Wilayah dan Kota*, Vol. 20(1), pp. 15-33; Firman, T. (2009), "Decentralization reform and local-government proliferation in Indonesia: Towards a fragmentation of regional development", *Review of Urban and Regional Development Studies*, Vol. 21(2-3), pp. 143-157.

Improving the connectivity, reliability and safety of existing para-transport

In the BMA, paratransit options and private vehicles are the primary modes of transport, which has caused crippling traffic congestion (Tarigan, 2016). Minibuses (*angkot*), motorcycle taxis (*ojek*), non-motorised pedicabs (*becak*) and even horse-drawn buggies (*delman*) provide an essential service for moving people about the city (Syabri, Pradono and Soegijanto, 2013). The minibus, the central mode of public transit, accounted in 2009 for about 31% of all motorised trips. In total, a fleet of 15 000 minibuses (with 12 to 14 seats) covered 84 fixed routes in the BMA, while only 97 buses (with 45 to 50 seats) covered 7 routes in Bandung City, and it is estimated that a further 35 000 paratransit units operate countless non-fixed routes across the city (SNCF, 2010). Although they are not yet authorised legally, motorcycle taxis are also gaining popularity (20 000 operators in 2009) because they can slip through congested traffic and because of the wide range of destinations they service (Syabri, Pradono, Soegijanto, 2013). Due to heavy traffic, low comfort levels and average speeds, the minibuses are unreliable. The large number of them and motorcycle taxis on Bandung's streets obstruct traffic flows and cause congestion.

Despite these problems, there is much potential to improve use of existing transport modes in Bandung. Urban transport systems must be integrated holistically in what is referred to as "last half-kilometre" or "last mile" connectivity. This ideally means that a passenger should be able to leave home and walk less than 500 metres to reach a bus stop or train station connecting to a larger public transport network. Connectivity is the single most important characteristic of any fully functional and profitable urban public transport system. This includes both inter-city connectivity to high-speed trains or regional airports, in addition to homes, businesses or shopping/recreational destinations. Bandung's *becak* offer an environmentally friendly last-mile service that transport clients on short local trips, as well as a critical source of employment for about 20 000 unskilled workers (Syabri, Pradono and Soegijanto, 2013). Bandung City should consider integrating the planned large-scale public transport system, such as light-rail transport (LRT) or the electric bus rapid transport (TMB) system, into a broader network serviced by local feeder buses and taxi services. Paratransit may be viewed as an inferior service to conventional and more sophisticated mass public transit systems, but it could form the basis of a complementary system to Bandung City's proposed LRT and TMB networks in the medium term. In addition, paratransit can navigate Bandung's narrow roads and mountainous geography, providing access to neighbourhoods that larger vehicles may not be able to service. This would go some way toward reducing resistance from *angkot* associations.

To unleash such potential, **regulating paratransit for reliability and safety is an issue the city needs to address immediately**. These initiatives must be pursued at the metropolitan level, because, as Bandung City's previous efforts to reduce congestion suggest, in its attempt to regulate the number of minibuses (*angkot*) within its municipal borders, the policies of neighbouring municipalities will have a direct effect on the outcome (GIZ, 2002). Minibuses licensed outside the city were freely able to drive into Bandung City, negating its efforts to reduce congestion through regulation. Such a proposal should be complemented by an integrated financial payment system using a single transport card, like the Oyster card in London, which functions across the metropolitan area's entire public transport network. This would incorporate future MRT, LRT or BRT lines and local bus services. The French Development Agency (AFD) is currently investigating low-carbon modality options for Bandung and the reorganisation of Bandung's central railway station to improve accessibility and the potential for an intermodal development project. Such studies should include options to improve use of existing paratransit modes.

Managing the increasing demand for private vehicles through pricing mechanisms

Bandung also needs to manage the increasing demand for private vehicles. Pricing mechanisms such as parking fees can be an effective tool. The City of Bandung is currently considering increasing the city's parking tax, which will be applied to all the city's private parking facilities. This will not only facilitate the use of public transport but raise revenues that allow the city to increase green investment. Parking taxes/fees are one of a few revenue sources from which city governments can benefit. ICT could further improve the instruments' effectiveness; for example, the city could apply dynamic pricing (applying a higher tax/fee for peak hours) for greater impact. The city could also reduce the taxes/fees for low-emission vehicles, to encourage their use. However, such traffic demand management mechanisms must be combined with the provision of alternative public transport modes for political buy-in and general public support. This underlines the importance of focused investment in public transport and of a comprehensive policy approach on land use and transport. The experience of congestion charges in London and Stockholm could provide useful insight (OECD, 2013).

Tackling transport-related air pollution

Bandung's streets have become heavily congested because of the large number of commuters reliant on private motor vehicles during the week and from visitors from Jakarta and other cities in West Java on weekends. This has resulted in rising air pollution levels, with the accompanying health and economic costs, in the form of lost time and productivity. Air pollution in Bandung is mostly attributed to transportation (Oanh, 2012). Given the serious risks to public health, the government must do more to address Bandung's air pollution levels. In 2015, Bandung City received a Blue Skies Award as the least polluted metropolitan area in Indonesia (Puspitasari, 2015). This represents a sharp turnaround from 2006 and 2008, when it was designated by the government as Indonesia's "dirtiest" metropolitan area (Prihandrijanti and Firdayati, 2011). Nonetheless, Bandung's current air pollution levels still substantially exceed the World Health Organisation's (WHO) air quality standards. Besides, Indonesia's transport sector was the source of 23% of all energy-related GHG emissions in 2010, of which 91% derived from the road network (MoT and GIZ 2014).

Air quality in the BMA is managed through a range of municipal government acts and regulations. The national and provincial government also plays an important role in regulating air quality (Sukenjah, 2014). In 1999, the Ministry of the Environment established the National Ambient Air Quality Standards (NAAQS) to regulate air pollution in Indonesia. Contemporaneously, a national air quality monitoring network system (AQMS) was established in ten large cities across Indonesia, including Bandung, to continuously monitor carbon monoxide (CO), sulfur dioxide (SO_2), nitrogen dioxide (NO_2), ozone (O_3) and particulate matter of less than or equal to 10 micrometres (PM_{10}).[2] However, data on $PM_{2.5}$ is not collected. In Bandung City, five continuous air quality monitoring stations were installed as part of the AQMS (Dago Pakar, Aria Graha, Tegallega, Batununggal and Cisaranten Wetan). Soon after they were installed, two of these units ceased to function due to a lack of maintenance (Sukenjah, 2014) and only three of the five pollutants are measured, because the instruments have been damaged (CAI-Asia, 2009).

Table 2.1. **Indonesia's national ambient air quality standards and WHO guidelines**

Pollutant	Average time	NAAQS (µg/m3)	AAQS in Jakarta (µg/m3)	WHO Guidelines
SPM	24 hours	230	230	-
	1 year	90	90	-
PM_{10}	24 hours	150	150	50
	1 year		-	20
SO_2	1 hour	900	900	-
	24 hours	365	260	20
	1 year	60	60	-
NO_2	1 hour	400	400	200
	24 hours	150	92.5	-
	1 year	100	60	40
O_3	1 hour	235	200	-
	8 hours	-	-	100
	1 year	50	30	-
Pb	1 year	1	-	0.5
CO	1 hour	30 000	26 000	30 000
	8 hour	-	-	10 000
	24 hours	10 000	9 000	-

Note: SPM = suspended particulate matter; PM_{10} = particulate matter of a diameter less than or equal to 10 micrometres; SO_2 = sulfur dioxide; NO_2 = nitrogen dioxide; O_2 = ozone; Pb = lead; CO = carbon monoxide; WHO = World Health Organisation.

Source: CAI-Asia (2009), *Indonesia Country Profile: Focus on Smaller Cities*, www.citiesforcleanair.org/documents/FINAL%20DRAFT%20Indonesia%20GTZ%20Country%20Profile%205Oct09.pdf (accessed 8 December 2015); CAI-Asia (2010), *Clean Air Management Profile: Indonesia*, http://cleanairasia.org/wp-content/uploads/portal/files/documents/CAMP_Indonesia_-_2010_Edition.pdf (accessed 15 September 2016); Krisnawati, L. (2008), *Implementation of Environmental Sustainable Transport, Indonesia*, www.unep.org/transport/pcfv/PDF/pathumbai_ESTinIndonesia.pdf (accessed 15 September 2016).

Systematic air pollution monitoring framework for the BMA should be established urgently as a collective effort of all levels of government. The Ministry of the Environment could consider adding $PM_{2.5}$ to the current NAAQS framework. It could also revise the standards so that they are more coherent with global standards. The NAAQS standards are well below WHO standards for some pollutants (Table 2.1). Since provincial governments can set more aggressive air pollution standards than the NAAQS, an option for the BMA is to co-ordinate with the West Java Province and consider strengthening their standards for vehicles and industries as well as ambient air quality standards as implemented in Jakarta (Table 2.1).[3] This is most pressing considering the peculiar local contexts of the city of Bandung -a basin surrounded by high rise mountains where air pollutants are trapped. Alternatively, Bandung and other four municipalities could be given flexibility in setting more stringent air quality standards than provincial and national regulations. Cities lack the mandate to set such standards under the current regulation. The importance of this is to empower city governments which generate the highest amounts of emissions to take action. In fact, Bandung manages air quality control through their own legislation and regulations (bylaws). This is achieved through regular vehicle emission test, car free days on Sundays lasting for a period of four hours from 06:00 a.m. to 10:00 a.m. in some streets, clean emission zones exclusively accessible to low emission vehicles and regular air quality modelling with research universities (Sukenjah, 2014). Successful implementation of such programmes by cities could encourage the national government to introduce such decentralised mechanisms. Besides, Bandung City should address the maintenance of AQMS immediately.

Several government agencies do conduct their own monitoring initiatives in addition to the two monitoring networks mentioned above. The Ministry of Health and Ministry of Transport collect data using mobile devices in 16 locations. The data that is collected is not shared between different agencies, however. The BMA's five local government units (LGUs) could share the data and co-operate with other government bodies to improve public health. The use of ICT could provide useful options (see Chapter 3). Bandung City will soon begin real-time air quality monitoring linked to the city's command centre (Bandung City, 2016). A central challenge, however, is the cost of equipment.

Innovative ideas are also needed to reduce air pollution from private vehicles. Bandung's **Blue Skies programme**, initiated by the Ministry of Forestry and the Environment, aims to reduce the levels of air pollution. This promotes low-emission vehicles by awarding a certificate to cars that meet certain emission standards. Preference is given in Bandung City in designated public parking areas to cars that have the certificates. Such initiatives could be expanded to the surrounding LGUs in the BMA as well as to private parking facilities. The BMA should also consider active participation in national and international initiatives for sustainable urban transport (Box 2.3).

Box 2.3. **National and international initiatives for sustainable urban transport**

Indonesia's **medium-term development plan 2015-2019** identifies several strategic urban transport challenges. It seeks to develop environmentally friendly transport infrastructure resilient to the impact of climate change. The medium-term plan also prioritises renewable fuel sources as well as the introduction of Euro 4 fuel standards (replacing Euro 2) and better managed transport networks (Bappenas, 2014). The medium-term plan also specifically targets the declining role of urban public transport and encourages a modal shift from private vehicles through Transport Demand Management (TDM) and scaling up of Bus Rapid Transit (BRT) and Mass Rapid Transit (MRT). For example, the national government is underwriting 49% of the costs of Jakarta's new MRT line. It also seeks to improve accessibility by enhancing pedestrian facilities and non-motorised transport (NMT).

Indonesia's **Sustainable Urban Transport Programme (NAMASUTRI)** targets urban transport and urban passenger transport in particular, such as commuter rail or bus rapid transit, to encourage development of transport infrastructure that will serve the needs of Indonesia's rising urban population.

Complementing the medium-term plan, the national climate change policy will also play an important role in the shift towards energy-efficient transport modes and non-motorised transport (NMT). The development of public transport systems and NMT infrastructure requires sectoral strategies and government regulation, such as the Minister of Transport Decree #7/2010 strategic transport plan (Renstra).

There are also several programmes funded by international donors that reinforce city governments' capacity to improve urban transport options. One is the **Sustainable Urban Transport Project (SUTIP)** funded by *Deutsche Gesellschaft für Internationale Zusammenarbeit* (GIZ) in close co-operation with Bappenas. The SUTIP initiative began in 2009, and has provided legal and regulatory policy advice. It has also contributed to preparation for the National Road Map on CO_2 mitigation, the Grand Design in Urban Transport (National Urban Transport Policy) and the preparation of National Medium Term Development Plan for urban transport. The SUTIP initiative is currently working with four partner cities (Palembang, Bogor, Solo and Yogyakarta) and provides training, advice on public transport restructuring and improvement schemes, TDM measures and non-motorised transport development.

Source: Based on Bappenas (2014) National Medium Term Development Plan 2015-2019 (RPJMN 2015-2019), http://www.bappenas.go.id/files/7714/1557/5291/RT_RPJMN.PDF (accessed 13 October 2016).

2.2. Accelerating investment in water and solid waste as essential urban services

The provision and management of essential urban services should form the basis of the BMA's urban green growth agenda. In some areas of the BMA, water supply, wastewater treatment and solid waste management need development. The lack of wastewater treatment capacity has resulted in local waterways that are considered to be among the most polluted in the world and ground water levels are declining and under great pressure. The resulting negative urban environmental externalities have included land subsidence and the associated impacts on Bandung's built environment and local infrastructure (Gumilar, 2013). The deficit in urban service provision is more pronounced in outlying districts, where urban development has been greatest. The **BMA-wide master plan** defined by the West Java governor's law in 2015, including sectoral plans on water and solid waste, is a positive development. It should be used as the basis to develop further metropolitan policies. These essential urban service sectors fall under the purview of local government in Indonesia and thus represent an opportunity for green growth in the BMA. Prioritising them could help BMA become a more inclusive, resilient and sustainable city.

This section deals with water resource and solid waste management together, as many of the challenges they face, and many of the approaches for solving them, are interconnected. Policies to enhance urban resilience against floods are also discussed.

Ensuring a clean water supply

In Indonesia, the government of Indonesia is responsible for water resources, provincial governments purchase this water in bulk for treatment, and city governments (municipal water utilities) buy the treated water for distribution to end users. In the BMA, there are three local water supply companies (*Perusahaan Daerah Air Minum, PDAM*).[4] They service approximately half (48.2%) of the BMA's urban areas through the city's network of running water, and 8.91% of households in peri-urban areas (Maryati and Humaira, 2015). In addition to PDAMs, water services are provided through (Komarulzaman, 2013): i) direct government provision via the public works department for populations not served by PDAM due to profitability issues, usually in the form of a small-scale water facility at the village level; ii) the private not-for-profit sector; and iii) private sources at the household level. In Bandung Regency, the number of people served in this way exceeds those served by PDAMs. The number of households with running water provided in Bandung City by PDAM Tirtawening Bandung covers 62% of the LGU's population (Moersidik et al., 2015). The comparable figure for residents in West Bandung Regency was only 8.3% (Komarulzaman, 2013). The wide disparity between Bandung City and other districts in the BMA is exacerbated by a waiver that new customers must sign agreeing not to contest PDAM's inadequate service levels before any new connection is established.

In recent years, the BMA's population and built environment have expanded rapidly, at the expense of water and sanitation infrastructure. Bandung City's municipal water utility, PDAM Tirtawening Bandung, expanded its service coverage by 0.65% annually in the past ten years, while the population grew by 1.42% each year, and has never achieved its service coverage expansion targets (Moersidik et al., 2015). Thanks to a service coverage deficit and substantial variation between districts, the number of people reliant on informal water services continues to grow (Statistics West Java, 2011). Even those who do enjoy access, only have as little as two hours of water supply daily and are reliant on filling tanks during this short period to store sufficient water for the rest of the day. The study of Masterplan Drainage in the BMA (2009) notes that the availability of raw water for the source of water supply will slightly decrease, given the increase of population and environmental problems such as: land subsidence, ground water extraction, river pollution, changes in conserved land, etc. This study also recommended an integrated policy for conserving catchment areas in BMA by developing 4 dams and 13 water ponds to serve as flood control and raw water sources, but this policy has not yet in fact been implemented.

Land subsidence is a serious challenge. Despite per capita water consumption levels that are lower than those of other Southeast Asian cities, increased ground water extraction has led to the rapid decline of the local ground water table, which has been linked to land subsidence in the Bandung basin (Gumilar et al., 2013). This comes in addition to subsidence due to Bandung's built environment. The long-term impact on Bandung's built environment may be costly, because it affects the city's building stock and infrastructure, such as roads and bridges, and will probably increase the risk of flooding in certain parts of the city.

Much can still be done to address the poor and inconsistent service provision. More attention should be paid to managing water resources at the scale of the Bandung Basin, and the first step towards this could be a **BMA-wide water assessment** to establish how much water is being extracted and from where, as well as when and by whom. This is especially pertinent to local industry, which is not monitored, and could mitigate the negative impacts associated with ground subsidence. Another promising option is to introduce **online, real-time water quality monitoring** tools for both drinking water and wastewater treatment. These represent a proven method for more effective water resource management. One key benefit would be the opportunity to monitor and measure water consumption or pollution levels, providing invaluable assistance to policy makers, while allowing the public to avoid potentially harmful consequences. Monitoring and evaluation would also show how much ground water is being extracted annually and could lead to more sustainable practices. It is not certain precisely how much water industry consumes, and more effective monitoring equipment could clarify this, to determine where it is used and by whom. High non-revenue water (NRW) loss, coupled with declining water resources, places great strain on the water supply. Bangkok's real-time tap water quality project, part of the Metropole Watch programme, is a positive example the BMA might consider (Box 2.4). Such monitoring tools should be a part of Bandung City's smart city strategy (see Chapter 3).

The BMA should then consider **reforming the water fee structure**. Because the volume of water supplied remains in the hands of the national and provincial governments, it is difficult for the city to meet the rising demand. However, PDAMs retain control over water tariffs, an important policy tool. The present water tariff structure is not financially viable, and does not allow for full-cost recovery principles, because PDAMs do not charge customers for the volume of water they consume. Instead, residential water tariffs are based on house size and their location. A **full cost-recovery water tariff structure** would discourage excessive water consumption, conserving water resources, while mobilising financial resources that could be invested in repair and extending the pipeline network. Investment in this essential urban service should aim to ensure every citizen has basic service. Indonesia's Ministry of Public Work has strict pricing laws limiting water tariffs to 4% of a residential area's income, which could be replaced by marginal use price signals, income-based fee rebates and or other distributional mechanisms. Industrial water use should be monitored, which it is not at present, to ensure that industry pays for the volume of water actually consumed. Of course, rationalising water tariff structure must take into consideration socio-economic concerns, particularly of the urban poor. Given the national subsidy system for low-income households, a progressive water tariff structure could still be imposed, using smart metering, although such a measure needs to be supported politically and by the public.

Rationalising the number of local water suppliers could also be an option, as the provision of water in Bandung is complicated by fragmented water suppliers as well as a convoluted policy structure shared between national and sub-national governments. The BMA could streamline them into one institutional entity for the entire BMA, with separate regional units focusing on different geographic focal points and service requirements.

Box 2.4. **Metropole watch programme: Toward open source water quality monitoring in Bangkok**

Infrastructure improvement (construction of sewage treatment facilities) is one of the strategies developed to tackle the issue of water quality in the Chao Phraya River and its canals. An advanced water quality surveillance system is also being implemented. From 2002-05, the Fugro OCEANOR-OTC Consortium developed the Metropole Watch monitoring system, which consists of 12 automatic real-time monitoring stations based along the Chao Phraya River and selected channels in the city of Bangkok. Water is pumped into the stations and analysed, and the results are subsequently transmitted via phone to the main servers and database system (an Environmental Surveillance and Information System, or ENSIS, as supplied by the COWI consulting group and the Norwegian Institute for Water Research/Norwegian Institute for Air Research). All stations measure the same basic parameters: water temperature, water level, conductivity (salinity), dissolved oxygen, pH and turbidity, while other parameters such as chemical oxygen demand, nitrates, oxidation-reduction potential, chlorophyll-A and trace metals (zinc, cadmium, lead, thallium, copper and nickel) are measured in the selected location. Information gathered between different monitoring points allows technicians and managers to map water quality patterns in Bangkok and identify strategic areas where additional wastewater treatment facilities can be constructed. This reduces uncertainty about pollutant loading and helps identify polluters. Particular focus has been placed on flushing pollutants through the network of channels and minimising saltwater intrusion. For an advanced monitoring system to be efficient in the long term, attention must be paid to maintaining investments in infrastructure and trained personnel.

The Metropole Watch programme, developed as the "real-time tap water quality monitoring system", is accessible at: http://twqonline.mwa.co.th/map.php?type=cl.

Source: Dutch Water Sector (n.d.), www.dutchwatersector.com/solutions/projects/187-metropolewatch.html (accessed 22 January 2015).

Tackling water pollution

BMA is crossed by 15 rivers, with a total length of 265 kilometres. Most of them are highly polluted, due to the lack of community awareness, waste disposal and wastewater discharge directly to the river. Much wastewater flows untreated into local rivers and water courses, adding to the high levels of pollution, and severely impacting residents and the local environment. For example, Bandung City faces challenges of riverbank management along the Cikapundung River, which crosses the city, a tributary that forms part of the Citarum River Basin (Box 2.5). The water quality is polluted and has lost its ecological function. The problems are caused by the lack of law enforcement on industrial wastewater discharge to the river and solid waste disposal from settlements along the river's banks. Some locations are prone to inundations given the limited capacity of the micro-drainage system.

The information collected for this case study does not permit an accurate assessment of the extent of different types of untreated liquid wastes, their sources and destinations, or the level of treatment provided. Bandung City acknowledged that surface water quality is deteriorating, but could not quantify how or provide specific levels for common household water contaminants. No programme exists to check if septic systems are functioning in the city and surrounding areas, and they are believed to be used by fewer than 10% of total households in the city; no mention is made of their use in rural areas in the BMA. It should be noted that these figures do not include "household-like" liquid wastes from commercial facilities and stores or hazardous liquid wastes from local industry, such as the large textile industry, agricultural waste from pig and poultry farms, as well as run-off irrigation waters containing pesticide residues. Estimated quantities of this wastewater are not known. Factories and farms conduct "self-monitoring" spot-checked by city environmental staff. Nonetheless, no figures are disclosed on the results of self-monitoring It is not clear whether monitoring data must be submitted to state, regional, or national environmental authorities for analysis.

In this regard, developing a **comprehensive monitoring framework for wastewater** should be first tackled by the BMA. A real-time surface water monitoring system could be considered, as is implemented in Bangkok, Thailand (Box 2.4). Banding city could also use its growing ICT systems to monitor the condition of the city's drainage system (e.g. intakes, culverts and canals). Jakarta uses an Android-based application, "Qlue", to allow citizens to report infrastructure and social problems to city authorities by submitting photos (Maulani, 2015). Citizens could identify areas where vegetation is overgrown, garbage is present, or where damage has occurred to the drainage system, which impedes the flow of water and prioritises their swift remediation.

The BMA should then accelerate **investment in wastewater infrastructure**. The small proportion of the BMA's black and grey wastewater that is processed demonstrates the inadequacy of the centralised sewerage network. The existing wastewater treatment in Bojongsoang (IPAL) has the capacity to serve a population of only 500 000, while the BMA's total population is 8.6 million. Both centralised and decentralised wastewater treatment systems represent viable options for the BMA. In the near term, decentralised wastewater treatment systems (DEWATS) operating on a neighbourhood scale may be advantageous in Bandung. Non-centralised systems offer other benefits, such as flexibility and adaptability, and may be better able to meet the changing needs of growing local populations. Although the capacity of Bandung's wastewater treatment plant may be considered sufficient by the city government, the real problem lies with the inadequate and poorly maintained system of sewage pipes and septic tanks. Improving oversight and expansion of septic systems would probably be the most cost-effective measure to tackle first, to ensure that existing infrastructure and associated investments are not under-utilised. In the longer term, the city's growing population will require upgrades to the centralised system as well. Under Mayoral Decree No. 185/2015, Bandung City has already effectively delegated some authority to co-ordinate and facilitate maintenance of urban infrastructure to a sub-district (*Kecamatan*). The same approach could be extended to decentralised wastewater treatment systems. Bandung City should consider providing financial support to sub-districts through a *Kecamatan* grant, while delegating responsibility to them as well.

In addition to investing in hard infrastructure, **soft infrastructure and community engagement may require more attention**, as the general public must buy into any reform. For example, there is some potential to reuse sewerage sludge for agricultural purposes, although this is limited, because household waste is mixed with industrial effluent, which results in higher concentrations of heavy metals. Moreover, a paradigm change favouring a cyclical approach is required that would seek to reuse waste by-products instead. Due to the lack of adequate infrastructure, informal and needs-driven practices and strategies substitute for formal service provision. Another innovative approach, "condominial sewerage", engages communities and households in the installation and maintenance of water and sanitation systems and has dramatically lowered costs in other developing countries. Such systems, installed with local in-kind labour as part of the counterpart's contribution, are typically better maintained by the residents if they have developed ownership of the system. The approach also develops social capital among participating neighbours that can be expanded to other social concerns, such as local transport measures, improved educational and health services and other public services. This process has also been shown to generate greater trust and co-operation between ordinary citizens and local government, especially among poorer, marginalised groups who have hitherto been passive recipients of city resources, making them active partners in decisions and actions that affect them directly. This can be a more important achievement than any concrete structure or donor-designed activity (World Bank/GFDRR, 2013a). Bandung could also help citizens develop ideas to improve water and sanitation systems by forming participatory local working groups empowered by the city and aided by local and external experts. It could also look for ways to generate seed money for low-interest micro-financing mechanisms with low transaction costs and lending/underwriting requirements that "recycle" loans through regular repayments of revolving loan programmes. This sort of financial support has dynamically changed the lives of many of the world's poorest people living in developing countries.

Box 2.5. **Revitalising the Citarum River Basin**

The Citarum River is one of Java's largest rivers, and contributes significantly to Bandung City's drinking water supply. This valuable water resource is one of the most polluted rivers in the world and epitomises the BMA's surface water challenges. Nearly 5 million people live in the Citarum basin, and households often dump unwanted refuse into it, given the limited municipal solid waste (MSW) services, while sewerage flows untreated into its tributaries. A holistic approach incorporating municipal solid waste and wastewater treatment strategies must be combined to improve this critical environmental resource. Bandung could facilitate efforts to convert these areas into attractive and widely used public spaces to prevent them from being used illegally to dump waste or from resettlement by squatters. Bandung is located in the Citarum River Basin and the Citarum River tributaries passing through the BMA are heavily polluted by human waste and by toxic waste containing lead, mercury, arsenic and other toxins.

In 2008, the Asian Development Bank approved a USD 500 million loan to clean up the Citarum River. Work did not begin until late 2011, when a much larger (USD 4 billion) and more comprehensive project to revitalise 180 kilometres from Mount Wayang through eight regencies and three cities, including Bandung, was initiated. As yet, the area running through the Bandung has not been developed into a showpiece of urban renewal efforts. It offers an opportunity for Bandung to use it for the dual purpose of providing much needed space for urban recreation and respite while retaining its flood-protection properties. Multipurpose public spaces, such as below-grade parks, playing fields and underground parking lots, can also be used for their temporary water storage capacity, which could significantly improve Bandung's resilience to periodic floods.

Source: Asian Development Bank (2014), "Cleaning up Indonesia's Citarum Basin", www.adb.org/features/cleaning-indonesias-citarum-basin, (accessed 28 June 2016).

Rationalising municipal solid waste management

While Indonesia's comprehensive waste policies leave municipalities responsible for designing and implementing their own policies (Box 2.6), the BMA continues to wrestle with the challenges of managing municipal solid waste (MSW). In Bandung City, it is managed by the city-owned municipal waste department (*Perusahaan Daerah Kebersihan*). In the four other municipalities, solid waste is managed by the respective public cleaning agency.

Three issues affect MSW management in the BMA: i) **the limited proportion of waste collected**, ii) **the lack of recycling**, and iii) **the dearth of final disposal sites**. First, it is estimated that 30-40% of the BMA's MSW is not collected or disposed of at landfill (Damanhuri, 2009). Waste that is not collected by the government is burned or discarded in open spaces, streams or rivers. The burning of solid waste by communities is an ongoing challenge, because it exacerbates air pollution, while discarded solid waste blocks drains and has led to severe pollution of the Citarum River (Box 2.5). Secondly, in the BMA, as little as 5% of inorganic waste is recycled (Damanhuri et al, 2009). Finally, Bandung relies solely on landfill and one disposal site (*Sarimukti*) to manage its solid waste. No alternative landfill site exists, and this is one of the city's primary challenges. At a sub-district level in Bandung City, MSW is first transferred to one of the municipality's 202 temporary waste facilities (Tarigan et al., 2016). A "collect-haul-dispose" system utilising manual labour and non-specialised trucks irregularly collect the 1 550 tonnes of waste produced daily from these sites (Chaerul et al., 2014). Eventually, 1 000 tonnes of MSW is transported 45 kilometres to the interim Sarimukti landfill site. This site has been repeatedly scheduled for closure, most recently in 2015 (IGES and City of Kawasaki, 2015).

To tackle the challenges, Bandung City has set ambitious visions. Sustainable MSWM is a central pillar of Bandung City's **Low-Carbon City Plan**. The plan includes a target to reduce the proportion of waste going to landfill from 69% to 25% between 2013 and 2018, and proposes two key measures to achieve this goal: promotion of 3 Rs – reduce, reuse and recycle – and waste-to-energy, which are informed by **Bandung City's medium-term development plan** (Bandung City, 2014) (Table 2.2).

Table 2.2. **Bandung City Medium-Term Plan 2014-18**

Index	2014 target (%)	2018 target (%)
Percentage of waste treated by the municipal government	77	90
Disposal by landfill	69	25
Waste reduction	7	65
Waste reduction by 3 R treatment	7	30
Waste reduction by waste power generation	1	35

Source: IGES and City of Kawasaki (2015), Feasibility Study on FY2014 Large-Scale JCM Project for Realizing Low-Carbon Development in Asia – Developing a Low-Carbon Society Under Collaboration between Bandung City and Kawasaki City, www.env.go.jp/earth/coop/lowcarbon-asia/english/project/data/EN_IDN_2014_03.pdfb.

Box 2.6. **Solid waste management strategies in Indonesia**

After the 2005 Leuwigajah landfill disaster, which killed 143 people, the government of Indonesia recognised the urgency of the situation, passing comprehensive waste management legislation (Munawar and Fellner, 2013).

The **Solid Waste Management Act**, 18/2008 has transformed municipal solid waste (MSW management across the nation. This comprehensive policy established a legal framework for the effective governance and management of solid waste in Indonesia. It defines MSW as the residues of daily human activities in reference to i) domestic waste, ii) domestic waste equivalents and iii) other specific non-hazardous wastes. The act attempts to encourage a paradigm shift perceiving the waste stream as a resource, while resulting in an annual 7% reduction in urban waste (Kasih, 2013a). It also prohibits open dumping and unregulated burning of waste. Prior to its implementation, Indonesia had no central regulation of municipal solid waste, with a fragmented system overseen by local governments. This led to wide variation in MSW management between regions, and sub-optimal performance (Munawar and Fellner, 2013). A 2012 presidential decree focusing on Domestic Solid Waste Management and Solid Waste set up new regulations to introduce sanitary landfill practices and improve management of landfill sites.

The Solid Waste Management Act divides municipal solid waste management between local and central government. The central government is responsible for Indonesia's national waste strategy and policy, encouraging co-operation between local governments (Kasih, 2013a). On the other hand, municipal and city governments are free to establish their own local waste policies in accordance with the national policy framework, as well as implementation and ongoing management. They are also charged with the monitoring and evaluation of waste management systems. In addition, the act emphasised the importance of environmentally sound waste practices and ordered the closure of all non-compliant landfill sites operating as open dumps within five years.

The act is guided by two underlying principles that assign responsibility to individual sources, such as households and industry, to reduce the waste generation burden on the system as a whole: i) extended producer responsibility (ERP) is "a policy approach under which producers are given a significant responsibility – financial and/or physical – for the treatment or disposal of post-consumer products" (OECD, 2001); ii) the 3 Rs approach – reduce, reuse and recycle – is practiced across all waste management chains.

The complementary Environmental Protection and Management Act 32/2009 regulates industrial and other hazardous wastes to protect human health and the environment (Kasih, 2013a). The act defines hazardous waste management as an activity covering the storage, collection, transport, utilisation and/or treatment of hazardous waste. It is based on a polluter-pay principle and bans the import of hazardous waste into Indonesian territories.

Source: Munawar, E. and J. Fellner (2013), "Injury time for Indonesia's landfills", https://waste-management-world.com/a/injury-time-for-indonesian-landfills (accessed 15 February 2016); Kasih, T. (2013a), "E-waste management in Indonesia (National Regulation Draft)", www.epa.gov/sites/production/files/2014-05/documents/indonesia.pdf; OECD (2001), *Extended Producer Responsibility, A Guidance Manual for Governments*, http://dx.doi.org/10.1787/9789264189867-en.

Revising pricing structure to increase the MSW service coverage

A primary aim for the BMA should be to increase MSW collection to 100%, but **financial constraints limit effective MSW management in the BMA** (IGES and City of Kawasaki, 2015). Limited local government budgets, in combination with waste collection fees that are too low to cover actual disposal costs, mean that MSW policies have not been fully implemented. The BMA's local governments transport the MSW from transfer stations to landfill sites and pay a tipping fee to the provincial government. Waste collection fees to ensure solid waste is moved to transfer stations offset some of these costs, but an average collection fee covers only an estimated 28% of the overall cost of waste management (Munawar and Fellner, 2013). Waste collection fees are determined not by the quantity of waste produced but other factors, such as housing type and location, or water and electricity consumption. Local governments can change the fee structure to lower charges if households reduce waste or increase levies for those who produce more, although such a pricing mechanism is not yet introduced. It is unlikely that any reforms will be successful unless these financial constraints are rectified and fees are raised in line with full-cost recovery principles.

Local governments in the BMA should consider increasing the collection fee to reflect the true cost of providing this critical urban service and to reinvest the increased revenue in improving the collection service. An option is to institute higher marginal costs as more rubbish is generated. However, if prices were to increase, those who would otherwise do so might be discouraged from having their waste transported to the transfer station, simply dumping it and contributing to the problem the government is seeking to curb. In view of the limited proportion of waste collected, any decision to increase the fee must be considered carefully and comprehensively. Creating the enabling conditions to discourage waste generation by providing households with recycling bins, as well as regulating open dumping and burning, should be explored.

It is also crucial to improve the efficiency of the collection services. The BMA's five local governments, with the support of West Java Province, could consider **integrating the MSW management** across the contiguous metropolitan area. Options include introducing a joint skill training programme for workers, sharing operational resource including workers and garbage trucks, and organise campaigns and event jointly to raise awareness of BMA citizens and promote waste separation.

Promoting source separation and formalise the informal collection to accelerate the three Rs

Composition of landfilled waste in the BMA, especially high proportion of organic matter and green wastes demonstrates high potential of recycling (Figure 2.2). Bandung's Low Carbon City Plan incorporates the 3 Rs – reduce, reuse and recycle – in an effort to increase recycling from 7% in 2013 to 30% in 2018. In order to achieve the goal, the first step must be to institute much better source separation at a household and business level. In the BMA, as in many Southeast Asian cities, most different types of waste are not effectively separated at the source, at the time of collection, so each type of waste cannot be properly recycled, composted or incinerated. A further problem is that, even if wastes are separated at the household level, they are mixed again at transfer or landfill sites (OECD, 2015). Campaigns by the BMA to raise citizen awareness of the need for municipal solid waste separation should be accelerated and expanded to all parts of the metropolitan area. The BMA could also consider requiring businesses, hotels, restaurants and bars, and large apartment complexes to recycle. A mandatory recycling system has been introduced in many cities in the state of California (United States). The city of San Carlos, for example, adopted a mandatory commercial recycling ordinance in 2010, which became operational within a year. The ordinance was phased in over two years and includes all types of recyclable materials: special wastes, food waste and green waste. It was adopted after extensive consultation with the business community (which supported the ordinance) and includes an extensive outreach programme to educate businesses (OECD, 2015).

Informal collectors make a critical contribution to the waste stream, especially in reusing and recycling. The collection of household waste and recycling is organised by local communities and undertaken primarily by informal collectors and waste pickers. The Ministry of Co-operative, Small and Medium Enterprises (MoCSM) estimated Indonesia had 1.2 million waste pickers in 2008 (Munawar and Fellner, 2013). The MoCSM also calculated that the annual financial value of recycled materials collected informally in Jakarta at more than USD 750 million, a figure almost equivalent to Jakarta's local government budget (Munawar and Fellner, 2013). Little of this financial windfall lands in the hands of informal collectors or pickers, who work in unhealthy and dangerous conditions. Much could be done to improve their working conditions. Despite their vital contribution to reducing the waste stream by recycling, the legal status of this work is uncertain (Chaerul et al., 2014).

Formalisation of the informal sector in the collection and recycling of municipal solid waste could be considered. This could be undertaken by providing financial incentives, training and providing targeted investment to new start-ups in the solid waste sector. Bandung City's new recycling programme also aims to co-operate with the city's active waste pickers. The further restructuring of the informal sector could also help to address some of these technical and financial constraints. Such a plan would not only guarantee income streams to low-skilled urban migrants, but supply industry and manufacturers with recycled materials and limit the quantity of waste produced and disposed. **Waste Bank (*Bank Sampah*)** is organised at a local community level and has been introduced in many Indonesian cities, including Bandung. The Waste Banks aim to collect non-organic waste (plastic, bottles, etc.) for recycling and organic waste to compost from households. In return, the waste bank converts residents' waste deposits into cash, which is transferred to savings accounts (Salim, 2013). **Waste Ventures** in India is one of several models that could be evaluated to develop a framework suited to Bandung's specific MSW needs and sociocultural context (Box 2.7).

Promoting waste-to-energy technology to reduce over-reliance on landfills

Bandung's landfill sites are managed by West Java Province, which is currently closing the only operating dumpsite (*Sarimukti*), while preparing two new sites (Nambo and Legok Nangka). The Indonesian government provides capital investment only in landfill sites, while operational and maintenance costs are paid for by the provincial government. The increasing volume of MSW, stringent national budget, neighbourhoods' resistance and poor co-ordination across levels of government have made a new landfill project extremely difficult at any location within the BMA. For example, due to the urgent need for additional spaces for landfill, Bandung City has tried to rent vacant lands in the neighbouring municipalities, but the negotiations were evidently not easy. Consequently, Bandung City has faced huge challenges in dealing with its MSW (Tarigan et al., 2016).

Bandung City has recently drawn up an ambitious plan to introduce **bio-digesters** to generate gas and fertiliser supported by the city of Kawasaki, Japan, and reduce waste going to landfill. The high proportion of organic matter and wet waste in the BMA's waste stream (Figure 2.2) makes it worthwhile to use this technology instead of waste-to-energy incineration plants. Source separation is crucial to make this technology viable, and the city needs to inform the public of the benefits to be gained from recycling and separating garbage at home or in the workplace. Bandung's urban agriculture initiatives will also have their own set of green co-benefits. Because such decision on the selection of MSW technologies could have a large-scale impact on the volume of wastes to be landfilled, strong policy co-ordination is needed across the national, provincial and local governments in the BMA. The proposed metropolitan governing mechanism will also play a key role in this area (Chapter 4).

Figure 2.2. **Composition of landfilled waste**

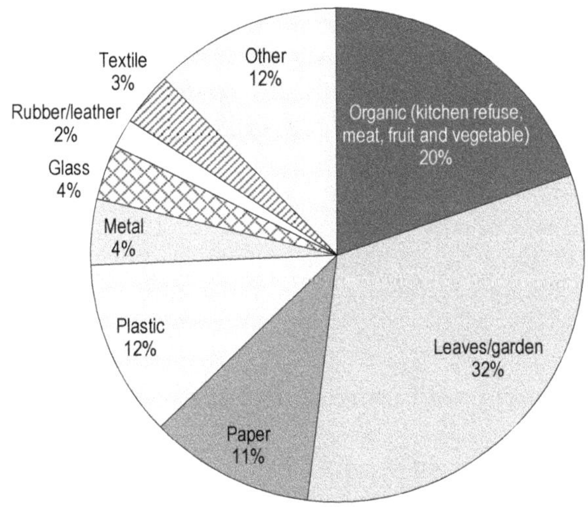

Source: Bandung City (2016), "Answers to the OECD case study questionnaire", internal document, unpublished.

Box 2.7. **Formalising the informal: Examining opportunities for municipal solid waste reduction**

In India, **Waste Ventures** provides door-to-door waste collection services and directly employs some of the poorest and most unskilled workers, whose livelihoods are put at risk by large-scale waste management operations that do not recycle sufficient waste or provide effective services. To date, the company has recruited 53 "pickers", who traditionally collect rubbish from roadsides and dump yards to earn their living. Providing employment and training, Waste Ventures equips them with skills and protective clothing so they can collect waste directly from the local households in the communities in which they work. The training gives them the skills to segregate waste on the spot into recyclable, organic and inert portions. Generally, 80% of the waste is processed for recycling, and by selling the by-products, additional revenue is generated from which Waste Ventures is able to pay the pickers a salary about twice that they would normally earn.

Waste Ventures also collaborates with households that are both customers and direct community stakeholders. Because the value of waste is higher the earlier it is segregated, Waste Ventures communicates to its customers on a regular basis the benefits of segregating waste before collection. The company distributes posters that illustrate best practice segregation methods, to raise awareness within the community. It also encourages late-adopters to take up its services, at educational events emphasising the environmental and public health risks of dumping or burning waste illegally. Both strategies directly target local residents in the communities in which the company works. Strategic preparation before services commence engages local government, in particular the municipal chairman, and ensures ongoing support. These public education campaigns can be measured in customer satisfaction, new skills and higher wages for the waste pickers and expansion of the waste collection services. Reducing urban pollution, its environmental impact and the risk this poses to public health contributes to a cleaner city.

Source: DECD (2014), "Skills Development by Green and Inclusive SMEs in India: Entrepreneurs' Approaches", www.enterprise-development.org/wp-content/uploads/DCED_GGWG_Skills_India_8_October_2014.pdf?id=2504 (accessed 12 October, 2014).

Leveraging investment in water and solid waste infrastructure to enhance urban resilience

Investment in the provision and management of essential urban services should be leveraged to build a more inclusive and resilient city. The BMA still faces annual flooding in the southern part of Bandung Regency and flash floods during heavy rainfall in several locations, such as Bandung Regency and Bandung City. Solid waste and wastewater management should be co-ordinated to effectively address the problem of flooding. Maintaining the BMA's drainage systems in flood prone areas in the BMA would be particularly important to minimise the risk of flooding. Several policies for rainwater harvesting have sought to increase the amount of rainwater managed on-site (see Section 2.4). Bandung is also located in an active earthquake zone that could destroy or seriously damage large sections of the sewage network or wastewater treatment plant. It would thus be advisable for the city to move toward a more distributed system to minimise the potential service disruption and serious repercussions on public health. Although less economically efficient than a unitary treatment plant system, a fail-safe approach would reduce the cost of repairs to get the system running again after a disaster (e.g. through flooding).

2.3. Investing in renewable energy and increasing energy efficiency

Investing in renewable energy in the BMA

As the energy sector is largely centrally managed by Indonesia's Ministry of Energy and Mineral Resources (MEMR), municipal governments in Indonesia have been little preoccupied with energy policies. Given the pressing need for increasing the energy supply, exploring renewable energy (RE) options is timely and relevant in promoting urban green growth. RE strategies can bring many other direct benefits to the city, such as more secured energy provision, reduced air pollution and reduced municipal solid waste going to landfills.

This is a timely moment for the BMA to explore RE. At the national level, the Indonesian government has demonstrated a commitment to promote the use of clean and RE. Indonesia's medium-term development plan 2015-2019 aims to increase the share of new and et al. sources and views this goal as one of its key development objectives. The National Energy Policy, as stated in the 2014 regulation No. 79, sets a target for new and RE to contribute 23% to the national energy primary mix in 2025 (Tharakan, 2015). This means that the installed RE capacity would need to increase by an ambitious 8.6 GW to 46 GW by 2025 to meet the target. The MEMR is managing a number of programmes to accelerate clean and RE development, although developing a RE sector is currently targeted especially for "under-developed, remote and rural areas" (London School of Economics, 2016b):

- At least 3.7 GW of the additional 35 GW the Indonesian government aims to bring online by 2019 will be generated using renewable sources, mainly hydropower (2.4 GW) and geothermal energy (1.2 GW). Nonetheless, the majority of this additional capacity will be sourced from coal-fired power plants (20 GW) and gas-fired projects (13 GW) (Enerdata, 2015).
- Enhancing the development of geothermal, bioenergy (municipal solid waste, biomass and biogas), hydro, wind- and solar-based power plants by putting feed-in tariffs (FiT) in place.

- Setting up a series of feed-in tariffs (FiT) to accelerate the development of RE.
- Providing an **Energy Security Fund** to accelerate the development and use of RE. The fund was developed throughout 2015, primarily as a means to support oil, but has also undertaken a development project related to RE sources. The legal framework for the fund was established in Law No. 30 of 2007 on Energy which stipulates that "development and utilisation of research output on new and RE shall be financed from state revenue from non-RE".
- Enhancing international co-operation in the development of RE technologies and energy conservation.
- Intensifying an energy-saving campaign as a massive national movement.

Although it does not appear that sub-national governments in Indonesia are taking an active role in achieving the national target, Bandung could take a leading role by introducing RE in its city operations. **Solar energy** presents a highly promising and practical option. The city government could support expansion of the solar industry by creating local demand. It could provide financing for solar collectors (for electricity and hot water) on large-scale residential and commercial buildings, for example. Greater use of solar energy for locally procured public goods, such as street lights, advertising billboards and lighting for public buildings, could also be promoted. Bandung has made substantial investments in high-tech industry, including solar panel manufacturing, which would provide the basis to develop these RE industries. The presence of the aerospace industry could also help the development of other renewable industries related to wind technology. Currently, there is no feed-in-tariff mechanism on wind energy, which creates relatively unfavourable market conditions for wind energy. The central government should co-ordinate with the private sector and consider introducing a feed-in-tariff mechanism for wind energy, so that such options become more competitive.

Another promising option for Bandung is waste-to-energy. Planning is under way to build a **waste-to-energy incinerator** in the BMA after a 2016 Presidential Decree (No. 18) which seeks to accelerate the development of a waste-based electricity power plant in Bandung, as well as Jakarta, Surabaya, Tangerang, Semarang, Surakarta and Makassar, to curtail the amount of waste sent to landfill (Wijaya, 2016). However, incinerators have been strongly resisted by the public in Bandung (Dipa, 2013). In addition, the city's waste contains a high proportion of organic matter and wet waste (Figure 2.2), in contrast to many OECD cities, where incinerator technology is used. Recently, consideration has been given to the introduction of pilot **bio-digesters**, as noted in the previous section. A thorough investigation of policy options, in particular in partnership with the Bandung Institute of Technology and other universities, should be explored to develop locally suitable technological solutions. Strong co-ordination among central, provincial and municipal governments, as well as engaging citizens and community groups in the discussion, would benefit Bandung in the long run.

Accelerating cities' action to curb increasing energy consumption

Curbing the increasing energy consumption is an urgent policy challenge for Indonesia, and cities have an important role to play in this. The National Energy General Plan (RUEN), promulgated in 2014, requests the formulation of energy plans at provincial and municipal levels of government in the future. The draft National Energy Conservation Master Plan (RIKEN) envisages a decline in energy intensity (the amount of energy required to produce one unit of GDP) of 1% per annum. To put this in historical perspective, in the period 2000-09, energy intensity fell by more than 1% each year, in both primary and final energy consumption. In 2010-11, however, the reduction in energy intensity was closer to 0.9% on both measures. Meeting the 1% target would require reduction in energy consumption of around 19.6% compared to business-as-usual scenario in 2025, and concerted efforts in different sectors are called for (Table 2.3).

Cities have a number of tools at their disposal to make their economic activities more energy efficient and contribute to national targets. As part of Bandung City's **low-carbon society initiative**, the administration has targeted a 20% reduction in energy use. The city has also taken the lead in energy conservation activities targeting government buildings, with as many as 30 different initiatives (IGES and City of Kawasaki, 2015). To scale up energy-efficiency measures, the city could use new urban development such as Teknopolis as a pilot project. Ambitious targets applying high standards of energy efficiency in buildings could be experimented with to guide private developers. Stockholm's experience with Hammarby Sjostad and Royal Seaport is one such example (OECD, 2013).

Cities can also collaborate with the private sector to reduce energy consumption from electric appliances. Bandung City has already mounted campaigns to encourage businesses and citizens to switch from incandescent lightbulbs to compact fluorescent lightbulbs (CFLs) or light-emitting diodes (LEDs). Subsidised or free CFLs and LEDs could be given away at public events to raise awareness, and businesses could support such campaigns, as they would benefit from increased sales. By collaborating with the private sector, these campaigns can easily be replicated by other cities in the BMA, not necessarily with formal co-ordination among the local governments. Cities could also co-ordinate with the private sector and launch regular information and educational campaigns to explain advantages of buying energy-efficient equipment, particularly air-conditioning, as well as household appliances, especially refrigerators and water heaters, which consume electricity continuously. This approach could also be combined with a **labelling programme** indicating the efficiency rating of a product, and the energy and financial savings to be gained annually. Neighbouring countries, such as Thailand, already have such programmes (OECD, 2015).

Curbing energy consumption from industry is equally important as it accounts for 40% of total energy consumption in Indonesia (Table 2.3), and cities also have many roles to play. City of Hai Phong, Viet Nam, has formulated Hai Phong Green Growth Strategy for Industry in 2020 (with the target for 2030), which is a vision for modernising industry and encourages energy-effective production. Based on this plan, the city will help the 120 casting companies that use coal to transform their manufacturing process. The city is already supporting firms in energy auditing and has provided consulting solutions to save energy. According to the Energy Conservation and Cleaner Production Centre of Hai Phong City (ECCH), the energy audit activities have saved a total of 50.3 million kWh per year, equivalent in monetary terms to more than USD 3 million and a reduction in carbon emissions of 42 000 tonnes per year (ECCH, 2014). Bandung City and other local governments in the BMA could send experts who provide technical advice to small- and medium-sized manufacturing firms and finance a part of the costs of high-energy-efficiency production facilities. Energy-efficient production systems can cut the cost per unit of production and increase price competitiveness, in addition to consuming less energy. Continuous investment to improve productivity and energy efficiency will help industries become more competitive and environmentally friendly (OECD, forthcoming).

Table 2.3. **Energy savings target in the Master Plan of National Energy Conservation**

Sector	Energy consumption by sector, 2012 (million BOE)	Potential for energy savings (%)	Target for potential energy savings, 2025 (%)
Industry	305 (39.7%)	10-30	17
Transport	311 (40.4%)	15-35	20
Household	92 (12%)	15-30	15
Commercial	34 (4.4%)	10-30	15
Others (farming, construction and mining)	26 (3.4%)	25	-

Source: Ministry of Energy and Mineral Resources (2012), *Master Plan of National Energy Conservation (RIKEN)*, Government of Indonesia, Jakarta. BOE stands for barrel of oil equivalent.

2.4. Promoting green buildings and combatting urban slums

The housing and building sectors present opportunities for green growth in Bandung, as many new housing and commercial developments will take place in the next decades. Given the share of energy consumption in the household and commercial sectors (Table 2.3), reducing energy consumption in buildings should be prioritised. Building policies are particularly relevant for local governments in most of Southeast Asian cities, as they typically have authority to control development by through building permits. In addition to reducing energy consumption, building policies could offer many other benefits to urban environment including reduced air pollution (due to improved heating systems), alleviating heat island effects, etc. Improving the quality of existing housing stocks is equally important for urban quality of life, given the fact that urban slums present an urgent challenge in Bandung and many other Southeast Asian cities.

Ensuring effective implementation of green building requirements

Bandung City has recently announced that a **green building certificate** will be a requirement, not simply a recommendation, as it was previously, for obtaining a city building permit (Izin Mendirikan Bangunan/IMB). This is intended to promote energy-efficiency savings and eco-friendly building in the city. A green building certificate will be issued for buildings that meet Bandung City's criteria as part of the green building regulations. It will incorporate all building types, such as residential, commercial, socio-cultural and religious buildings. However, during the first stage of implementation, the regulation will only be applied to new buildings with a floor area of more than 5 000 square metres and to the extension of existing buildings with an additional minimum floor area of 5 000 square metres. Smaller buildings will be included in the next phase of the programme. The green building requirements include electricity energy saving, using materials that reduce energy use, prioritising local resources, reducing the carbon footprint and planting vegetation for a greener city. The aim is to incorporate green architectural design principles into new developments. The city will not issue permits to development projects if they do not meet these green certification requirements.

While the policy holds promise, it has yet to be put into action, and progress must be made on the second phase for smaller buildings. To ensure effective implementation, it is crucial for Bandung City to ensure capacity for enforcement including on-site inspections. In addition, a number of supporting mechanisms for developers and building owners could be considered. For example, the city can co-operate with the private sector and provide training programmes on the green building requirements. The city can also provide support to local Energy Service Companies (ESCOs), which could allow building owners to improve building energy efficiency without upfront investment or special loans. This could create business opportunities for green services. The city could also consider financial incentives for developers who introduce RE and other environmental friendly building design. Finally, the policy should be scaled up beyond the municipal border. Bandung City and other local governments in the BMA should co-operate to extend the policy benefit to the entire BMA.

Managing rainwater on-site to make Bandung more resilient to floods

In 2014, Bandung received more than 2.3 metres of rainfall and averaged 19 rainy days per month. The area now at risk of flooding increased from 8 square kilometres in 1990 to 15 square kilometres in 2010 (Chapter 1), partly due to increasing impermeable built-up areas. In this regard, increasing ground water absorption through retention ponds and permeable surfaces in urban development should be considered to decrease flood risk and increase aquifer recharge, potentially allowing the city to meet its long-term water needs.

Rainwater harvesting is a viable option for remediating the limited drainage infrastructure put in place in Bandung. There are already several policies pertaining to rainwater harvesting that have sought to increase the amount of rainwater managed on-site, such as i) government regulation No. 33/2011 on national water resource management; ii) Ministry of Environment Decree No. 12/2009 on the use of rainwater; iii) Ministry of Public Works and Housing Decree No. 11/2014 on rainwater management in building and its land plot. In Bandung City, households are required to retain rainwater on-site, and in commercial buildings, this water is mandated to be used in toilets and gardens. Such initiative is complementary with water supply policies, as it alleviates the demand for piped water. The city should work together with the surrounding municipalities and encourage them to introduce similar initiatives. Bandung City's effort to increase water capture and storage and make cities more flood-resilient can only be effective if introduced across the BMA.

Upgrading urban slums and integrating them into the existing urban fabric

Although Indonesia has been combatting urban slums since its Kampung Improvement Program in the 1970s, the challenge persists and remains urgent. Current best practices advocated globally seek to enhance infrastructure in place where possible, since it is both economically unrealistic and socially destabilising to move communities to other parts of the city (Cities Alliance, 2016). It requires a comprehensive approach, especially co-ordinated with its urban resilience strategy, especially since many urban slums are in flood-prone areas.

The government of Indonesia aims to eradicate urban slums as part of the national medium-term development plan by 2019. It is anticipated this will be implemented through several national service delivery platforms. Ministry of National Development Planning (Bappenas, 2013) has launched a collaborative platform to revitalise slum settlements that clearly outlines the need for sectoral integration and central-local responsibility. Several slum alleviation programmes are being implemented, including a neighbourhood upgrading and shelter project (NUSP-2); a collaborative program for slum alleviation and self-help housing assistance.

As noted in Chapter 1, informal settlements in Bandung have increased, with at least 26 000 dwelling units and 120 000 inhabitants. They are dispersed in various slum spots within the city. More than 50% of the districts in Bandung City still contain slum areas, concentrated into densely populated neighbourhoods. The dwellings are mostly semi-permanent, improper and vulnerable to floods, because some locations are along the Cikapundung Riverbank that flows through the city (Tarigan et al., 2016).

Bandung City has made continuous effort in upgrading informal settlements and integrating them into the existing urban fabric. In 2014, the Ministry of Public Works and Housing selected Bandung for an Adiupaya Puritama award recognising its innovative programme to revitalise urban slum areas. For example, neighborhood development in Tamansari along riverside of Cikapundung is an example of sustainable residential development creating public space, providing public housing, and improving the riverbank and drainage systems. At least three slum revitalisation programmes are underway including: i) short-term provision of infrastructure, basic services and utilities for exceptionally dense populations at *Babakan Ciamis*; ii) medium-term slum improvement along the riverbanks at *Babakan Surabaya*; iii) long-term public apartment housing and area revitalisation without eviction at the *Babakan Siliwangi*, *Sadang Serang* and *Paldam* area in Jakarta Street. Despite the abovementioned efforts, little reduction to the slum areas has been detected in Bandung. The main reason behind this situation is the migration flow of unemployed individuals to Bandung. Individuals who have left slum areas are often replaced by newcomers from the neighbouring municipalities searching for better opportunities in the city, leaving the number of slum residents and areas unchanged (Tarigan et al., 2016). This demonstrates the strong need for a co-ordinated policy approach among the five local governments in the BMA.

Main policy recommendations

- Develop a metropolitan spatial land-use plan to guide urban development and a transport policy to co-ordinate urban mobility across the BMA. Conduct a BMA vulnerability and risk assessment and asset inventory in tandem with land use planning in the BMA, to enhance urban resilience.
- Encourage public-private partnerships and private sector finance to leverage public funds and accelerate transport infrastructure development.
- Incorporate the BMA's informal transport infrastructure (minibuses, motorcycle taxis, non-motorised pedicabs) as part of a feeder system. Increase their reliability and safety.
- Repair the installed monitoring stations in Bandung City and maintain them regularly. Provide more incentives to low-emission vehicles by expanding priority parking to private parking facilities. Extend Bandung's **Blue Skies programme** further in the BMA. Make all air pollution data publicly available in real time, using ICT.
- Consider including PM2.5 as one of the continuously monitored pollutants in the NAAQS. Set more aggressive ambient air quality standards than NAAQS for the BMA.
- Undertake BMA-wide water assessment to establish how much water is being extracted and from where, as well as when and by whom.
- Revise the water and solid waste tariff structures to reflect the true costs and reinvest the increased revenue in improving the service coverage. Introduce higher fees for customers who consume more water and generate more waste.
- Introduce online, real-time water-quality monitoring tools.
- Enhance source separation by formalising the work of the informal sector and introducing better working conditions to promote a decent workplace.
- Provide financing for solar collectors (for electricity and hot water) on large-scale residential and commercial buildings. Promote greater use of solar energy for locally procured public goods, such as street lights, advertising billboards and lighting for public buildings.
- Consider introducing a feed-in-tariff mechanism for wind energy.
- Use the national government's Energy Resilience Fund to finance the BMA's local energy policy study, when it becomes available.
- Incorporate principles of good architectural design to boost energy efficiency in the built environment.

Notes

1. *Bandung Berkebun* is a programme under *Indonesia Berkebun*. Started in 2011, *Indonesia Berkebun* has spread to 30 cities in Indonesia. This programme is run by communities in each city without government intervention.

2. Government Regulation No 41/1999 on Air Pollution Control stipulates general rules on ambient air quality, specifying standards for pollutants including suspended particulate matter (PM), Carbon Monoxide (CO), nitrogen oxides (NOx), Sulphur dioxide (SO2) among others.

3. West Java Province has set its air quality standard parameters (Peraturan Gubernur no 78 tahun 2013 tentang Petunjuk Pelaksanaan PERDA no 11/2006 tentang Pengendalian Pencemaran Udara), although they are at par with national standards (Government Regulation No 41/1999 on Air Pollution Control)

4. PDAM Tirtawening (*Kota Bandung*); PDAM Tirta Raharja (*Kota Cimahi, Kabupaten Bandung, Kabupaten Bandung Barat*) and PDAM Tirta Medal (*Kabupaten Sumedang*). In addition, PT. Tirta Gemah Ripah supplies untreated water to the PDAMs.

Bibliography

AFD (2014), "Finding Urban Transport Solutions: The Challenges of Financing and Integration of Networks", seminar held in Bandung on 23 June 2014.

Ardiwijaya, V. S., Soemardi, T. P., Suganda, E., & Temenggung, Y. A. (2014), "Bandung Urban Sprawl and Idle Land: Spatial Environmental Perspectives", in *APCBEE Procedia*, *10*, 208-213.

Asian Development Bank (2014), "Cleaning up Indonesia's Citarum Basin", www.adb.org/features/cleaning-indonesias-citarum-basin, (accessed 28 June 2016).

Bandung City (2016), "Answers to the OECD case study questionnaire", internal document, unpublished.

Bandung City (2014), *Low Carbon City Planning in Bandung*, www.iges.or.jp/isap/2014/PDF/pl11/pl11_07_ayu%20sukenjah.pdf (accessed 15 February, 2016).

Bappenas (2014) *National Medium Term Development Plan 2015-2019* (RPJMN 2015-2019), www.bappenas.go.id/files/7714/1557/5291/RT_RPJMN.PDF (accessed 13 October 2016)

Bappenas (2013), *National Action Plan for Climate Change Adaptation (RAN-API): Synthesis Report*, https://gc21.giz.de/ibt/var/app/wp342deP/1443/wp-content/uploads/filebase/programme-info/RAN-API_Synthesis_Report_2013.pdf.

Bangkok Metropolitan Administration (BMA) (2009), statistical Profile of Bangkok Metropolitan Administration 2009.

CAI-Asia (2010), *Clean Air Management Profile: Indonesia*, http://cleanairasia.org/wp-content/uploads/portal/files/documents/CAMP_Indonesia_-_2010_Edition.pdf (accessed 15 September 2016).

CAI-Asia (2009), *Indonesia Country Profile: Focus on Smaller Cities*, www.citiesforcleanair.org/documents/FINAL%20DRAFT%20Indonesia%20GTZ%20Country%20Profile%205Oct09.pdf (accessed 8 December 2015).

Chaerul, M., A.R. Fahruroji and T. Fujiwara (2014), "Recycling of plastic packaging waste in Bandung City, Indonesia", in *Cycles Waste Management*, Vol. 16(3), pp. 509-518.

Cities Alliance (2016), *About slum upgrading*, www.citiesalliance.org/About-slum-upgrading (accessed 30 March 2016).

Damanhuri, E., W. Handoko and T. Padmi (2014), "Municipal solid waste management in Indonesia", in A. Pariatamby and M. Tanaka (2014), *Municipal Solid Waste Management in Asia and the Pacific Islands*, Springer, Singapore, pp. 139-155.

Damanhuri, E. et al. (2009), "Evaluation of municipal solid waste flow in the Bandung metropolitan area, Indonesia", in *Journal of Material Cycles and Waste Management*, Vol. 11(3), pp. 270-276

Dipa, A. (2013), "Bandung residents reject garbage-based power", *Jakarta Post*, www.thejakartapost.com/news/2013/08/30/bandung-residents-reject-garbage-based-power.html (accessed 28 June 2016).

Dorodjatoen, A.M.H. (2009), "The emergence of Jakarta-Bandung Mega-Urban Region and Its future challenges", in *Jurnal Perencanaan Wilayah dan Kota*, Vol. 20(1), pp. 15-33.

ECCH (2014), "Activities of Hai Phong Energy Conservation and Cleaner Production Centre associated with green growth and sustainable development", Energy Conservation and Cleaner Production Centre, http://ecchaiphong.gov.vn/defaulte.aspx?pageid=newsdetailsE&catID=6&id=131 (accessed 12 June 2016).

Enerdata (2015), *Indonesia releases its 35 GW power capacity addition plan*, www.enerdata.net/enerdatauk/press-and-publication/energy-news-001/indonesia-releases-its-35-gw-power-capacity-addition-plan_32605.html (accessed 4 April 2016).

Firman, T. (2009), "Decentralization reform and local-government proliferation in Indonesia: Towards a fragmentation of regional development", in *Review of Urban and Regional Development Studies*, Vol. 21(2-3), pp. 143-157.

Maryati, S. and A.N.S. Humaira (2015), "Extending public water supply in peri-urban areas: Technical, engineering, economic, and environmental considerations", the fifth International Conference of Euro Asia Civil Engineering Forum (EACEF-5), http://dx.doi.org/10.1016/j.proeng.2015.11.035.

Maulani, A.M. (2015), *Qlue*, the app that keeps officials in Jakarta accountable. https://e27.co/qlue-the-app-that-keeps-officials-in-jakarta-accountable-20150922/ (Accessed 12 October, 2016).

GIZ (2002), *Sustainable Transport: A sourcebook for Policy-makers in Developing Cities Module 1b - Urban Transport Institutions*, www.sutp.org/files/contents/documents/resources/A_Sourcebook/SB1_Institutional-and-Policy-Orientation/GIZ_SUTP_SB1b_Urban-Transport-Institutions_EN.pdf (accessed 24 June 2016).

Global Commission on the Economy and Climate (2014), *Better Growth, Better Climate: The New Climate Economy Synthesis Report,* World Resources Institute (WRI), Washington, DC.

Government of Indonesia (2015), "Delivering green growth in Indonesia: A roadmap for policy, planning and investment decision makers", http://issuu.com/governmentofindonesia-gggigreengrow/docs/green_growth_roadmap_english (accessed 15 March 2016).

Government of Indonesia (2011), *Presidential regulation of the republic of Indonesia,* No. 61, http://forestclimatecenter.org/files/2011-09-20%20Presidential%20Regulation%20No%2061%20on%20The%20National%20Action%20Plan%20for%20Greenhouse%20Gas%20Emission%20Reduction.pdf.

Government of West Java (2015), *Government Planning Documents*, http://jabarprov.go.id/En/index.php/pages/id/87 (accessed 15 March 2016).

Gumilar, I. et al. (2013), "Land subsidence in Bandung Basin and its possible caused factors", in *Procedia Earth and Planetary Science*, Vol. 12, pp. 47-62.

Hudalah, D., H. Winarso and J. Woltjer (2010), "Planning by opportunity: An analysis of periurban environmental conflicts in Indonesia", *Environment and Planning*, Vol. 42(9), pp. 2 254-2 269.

IGES and City of Kawasaki (2015), *Feasibility Study on FY2014 Large-Scale JCM Project for Realizing Low-Carbon Development in Asia – Developing a Low-Carbon Society Under Collaboration between Bandung City and Kawasaki City,* www.env.go.jp/earth/coop/lowcarbon-asia/english/project/data/EN_IDN_2014_03.pdf.

Kasih, T. (2013a), "E-waste management in Indonesia (National Regulation Draft)", www.epa.gov/sites/production/files/2014-05/documents/indonesia.pdf.

Kasih, T. (2013b), "Indonesia country paper analysis", Fourth Regional 3R Forum in Asia, Ha Noi, Viet Nam, www.uncrd.or.jp/content/documents/Hanoi%203R%20Forum%20PS5_Indonesia.pdf.

Komarulzaman, A. (2013), "Global Development Network Report: Increasing access to water services in Bandung Regency: A policy simulation exercise", Center for Economics and Development Studies, http://118.139.174.39/admin/uploads/editor/files/GDN_PEM_report_cbps_bandung.pdf (accessed 5 October 2016).

KPPN (2014), *The National Medium Term Development Plan*, (RPJMN 2015-2019).

Krisnawati, L. (2008), *Implementation of Environmental Sustainable Transport, Indonesia*, www.unep.org/transport/pcfv/PDF/pathumbai_ESTinIndonesia.pdf (accessed 15 September 2016).

London School of Economics (2016a), *Law 30/2007 Regarding Energy,* www.lse.ac.uk/GranthamInstitute/law/law-302007-regarding-energy/ (accessed 15 March 2016).

London School of Economics (2016b), *National Medium Term Development Plan 2015-2019 (RPJMN 2015-2019)*, www.lse.ac.uk/GranthamInstitute/law/national-medium-term-development-plan-2015-2019-rpjmn-2015-2019/ (accessed 11 March 2016).

Lubis, H., M. Isnaeni and S. Nurjaya (2003), "Urban transport and land use planning toward the sustainable development (Case study of Bandung metropolitan area)", *Journal of the Eastern Asia Society for Transport Studies*, Vol. 5, pp. 1702-1717.

Ministry of Energy and Mineral Resources (2012), *Master Plan of National Energy Conservation (RIKEN)*, Government of Indonesia, Jakarta.

Ministry of Public Works (2008), *Slum Settlements Profile*, Directorate General of Human Settlement.

Moersidik, S.S. et al. (2015), "Project portfolio management to increase PDAM Tirtawening's Service Coverage Area", *Water Resources Management VIII,* Vol. 196(12), pp. 65-76.

MOT and GIZ (2014), Sustainable Urban Transport Programme Indonesia (Nama Sutri). http://transport-namas.org/wp-content/uploads/2014/11/Overview_IND_SUTRI-NAMA.pdf (Accessed 12 October, 2016).

Munawar, E. and J. Fellner (2013), "Injury time for Indonesia's landfills", https://waste-management-world.com/a/injury-time-for-indonesian-landfills (accessed February 2016).

Oanh, N. T. K. (ed.) (2012), *Integrated Air Quality Management: Asian Case Studies*, CRC Press.

OECD (forthcoming), *Green Growth in Hai Phong, Viet Nam,* OECD Publishing, Paris.

OECD (2015), *The Metropolitan Century: Understanding Urbanisation and its Consequences*, OECD Publishing, Paris, http://dx.doi.org/10.1787/9789264228733-en.

OECD (2013), *Green Growth in Cities*, OECD Publishing, Paris, DOI: http://dx.doi.org/10.1787/9789264195325-en

OECD (2012a), *Compact City Policies: A Comparative Assessment*, OECD Green Growth Studies, OECD Publishing, Paris, http://dx.doi.org/10.1787/9789264167865-en.

OECD (2012b), *OECD Reviews of Regulatory Reform: Indonesia 2012: Strengthening Co-ordination and Connecting Markets*, OECD Publishing, http://dx.doi.org/10.1787/9789264173637-en.

OECD (2001), *Extended Producer Responsibility, A Guidance Manual for Governments*, OECD Publishing, Paris, http://dx.doi.org/10.1787/9789264189867-en.

Parlina, I. (2016), "High speed train to integrate with LRT, break ground this month", *Jakarta Post*, www.thejakartapost.com/news/2016/01/05/high-speed-train-integrate-with-lrt-break-ground-month.html (accessed 30 March 2016).

Prihandrijanti, M. and M. Firdayati (2011), "Current situation and considerations of domestic wastewater treatment systems for big cities in Indonesia (Case study: Surabaya and Bandung)", in *Journal of Water Sustainability*, Vol. 1/2, pp. 97-104.

PT PLN (Persero) (undated), *Executive Summary of Electricity Supply Business Plan 2013-2022.*

Puspitasari, M.A. (2015), "Bandung named as least polluted metro area in Indonesia, Tempo.co" http://en.tempo.co/read/news/2015/12/18/206728810/Bandung-Named-as-Least-Polluted-Metro-Area-in-Indonesia (accessed 5 October 2016).

Salim, R. (2013), *Waste Not, Want Not: "Waste Banks" in Indonesia*, http://blogs.worldbank.org/eastasiapacific/waste-not-want-not-waste-banks-indonesia (accessed 28 June 2016).

Schneider, A. et al. (2015), "A new urban landscape in east-Southeast Asia, 2000-2010", in *Environmental Research Letters*, Vol. 10(3), http://dx.doi.org/10.1088/1748-9326/10/3/034002.

SNCF (2010), 'Integrated master plan for public transport system in metropolitan Bandung', in *Kerjasama Badan Perencanaan Daerah Jawa Barat dan Yayasan Lembaga Afiliasi dan Penelitian Industri*, unpublished report

Statistics East Java (2015), *East Java in Figures*. BPS – Statistics of Jawa Timur Province. Publication Number : 35000.1501

Statistics West Java (2011), *West Java in Figures 2012,* http://jabar.bps.go.id (accessed 19 October 2015).

Sukenjah A. (2014), "Air Pollution and Transportation Management in Bandung City, Indonesia", http://hls-esc.org/documents/5hlsesc/Bandung.pdf.

Syabri, I., Pradono and B.T. Soegijanto (2013), *Embracing Paratransit in Bandung Metropolitan Area, West Java, Indonesia: Case study prepared for Global Report on Human Settlements 2013*, http://unhabitat.org/wp-content/uploads/2013/06/GRHS.2013.Case_.Study_.Bandung.Indonesia.pdf (accessed 23 June 2016).

Tarigan, A.K.M. et al. (2016), "Bandung City Indonesia", in *Cities*, Vol. 50, pp. 100-110.

Tharakan, P. (2015), "ADB papers on Indonesia: Summary of Indonesia's energy sector assessment", www.adb.org/sites/default/files/publication/178039/ino-paper-09-2015.pdf (accessed 8 April 2016).

UCLG – CISDP (2010), Bandung, Indonesia: An inclusive approach to developing the future Bandung community, www.uclg-cisdp.org/sites/default/files/Bandung_2010_en_final.pdf.

UNDP (2015), "Converging development agendas: 'Nawa Cita', 'RPJMN', and SDGs", United Nations Development Programme, New York, www.id.undp.org/content/dam/indonesia/2015/doc/publication/ConvFinal-En.pdf (accessed 15 March 2016).

Wijaya, C.A. (2016), "Jakarta to develop first waste-to-energy plant in Sunter", *Jakarta Post*, www.thejakartapost.com/news/2016/02/13/jakarta-develop-first-waste-energy-plant-sunter.html (accessed 28 June 2016).

World Bank (2015), *Turning the Right Corner: Ensuring Development through a Low-Carbon Transport Sector* (WRI's new on-line series, *Moving Beyond Cars?*), World Bank, Washington, DC.

World Bank/GFDRR (2013a), *Building Resilience: Integrating Climate and Disaster Risk in Development*, World Bank, Washington, DC.

World Bank (2013b), *Planning, Connecting, and Financing Cities – Now, http://siteresources.worldbank.org/EXTSDNET/Resources/Urbanization-Planning-Connecting-Financing-2013.pdf* (accessed 5 October 2016).

Yachiyo Engineering (2012), "Feasibility Study for Promotion of International Infrastructure Projects in FY2011: Study on the High Speed Railway Project (Jakarta-Bandung Section), Republic of Indonesia", www.jetro.go.jp/ext_images/jetro/activities/contribution/oda/model_study/infra_system/pdf/h23_result03_en.pdf (accessed 14 March 2016).

Chapter 3

The smart city vision and green growth in Bandung

Chapter 3 examines opportunities offered by smart city tools, and in particular digital technologies, to encourage green growth in the Bandung Metropolitan Area (BMA). "Smart City Bandung" is one of the driving visions developed by the City of Bandung to enhance the attractiveness and performance of the city. In this context, it is worth exploring how existing smart city projects can support BMA's green growth and how they can be enhanced. This chapter is structured into the following five sections:

1) tailoring Bandung's smart city vision to green growth objectives

2) enhancing data and knowledge on green growth Bandung

3) enhancing transport and energy infrastructure's performance

4) making Bandung resilient to natural disaster risk

5) ensuring inclusive development.

This chapter benefited from discussions at the third OECD Knowledge-Sharing Workshop on Urban Green Growth in Dynamic Asia, held in Bandung on 7-8 May 2015 and supported by the OECD Knowledge Sharing Alliance.

Key findings

- **A smart city uses Information and Communication Technologies (ICT) and digital technologies to support** real-time data production, automated utility systems and digital communication tools, **with the objective of making critical urban infrastructure components and services more efficient and interconnected.** It is expected that the global market for smart urban services will reach USD 400 billion per year in 2020, and many cities have already adopted these new opportunities. Bandung is aiming to be a smart city, and the first digital technologies acquired or developed show the potential of the city to become a smart city model in the developing world. The city should continue its efforts and tailor its smart city vision and projects to urban green growth performance. Transport, energy, water, flood resilience and solid waste systems all offer opportunities.

- One of the most important applications of smart city tools is the **production, collection and diffusion of urban data and knowledge.** The Bandung Command Centre, the flagship smart city project, aims to collect data on the traffic and traffic violations, emergency needs and location of public utility vehicles. Citizens' input can be collected on a range of issues through social media, helping to identify problems more rapidly. Data collection through digital technology should, however, be undertaken within a more comprehensive framework tailored to green growth objectives. This is all the more important since the city has insufficient data to assess policy needs and track progress towards green growth.

- **Smart city initiatives in Bandung have mainly targeted the transport sector.** A third-generation bicycle-sharing programme, an electronic parking system, smart cards and traffic visualisation are being developed, although they are still in the pilot or design stage. Digital technologies could also be used to analyse traffic congestion and commuting flows. **The energy sector is not currently included in the smart city vision,** although it is one of the areas worldwide where digital technologies have been most developed. They can be particularly useful for reducing energy consumption and helping deploy renewable energy facilities.

- **Making Bandung resilient to disaster risk,** and in particular the frequent floods, is another potential application for smart city tools. While the command centre will be useful for co-ordinating emergency response teams in case of disaster, a more comprehensive smart resilient strategy is needed. Digital technologies can help make urban planning more resilient through flood simulation tools, to co-ordinate the response of infrastructure and to reach out to local communities and the private sector.

- **Finally, social inclusion** should also be a goal of smart city tools. Bandung has more than 120 000 slum dwellers, and 8% of its population lives below the poverty line. The smart city vision aims to improve education, health care, security, community outreach, Internet literacy and citizen engagement. It is not clear what role digital technologies will actually play and how they will target the urban poor, but it is critical not to leave low-income communities out of smart city projects. The local government should develop clear strategies for this, and ensure the input collection system from citizens is also used by the urban poor. This strategy could be coupled with the urban slum revitalisation programme started in 2014. Using smart technologies in consciousness-raising and education programmes can also help ensure that Bandung's smart city vision is inclusive.

3.1. Tailoring Bandung's smart city vision to green growth objectives

The expansion of ICT and digital technologies market for smart cities

"Smart City Bandung" is a new vision formulated by Bandung City Mayor Ridwan Kamil, based on growing worldwide interest and investment in this field. The smart city concept directly grew out of the sustainable cities movement and is widely considered to have the potential to transform cities. The label has often been used in inconsistent ways and may be confused with such concepts as the "digital city", "intelligent city" or "knowledge-based city", resulting in some confusion about its supposed added value. The common understanding of a smart city is a city monitored through information and communication technology (ICT) and digital technologies, the idea being that enhanced real-time data, automated utility systems and digital communication tools will increase the cost-effective provision of urban services (e.g. transport, energy, water) and governance. This report will consider the use of ICT and digital technologies as the main characteristic of a smart city. While the concept of the smart city is sometimes used to describe aspects such as innovation, creativity, entrepreneurship and good governance, these do not bring specific added value if they are not considered as technology, and are also less concrete in terms of investment and economic markets.

ICT and digital technologies supporting city management are at the heart of a global market in rapid expansion. The global market for smart urban (e.g. technology-supported) services is expected to reach an annual USD 400 billion in 2020, including USD 220 billion for the smart energy market alone, USD 156 billion for the smart transport market and USD 22 billion for the smart water market (Department of Business, Innovation and Skills [BIS], 2013). A few years ago, this market was almost non-existent. Another study estimates the revenues of the smart waste market at around USD 42 billion from 2014 to 2023.[1] These figures do not include other non-infrastructural use of smart city tools such as mobile applications, which are not necessarily urban-specific, and whose potential is likely to be higher than these figures suggest. The smart city market is mainly driven by global utility firms such as IBM, Cisco, Intel, Microsoft, Siemens and more recently Google, which increasingly partner with local governments to propose ICT and digital technology-based smart city services. At the same time, many cities are branding themselves as "smart cities" or willing to become worldwide leaders in smart city tool applications for urban management, such as Barcelona, Amsterdam and Singapore, which recently launched an ambitious smart city plan ("Smart Nation Singapore"). An increasing number of smart city events and competitions presenting awards to cities, such as Barcelona's Smart City Expo World Congress, are now held each year.

Bandung's smart city vision

Bandung's smart city vision was initially formulated within the Smart City Grand Design strategic document and was revised and incorporated into the 2013-2018 ICT Master Plan. The ICT Master Plan places great emphasis on e-government (including digital administration and public participation) and enhancing basic digital infrastructure (e.g. Internet connectivity and quality of servers) (City of Bandung, 2013). Bandung City's smart city approach is defined as: "the use of ICT to connect, monitor efficiently and effectively and control a variety of resources that exist within the city in order to maximise service to the citizens" (City of Bandung, 2015a). **"Teknopolis"**, a new city district planned to attract technology industries and businesses, is an important element of the smart city vision, although it is not explicitly specified in the ICT Master Plan (City of Bandung, 2015b). The **Bandung Command Centre** is the flagship project for achieving the smart city vision (Box 3.1). Initiated in early 2015, it is comparable to other existing intelligent operations centres in other cities. It consists of a digital control board collecting street-level data in a variety of sectors, whose intent is to improve city management (in terms of traffic, safety, flood and emergency response, and governance with citizens). It will collect information on traffic congestion and accidents through closed-circuit television (CCTV) cameras and Global Positioning System (GPS) devices installed in school buses, ambulances, public buses and garbage trucks. The information is automatically displayed on a digital screen in the Command Centre, allowing city staff to make informed decisions in the case of emergency or traffic violations. It also collects inputs from citizens on any concern they may raise about city management and functioning. The Centre is managed by the Information and Communication Agency of Bandung City, but each district of the municipality possesses a scaled-down version, as a strategy for local government to decentralise smart city actions.

Other smart city projects in Bandung City include the development of mobile applications in a range of fields (e.g. social networks, taxi service, amenities), in ad hoc infrastructure projects such as the development of electronic parking and third-generation bicycle-sharing systems, but also supporting strategies such as the introduction of digital tools in city schools and educational programmes focused on ICT. These projects are not always the sole responsibility of the City of Bandung; foreign companies (e.g. IBM) and local universities, in particular Bandung Institute of Technology (*Institute Teknologi Bandung,* ITB) have contributed to their development of smart city projects.

Box 3.1. **Bandung Command Centre**

The Bandung Command Centre is Bandung City's flagship project for its vision to become a smart city. It was initiated in early 2015, in partnership with IBM and Institut Teknologi Bandung (ITB), one of the top universities in Indonesia, and is similar to other existing command centres in Japan and Korea, aiming to improve public services. The centre consists of a digital control board that allows city staff to remotely monitor traffic and manage crisis situations in the city (in case of accidents, crime, etc.). Fifteen operators from the Bandung Telecommunication and Information Agency work permanently in the Command Centre, but it is also accessible to other city departments, such as fire brigades, police officers and transport agencies. It collects information from the street level to make informed decisions to improve such public services as ambulances, fire fighters and police intervention. The information is shown on a digital screen in the Command Centre. Two types of methods are used to collect street-level data:

- It uses CCTV cameras in streets and GPS tracking installed in school buses, ambulances, public buses and garbage trucks. For instance, a traffic violation could be easily spotted by the cameras and the information would be immediately transmitted to the Centre and appear on the screen.
- In addition to CCTV cameras and GPS tracking, social media is used by the Command Centre to collect information at street level. The Command Centre can be reached directly by citizens from Twitter, and they can transmit via their smartphones or computers any concerns they raise regarding safety and traffic (e.g. poor road conditions).

Box 3.1. **Bandung Command Centre** *(continued)*

Some of the information gathered by the Command Centre is also accessible to the public. The data collected through GPS devices in school buses can be viewed by the local population, so they can make an informed decision if a bus is held up by traffic. The Command Centre is being developed as a privileged interface of communication between governments and local communities in the city.

The Bandung Command Centre also works as a data bank, storing information on traffic violations, road infrastructure conditions, safety performance, disaster frequency and locations, etc. It makes it possible to visualise the types of problems most frequently encountered in every district of the city, and make a performance assessment for each of them. In future, smaller operations centres will be opened in each district, in a strategy to decentralise smart city tool management. The Centre is being developed in three stages, only the first of which has been completed, and it is expected to cover management of other sectors in future.

Identifying green growth benefits of Bandung's smart city vision and projects

Common applications of ICT-based smart city tools include the optimisation of transport, electricity and water networks, grassroots participation and government accountability. Opportunities to encourage urban green growth by increasing the competitiveness of urban utility systems and their environmental performance, and by enhancing governance, are therefore significant. It is not so far clear which development objectives the City of Bandung's smart city vision pursues, and to what extent the current and future projects, and the vision itself, aims to support green growth objectives. The ICT Master Plan lists environmental quality as an objective, but the document offers no clear details on how this can be achieved. The City of Bandung should thus identify more clearly, in the ICT Master Plan, the estimated development benefits of each smart city project, with an emphasis on environmental and economic performance. For instance, the Master Plan should identify benefits in terms of: environmental monitoring, reduction of air pollution, increase in green growth awareness among citizens, performance of utility systems with high environmental and economic dimensions (e.g. transport, energy, water, solid waste, land use) and look for potential direct economic benefits (e.g. employment and GDP output in smart city industries and services, green innovation).

To identify such benefits, the City of Bandung should explore how smart city tools can support its functioning and governance. Typically, smart city tools in the world have supported green growth in the following ways:

- They can be used to **produce new data or improve existing data** (qualitative or quantitative). Indeed, more and more technologies can now automatically and remotely measure, and therefore provide opportunities that did not necessarily exist before because of the lack of technical, human and financial capacities of governments – especially when it comes to producing real-time data. Existing initiatives tracking individual mobility patterns in public transport networks through smart card data are a good illustration. Data collected is commonly used to identify problems to help city staff make informed decisions. For instance, data on mobility patterns could help to adjust a public transport network. In New York City, fibre-optic sensors placed on the Brooklyn Bridge provide real-time information on the condition of this old infrastructure. In some cases, the purpose of data production is not to inform public authorities but citizens, such as smart water meters in households.

- In other cases, data production is not necessarily the objective of smart city tools. For instance, they have been largely used to effectively **ensure compliance** with new urban systems. One of the best examples is the third-generation bicycle-sharing system, found in many cities in the world (e.g. *Velib'* in Paris, France). The smart card used to unlock bikes at stations connects the bike in-use with the ID of the user, including its bank account. This has been successful in preventing theft, the main cause of failure of former bicycle-sharing systems.

- Smart city tools can provide new opportunities for local governments to **regulate urban systems**. A smart parking system in San Francisco automatically adjusts prices according to available parking space — to match demand. In Lyon, France, sensors placed in several locations of a new building block automatically adjust the heat or cold, depending on how many people are in the building. The electronic congestion toll of Singapore is an example of how smart city tools can help to regulate, ensure compliance and collect data at the same time.

- Smart city tools can help to increase **security**. A good example is the mobile banking system in Nairobi, Kenya, which has helped the urban poor secure their financial assets through mobile phones and save time to dedicate it to revenue-generating activities.

- Finally, smart city tools can be used to create digital and convenient **interfaces** between citizens and specific (public or private) services, or between citizens themselves. The objective is to facilitate access to some services or collective action. It is the case, for instance, of real-time data information about subway lines in Tokyo, of the Uber system, and of the online platform for car-sharing Blablacar, in France. A more extreme example is early warning systems, such as the one set up in Rio de Janeiro, Brazil.

The main smart city initiatives that have supported urban green growth in the world and in Bandung are listed in Table 3.1 below. The variety of projects shows the high potential for innovation in this field. In Bandung, environmental monitoring, improvement of transport systems, education and communication with citizens have been the most critical projects under development, centred around the Bandung Command Centre. However, the potential clearly exists to develop many more smart city projects in all sectors. This chapter will elaborate on three development and green growth strategies that can be supported through smart city tools: i) enhancing of data and knowledge on green growth in Bandung; ii) improving transport and energy systems; iii) ensuring resilience to natural disaster risks; and iv) ensuring social inclusion.

Finally, Bandung's smart city vision does not have a clear, comprehensive implementation and institutional framework. The contribution of Teknopolis to the smart city vision is still unclear and it is not explicitly referred to in the ICT Master Plan. Local government should try to institutionalise the smart city strategy, and incorporate it into development strategies, to ensure its viability. Chapter 4 will discuss this in detail.

Table 3.1. **Main smart city initiatives for green growth in the world and Bandung to date**

Sector	Main smart city initiatives in the world	Smart city initiatives in Bandung City
General environment	• Air pollution monitoring (Louisville, Kentucky; Chicago) • Greenhouse gas emissions sensors • Weather forecast sensors	• CO_2 and CO emissions sensors • Air pollution monitoring (in development)
Energy	• Smart electricity grid (China) • Street lighting regulation (Besançon) • Smart metering in households (Italy) • Home/Building Energy Management System (Lyon, Yokohama) • Renewable energy generation: smart shacks with solar charging for mobile phones (Stellenbosch, South Africa) • Resilience of the electricity grid (Maryland, Pennsylvania)	n.a.
Water	• Smart metering in households (Washington DC) • Flood management through simulation software (Paris, London, Rotterdam) • Control of water levels in canals and rivers (Bangkok) • Study of impact of sewer overflow due to storm water (Philadelphia) • Reduction of water leaks (Aquamatix; Leesburg, Virginia)	• Digitalisation of clean water disaster reports
Transport	• Smart card/integrated fare collection service (Paris) • Bicycle-sharing (Lyon) • Free-service car-sharing (Paris) • Online platform for car-sharing (France) • Smart parking system (San Francisco) • Electronic congestion toll (Singapore) • Smart taxi service (Uber) • Mapping informal public transport routes (Nairobi) • Maintenance of bridge conditions (NYC) • Traffic management centre (including forecast and distribution) • Emergency services	• Smart card (in development) • Bicycle-sharing (pilot stage in ITB) • Electronic parking system (in development) • Emergency services management
Solid waste	• Sensors in garbage trash to reduce waste consumption (Barcelona) • Smart bins (Groningen) • Improvement in the solid waste collection system (Maputo) • Smart optical sorters • Automated waste collection system (Singapore) • Radio Frequency Identification Swipe Card (South Korea) • Environmental reporting (London)	• GPS tracking of garbage trucks (10 currently operational, with plan to cover all garbage vehicle fleet)
Land-use	• Geographic information system (GIS) mapping • Cadastre improvement (Mexico)	n.a.
Governance	• Increase efficiency of social services (NYC) • Open Data (NYC, Chicago)	• Bandung Command Centre • Citizens' communication through social networks
Others	• Earthquake detection (Japan) • Early warning systems (Rio de Janeiro/Austin) • Resilience through safe banking (Nairobi) • Prediction of medical needs in case of disaster (USA) • Better identification of citizens in need of support in case of disaster (NYC) • Crowdsourcing post-disaster recovery (NYC) • E-learning • Electronic delivery to citizens • Video crime monitoring	• Video crime monitoring • Panic button • Digital classes • Digital education administration • Online administrative procedures (e.g. building permits, tax records)

3.2. Enhancing data and knowledge on green growth in Bandung through ICT

Bridging the data gap through smart city tools

A common problem faced by all fast-growing Asian cities, including Bandung, is a lack of data for assessing their performance on a variety of economic, social and environmental indicators. Data is often lacking on the current status and evolution of air quality and greenhouse gas (GHG) emissions, on commuting flows, on energy consumption, on the potential socio-economic damage a given natural disaster can generate, etc. This makes it difficult to evaluate the hazards citizens face daily (e.g. air quality and disasters), and obscures what policies are needed for urban green growth and planning public investment.

One of the smart city tools' main advantages is the production, collection and diffusion of such data. Modern technologies' capacity to measure and transmit complex information remotely in real time can help governments with technical, human and financial capacity issues to increase their understanding of their cities. Smart city devices can collect data in different ways: the smart device itself can collect the data, (as in smart meters for household water and electricity consumption), or, for example, mobile phones can offer data on mobility patterns through GPS. In Bangkok, sensors on water gates provide real-time data on water levels in the city, allowing the local government to control flood resilience infrastructure more efficiently. Smart devices can also help gather more legible information from existing data: for instance, with geographic information system (GIS) software mapping that uses information collected on the ground (Table 3.2).

Modern ICT can also collect crowdsourced data. This process allows citizens ("the crowd") to provide a service (or "outsource" a task) through data generated by the citizens (whether voluntarily or not). Digital technologies increasingly connect citizens directly (through smartphone applications, for instance) to the government and collect data on the ground on a specific issue. In 2011, Transport for London, the local transport agency that manages the London Underground system, collaborated with a group from the University College of London to study the Underground's daily operations. The study used data provided by commuters' Oyster smart cards to map the movement of users and congestion at major stations. The digital data visualisation allowed by the smart card system made it possible to model congestion patterns. This helped assess the impact of potential mechanical failures of trains on specific lines or other service failures.[2] In Louisville, Kentucky, the local government partnered with Propeller Health in 2012 to distribute 500 smart inhalers to asthmatic residents. As users activated the devices, data on time and location was sent to the patients' doctor and city officials. This helped generate a "heat map" of emergency asthma attacks. IBM analysis evaluated the data with a range of potential causes (e.g. air pollution, traffic congestion, pollen outbreak), identifying which areas were most at risk and needed intervention. The city now plans to install air quality sensors on bicycles to identify the routes most at risk for children.[3]

Crowdsourced data does not necessarily require intensive investment. Generally, open-source mobile applications can be used to collect data (while ensuring citizens' privacy) and have proven to be successful in developing countries. In Nairobi, the informal public transport network (*matatu*) was mapped using mobile phone data of *matatu* users (see Section 3 below).

Table 3.2.**Types of data collected by smart devices**

Sector	Type of data (general)	Data collected by Bandung
General environment	• Air pollution (sensor) • Greenhouse gas emissions (sensor) • Weather forecast (sensor)	• Humidity, temperature (sensor) • CO_2 and CO emissions (sensor) • Air pollution sensors (sensor, in development)
Energy	• Energy consumption in households (sensor) • Power outage in the electricity grid (smart meters)	n.a.
Water	• Water consumption in households (sensor) • Water quality (sensor) • Water levels and pressure in canals/rivers and pumps/gates (sensors) • Weather forecast modelling • Water flow patterns (simulation tools) • Water infrastructure condition (pipelines, dikes, gates, etc.) (sensors, GIS) • Sewer overflow (sensors) • Sea level rise map (GIS)	• Digitalisation of clean water disaster reports
Transport	• Transport users (smart cards) • Traffic situation (CCTV and sensors) • Parking congestion (electronic ticketing) • Automatic detection of traffic events (CCTV) • Traffic violations (radar) • Mobility patterns (mobile data) • Bridge and road condition (sensors, GIS, mobile apps, CCTV) • Real-time transport schedule (Tokyo)	• Traffic situation (CCTV) • Parking congestion • Detecting traffic events (CCTV)
Solid waste	• Amount of solid waste (sensors in garbage cans/trucks/landfills) • Location of garbage trucks (GPS) • Location of garbage in the city (mobile apps, sensors)	• Location of garbage trucks and efficiency of the collection system (GPS) • Digitalisation of reports on cleanliness
Land-use	• Vulnerability mapping (GIS software)	n.a.
Governance	• Data on citizens	• Tax records (e.g. parking tax)
Others	• Earthquake detection • Direct input from citizens (all sectors) • Mobile phone usage* • Ambulance turn-around times (computer software) • Emergency needs (mobile phones)	• Input from citizens • Emergency need (mobile application) • Digitalisation of land inventory and cadastral data

* This could reveal a need for public Wi-Fi spots, see:www.atelier.net/en/trends/articles/manycities-maps-urban-residents-daily-lives-produce-smarter-insights_437558?banner=1#ptlink.fid=23829&isc=1&did=bookmark.02e229d5ce938f892eaba8e6d031dffeb798e5b6&ctp=article.

Leveraging capacity to produce, collect, and monitor data in Bandung

Bandung City's smart city vision and the few projects being developed will help to enhance data production. The Bandung Command Centre works as a data bank collecting information on traffic violations and accidents through GPS and CCTV cameras installed in the streets and on public vehicles. The Centre also collects information directly from citizens on issues in the city (e.g. poor road conditions, crime). The Command Centre makes it possible to visualise the problems most frequently encountered in every district of the city, making a performance assessment for each. Smart devices in Bandung also monitor parking congestion (with the new electronic parking system) and the location of garbage trucks (Table 3.3). The ICT Master Plan also focuses on data collection, if not specifically for environmental and green growth purposes. The initiatives consist mainly of digitising existing, rather than producing new data (City of Bandung, 2013).

The Command Centre is a remarkable initiative for collecting data, but Bandung's smart city vision lacks comprehensive and clear objectives of data production on green growth. In many opportunity areas listed in Table 3.3, the Command Centre at this stage only slightly contributes to producing data. Energy sector data is not covered. The City of Bandung should ensure that its capacity to collect data is progressively reinforced through multiple smart devices. Efforts should be made not only to improve the data collected in the sectors covered by the Command Centre (e.g. traffic), but on air quality, water and energy consumption and solid waste generation, to provide city staff with an overview of Bandung's green growth performance. The city government can evaluate the smart data collection options listed in Table 3.3 and plan how each could be progressively developed over a given period, for instance, 10 years. The following sections will also list some of the most important data needed for green growth in Bandung that can be part of broader smart city initiatives. It will also be critical to centralise all the data collected in a single system, so knowledge is not fragmented in administrative silos. The Bandung Command Centre could easily undertake this task, since it collects data from a variety of sectors.

To complement this baseline data collection, the City of Bandung should undertake more complex research on urban dynamics, in partnership with local universities and data analysts from local technology companies such as IBM. Smart devices producing an increasing quantity of data on the interaction of urban systems will require advanced analytical capacity and could also be useful in informing the city government the next smart devices to develop. As a regional innovation and education hub, Bandung is well-suited to this task. Analytical research capacities could be developed through the creation of Teknopolis, the future state-of-the-art urban district in Gedebage, in the south-east of Bandung City. Details on the research capacity of the Teknopolis Master Plan are not well developed, or on how it will become a smart district, another objective of the Master Plan. The Transport Research Group (TRG) of the University of Southampton (UK) specialises in research on all aspects of the development and application of a wide range of Intelligent Transport Systems (ITS) (Department of Business, Innovation and Skills [BIS], 2013). Similarly, the Hong-Kong Transport Information System (TIS) is a centralised warehouse for the collection, processing and dissemination of data on transport. It also includes a Road Traffic Information Service for citizens, a Driving Route Search Service, and an e-Transport multi-modal portal (Department of Business, Innovation and Skills [BIS], 2013). Bandung could usefully study such initiatives in each green growth opportunity area. The Bandung Institute of Technology (ITB) could be a major partner for smart city research groups.

To encourage research on the city, and develop smart devices for collecting data, Bandung could create an open data website not only for city staff but researchers, citizens and the private sector. New York City's Open Data website, for instance, offers access to dozens of datasets in a range of sectors, such as GIS maps of building footprints, maps projecting the impacts of sea level rise, street tree census, time-series water consumption data, bicycle parking, demographic statistics, etc.[4] Such digital tools facilitate access to data and spur innovation and research. Bandung could adopt a similar strategy to make data more easily accessible to companies and universities and broaden the use of smart city tools in diffusing knowledge. This would support the city's strategies for smart open government and transparency, and reinforce public trust.

Another initiative Bandung City could adopt would be to collect best community practices and ideas/proposals that relate to green growth, using the Command Centre as a central database. The small Command Centres planned for each of the city's districts could be used as the primary collector of such information, relaying them to the mayor and his administration. **A mobile "green growth" application** could be used as an interface between citizens and the Command Centres. Inputs could also be directly uploaded in the centres by district officers. Along these lines, the **OECD's Observatory for Public Sector Innovation (OPSI)**, accessible online,[5] collects and analyses examples and shared experiences of public sector innovation, providing practical advice on how to make innovations work. Users interested in public sector innovation can access information on innovations, share their own experiences and collaborate with other users directly through the online platform. The Command Centres could replicate such a mechanism, focusing on community practices and green growth. This would help leverage existing practices, helping to avoid policies with poor prospects of success.

3.3. Enhancing the performance of green growth-related infrastructure

While data production is a significant achievement, smart city projects also aim to improve the management of urban infrastructure. The transport and energy sectors are the main beneficiaries of modern ICT. Many of the existing tools aim to alleviate traffic congestion, and in the energy sector, principally target energy efficiency and renewable energy development (although renewable energy (RE) is not always considered a smart city application). Bandung's efforts in this domain are not well-developed but have great potential. The key will be to identify the right tools for transport and energy management while contributing to urban green growth.

Smart transport opportunities for Bandung

Congestion, air pollution and GHG emissions from the growing numbers of private motorised vehicles are the two most important green growth challenges faced by Bandung City, along with solid waste management (see Chapters 1 and 2). Smart city tools for transport have great potential for urban green growth. The local government has already launched some ICT initiatives including:

- **An electronic parking ticketing system** is planned to rationalise the city's parking system. Electronic machines at the entrance of each parking area will ensure compliance with parking rules (time limits, payment). The aim is to discourage car use and raise municipal revenues; the local government is also considering raising parking taxes.
- **A smart card** has been created to ease citizens' access to services including public transport. It is currently only used for the parking system, so users can pay more easily (City of Bandung, 2015b). The card should become particularly useful when the new mass transit networks (cable cars, monorail) become operational, as it will be used to access several transport modes.
- **Smartphone applications** have been developed to give citizens better information on public transport routes and schedules (*angkot*, buses, taxis). These digital tools estimate travel time, give fares and suggest the optimal choice of transport mode. They have been developed with the help of Telkom Indonesia (PT Telekomunikasi Indonesia), the largest telecommunications services company in the country, which hopes to extend them across Indonesia.

The City of Bandung should continue its efforts to improve its transport system, which may not be sufficiently ambitious to solve the city's congestion and air pollution. Bandung's bicycle-sharing programme could be upgraded to a third-generation system like those that have been installed in many cities of the world since 2007 (e.g. Paris, Hangzhou). Its bicycle sharing still works on a cash payment basis,[6] which reduces its convenience. As noted, third-generation systems use ICT to digitally connect bike users to their ID and bank accounts, docking them electronically in case of theft or infringement of rules. This could significantly increase the impact of the programme, as it has in Paris and other cities.

Commuting flows could be more thoroughly analysed to evaluate potential transport needs. One study suggests that Bandung has a significant origin-destination mismatch, resulting in long and complex individual travel patterns (Tarigan et al., 2015). In examining the efficiency of the *angkot* system, currently the top paratransit option, city staff could take inspiration from Nairobi, Kenya, where a team of international and local analysts studied data from users' mobile and GPS units to map the city's 130 *matutu* routes (similar to the *angkot* system), identifying stops and congestion. The results were shown in a digital map accessible to citizens online.[7] The City of Bandung could undertake a similar project, not to map the 38 *angkot* routes but to study congestion, the location of stops, etc., to evaluate the network's efficiency. This could show whether some lines are underused and reveal commuting flows, which could help plan future transit network development. Alternatively, GPS devices could be placed in each *angkot* vehicle. Another measure to encourage the use of this mode of transport rather than private cars and motorcycles would be to set up free Wi-Fi hotspots in *angkot* vehicles, as an effective way to encourage the use of public transport, and to attract younger riders.

Traffic prediction is an increasingly popular smart transport initiative. In many cities, events are recorded in real time by cameras and sensors are analysed through modern technologies. In Singapore, the Land Transport Authority (LTA) has collaborated with IBM on a scheme to predict traffic flow in the Central Business District, using real-time traffic inputs and historic traffic data. The speed and volume results were highly accurate, and will help LTA's traffic controllers better anticipate and manage traffic (Department of Business, Innovation and Skills [BIS], 2013). Opportunities for a similar system exist at the Bandung Command Centre, which already manages some traffic information.

The local government should also continue to improve the parking and garage management system. Singapore's LTA launched the Parking Guidance System (PGS) in 2008 in response to rising congestion. The PGS collects data on the parking spaces available at various car parks, and displays the collated data on nearly 30 electronic information panels across the city. It allows car users to view parking options on the road, and reduce the time and fuel costs of parking in the most congested areas of the city (C40 Cities and Siemens, 2013). In San Francisco, a more ambitious project was initiated: information on occupancy from all the parking areas in the city is collected, centralised and integrated through digital technologies. This information is used to adjust the parking fees according to occupancy and availability in other parking areas, to balance parking throughout the city and alleviate congestion (Box 3.2).

An innovative practice for long-distance trips is a voluntary private car-sharing platform. In France, the Blablacar start-up website allows the owners of private cars to organise carpooling, to pool the cost of tolls and fuel. This can result in prices competitive with other transport modes, such as trains or air travel.[8] In addition, it could alleviate congestion on some long-distance commuting flows, reducing air pollution and GHG emissions. A congestion toll could also be set up, as in Jakarta, London and Singapore, using electronic devices to ensure compliance.

In the longer term, Bandung could develop more ambitious options to improve mobility. In addition to the bicycle-sharing system, an electric car-sharing system could be developed by the local government, relevant international partners and local stakeholders (e.g. Telkom and ITB, since they could provide local technical support). The

City of Paris, for example, set up the *Autolib'* programme jointly with *Bolloré* (an international French transport and logistics industrial group) in 2011. By July 2015, more than 3 300 vehicles and 975 stations were operational. The principles are very similar to the system of the third-generation bicycle-sharing: a user can borrow one of the electric cars parked in specific stations in the city, and return it to another station. The sustainability of the system is ensured by the digital identification that tracks the user, while an electronic deposit is linked to the user's digital ID. If a user misbehaves, the system will be informed and can automatically take action. The electric car-sharing system reduces the need for private cars in the city and avoids parking issues.

Box 3.2. **Smart parking management in San Francisco**

The San Francisco Municipal Transport Authority (SFMTA) SF*park* project uses new technologies and policies to improve parking in the city. The project was largely funded by the US Department of Transport, which provided 80% (USD 19.8 million) of the programme's total cost of USD 24.8 million. The project involved 6 000 metered on-street parking spaces (about one-quarter of the city's total supply) and 12 250 parking spaces in 14 city-operated garages (75% of the spaces managed by SFMTA). Around 11 700 parking sensors were deployed, along with 300 repeaters and gateways. The key strategic initiatives in SF*park* included:

- real-time parking availability information to make it easier to find a parking space
- demand-responsive pricing to create parking availability
- longer time limits at parking meters to make parking more convenient
- meters that make it easy to pay by credit card and other forms of payment
- garage facility upgrades to make garages more convenient.

The main principle of SF*park* is to use smart pricing so that drivers can quickly find open spaces. To help achieve the right level of parking availability, SF*park* periodically adjusts meter and garage pricing up and down to match demand. Demand-responsive pricing encourages drivers to park in underused areas and garages, reducing demand in overused areas. According to the SF*park* Pilot Project Evaluation, the amount of time that the target parking occupancy (60% to 80%) was achieved increased by 31% in pilot areas, compared to a 6% increase in control areas. In so-called high payment (HP) compliance pilot areas (where people tend to pay the meter most of the time), the 60% to 80% target occupancy rate nearly doubled. The amount of time that blocks were too full to find parking decreased 16% in pilot areas, while increasing 51% in control areas. HP zones saw a 45% decrease. SF*park* maintained consistent parking availability while increasing use of SF*park* garages. Use of these facilities grew by 11%, far exceeding that of non-SF*park* garages.

An estimated reduction in GHG emissions of 30% was realised, from 7 metric tonnes per day to 4.9 tonnes per day in the pilot areas. Vehicle miles driven also decreased by 30% (compared to a 6% decrease in the control areas), and traffic volumes fell 8%.

In addition to the parking information map available on the SFpark.org homepage, information on parking availability is distributed via a free SF*park* iPhone app, Android app and the region's 511 phone system.

Source: Woods, E. (2014), "Results in for San Francisco's Parking Experiment", Navigant Research Blog, www.navigantresearch.com/blog/results-in-for-san-franciscos-parking-experiment (accessed 30 August 2016); SF*park* (n.d.), SF*park* website http://sfpark.org/about-the-project/ (accessed 30 August 2016).

Smart energy opportunities for Bandung

At the local level, the energy sector has great potential for green growth. Unlike transport and solid waste, this sector is not considered a top priority by citizens, since the negative externalities of poor energy management (i.e. high GHG emissions) do not visibly and immediately impact citizens. However, reductions in GHG emissions and savings from higher energy efficiency should not be neglected. Digital technologies can support energy efficiency and consumption. It is an area where digital technologies have been most developed. These tools could help the Bandung City implement its green building regulations (see Chapter 2). Developing smart city tools in this sector would help align the city's strategy with national objectives: the 2011 National Action Plan for Greenhouse Gas Emissions Reductions (RAN-GRK) identifies energy management, including energy efficiency and energy conservation, as a critical pillar for implementation (RAN-GRK targets 17% energy savings in the industrial sector, 15% in the commercial sector and 15% in the residential sector). RAN-GRK is being reviewed by Bappenas for the period 2014-19. The review of RAN-GRK is conducted in accordance with Indonesia's Intended Nationally Determined Contributions (INDCs) as part of its contribution to the global community under the United Nations Framework Convention on Climate Change (UNFCCC).

The City of Bandung should look for opportunities to reduce energy consumption at the street level. Some cities have installed digital systems that remotely control street lighting depending on street traffic. In Besançon, France, the local government has set up a smart street lighting system (LUBIO) in co-operation with Schneider Electric. The objectives were to adjust street lighting during daylight hours, when lighting was not necessary, and to reduce the intensity of street lightning remotely between 10 p.m. and 6 a.m., when needs are lower. Street lights were also replaced by more efficient light bulbs. The project was mainly financed by the energy savings realised under this smart system, estimated at 42% to 50%.[9] In Bogor, Indonesia, the French Development Agency (AFD) is undertaking a smart street lighting project. Smart command of the lighting system could be integrated with the Bandung Command Centre, and financed at least in part through the Street Lighting Tax (PPJ), collected by the State Electricity Company Perusahaan Listrik Negara (PLN) as a percentage of customers' electricity bills and transferred to the local governments. The revenue is usually used to finance the installation and maintenance of lighting systems. Digital technologies can also realise energy savings at the household level. The French energy company EDF is developing home energy monitors that show past and present energy consumption and how much it costs, allowing users to make informed decisions about their energy use. Such smart metering systems (not only for electricity but water) will, however, require a national reform of PLN's tariff systems. Electricity pricing in Indonesia is based on installed capacity and not household consumption, which prevents real-time dynamic pricing.

Technologies can also support the production of RE. In Stellenbosch, a small town outside Cape Town, South Africa, an initiative has encouraged the construction of "smart shacks", easy-to-assemble fire-proof homes that produce off-grid energy through rooftop solar panels.[10] This could be particularly useful in Bandung's informal settlements. The City of Bandung could also start considering more ambitious and time-consuming projects for smart energy management, combining energy efficiency and RE smart tools. The City of Lyon has redeveloped an old industrial area into a new eco-district known as Confluence. In this new district, three buildings have been developed as positive-energy buildings. Combining smart architectural design, ICT sensors and energy-efficient technology, these buildings can produce more energy than they consume (Box 3.3).

Box 3.3. **Energy-positive eco-district in Lyon, France**

The new eco-district of Lyon Confluence, a 1.5 square kilometres project initiated in 2001, doubles the area of the urban peninsula between the rivers Rhone and Saone, in the commercial heart of Lyon. One of its objectives is to produce no more CO_2 in 2020 than in 2000, despite the construction of 1 million square metres of new buildings. Within the new eco-district, three buildings designed by the architect Kengo Kuma are connected through a common energy management system, whose aim is to produce more energy than it consumes. These buildings are named "Hikari" ("light" in Japanese). They are the first "positive-energy" building block in Europe, at a size of 12 800 square metres (similar projects were previously limited to the scale of an individual building). The project involved a partnership between Bouygues, NEDO (the Japanese public agency promoting environmental and industrial technologies and renewable energy) and Toshiba.

The concept underlying *Hikari* is a pooling of needs and resources. The three buildings, a mix of offices, housing and commercial areas, communicate with each other and distribute energy according to the needs of each building. Excess energy is stored and used in peak hours, thanks to a fuel cell, taking advantage of the fact that offices are empty at night, while housing occupancy is high. Energy produced in offices on non-working days can be reinjected into the apartments. In the basement, a central brain drives the system overall.

Energy is produced by solar panels on the roof and balconies of the 42 apartments. It is completed by a rapeseed oil fuel co-generator. The cooling requirements of the offices and shops are covered by an "absorption chiller" that produces ice water from the heat created by the co-generator and the cold from the water table. A geothermal system also contributes to cooling by drawing in the cool waters of the Saône. *Hikari* consumes 50% less than the standards of the current thermal regulations and produces a higher amount of energy than its consumption, about 0.2%. The building's architecture is also innovative: the building envelope adapts to the path of the sun, absorbs and controls the light radiation and energy intake. Large cuts carve the glass facades, wood, aluminium and stone to make the most of natural light inside the buildings.

ICT are at the heart of *Hikari*'s system. The buildings are full of sensors that measure temperature and CO_2, but also detect the presence of people in the rooms, monitor ventilation, lighting, etc. They record a series of parameters that allow the central "brain" to regulate the production of heat and cold in real time. Continuously calculating consumption, the system informs users of the performance of their office or home and the entire building. Each household is equipped with an energy-tracking tablet adjusting the temperature of an apartment to residents' needs.

The cost of housing in *Hikari* is high, the equivalent of housing in the most beautiful areas in Lyon. All housing units have been sold, however, partly because the new owners were attracted by the possibility of controlling and regulating their energy consumption.

Source: Le Monde (2015), "A Lyon, Hikari, le premier îlot urbain à énergie positive", www.lemonde.fr/planete/article/2015/09/17/a-lyon-hikari-le-premier-ilot-mixte-intelligent-a-energie-positive_4761665_3244.html (accessed 02 October 2015).

3.4. Making Bandung resilient to natural disaster through smart city tools

Urban resilience to natural disaster risks is a critical condition for ensuring long-term green growth in many Asian cities. The 2011 mega flood that hit the Bangkok Metropolitan Region and other parts of Thailand is reported to have been among the costliest natural disasters since the 1980s, resulting in losses in the global supply chain of USD 44.2 billion and significantly slowing Thailand's economic growth in the months after the floods (OECD, 2013). In the City of Bangkok alone, the damages reached USD 9.3 billion. Bandung is also routinely affected by floods, and although such events have not affected the city with comparable intensity, it must prepare for potential shocks, since climate change involves uncertainty about the occurrence and intensity of floods, hurricanes, etc. Floods, earthquakes, fires and landslides are the most common disasters in Bandung. Smart city tools can be an effective means to make Bandung more resilient to disaster risk. While the Command Centre will be useful for co-ordinating the action of emergency response teams, developing other smart initiatives could allow the city to tackle the lack of resilience more comprehensively, by enhancing urban planning, infrastructure management and the effectiveness of local community and private sector engagement before, during and after a disaster.

Mapping vulnerable urban areas through digital technologies

While Bandung has not been affected by a major natural disaster in recent years, the lack of comprehensive strategic planning for urban resilience suggests that the city is nevertheless vulnerable to potential threats. Lack of urban planning can make an important factor in such vulnerability. Other cities already use digital tools to inform urban planning decisions. This represents an opportunity for Bandung to promote its smart city vision while ensuring urban resilience.

One of the most common digital tools used for this purpose is geographic information system (GIS) mapping. For floods, it consists in overlaying different types of GIS maps (e.g. topography, rivers, infrastructure, land use) to identify populations physically exposed to floods and earthquakes. The City of Bandung has not developed a hazard map to identify such populations and take action to reduce the potential human and economic damages of floods or earthquakes. The City of Kumamoto, Japan, has set up a smart tool initiative to obtain data directly from local residents to inform hazard maps. Citizens can directly access a digital base map provided by the municipality and add information about the vulnerability of their own house.[11] A common obstacle shared by many developing cities is the difficulty of collecting data (e.g. the number and size of households) in the poorest areas of the city. These tend to be located in sites such as riverbanks that are vulnerable to floods or earthquakes. In Bandung, adopting a strategy like the City of Kumamoto's will require investments to engage the poorest communities, through ICT training, for instance. Recent projects in the developing world have shown this can be achieved. In Dar es Salaam, Tanzania, locally trained students equipped with tablets have roamed the slums and mapped them for the first time (see Section 3.5). Similar processes could be used to create vulnerability maps in Bandung.

GIS hazard maps are relatively static and do not allow for the dynamic impact of a disaster such as a flood. The City of Bandung could also consider complementary types of digital technologies to inform urban resilience. The Public Utilities Board of Singapore, for instance, is using a simulation software called 3Di[12] that not only measures real-time water levels in different places in the city, but analyses, models and forecasts potential water flows in case of flash floods. Such a system can help identify catchment-wide solutions to reduce the speed of surface run-off in urban areas, to identify which areas to monitor and to decide pro-actively on appropriate land-use and infrastructure strategies (Public Utilities Board of Singapore, 2013). Such technology should be distributed to the local authorities in the West Java Province and to the provincial government, to assess region-wide water flows and encourage a comprehensive regional approach. The software may help identify weaknesses in other local areas that are risk factors for Bandung. Another recently developed tool is the Aqueduct Global Flood Analyzer developed by the World Resources Institute (WRI), Deltares, the Institute for Environmental Studies, Utrecht University and the Netherlands Environmental Assessment Agency. This estimates the human and economic damages of floods, based on different scenarios and geographical scales. It estimates, for instance, that even in a scenario of moderate climate change and continuation of current socio-economic development trends, and assuming a 50-year infrastructure protection, the West Java State could suffer damages of more than USD 500 million by 2030, affecting more than 47 000 people. West Java is the smallest unit of analysis and does not produce detailed information on the City of Bandung or its metropolitan area. The local government could consider using such tool to produce data at the local level.

Evaluating the impact of disasters on urban infrastructure

Smart city tools for resilient urban infrastructure are also being developed. Many other cities rely on sensors to monitor water levels and seismic activities. In Southeast Asia, the Bangkok Metropolitan Administration created a Flood Control Centre (FCC) in 1990 using computer technology to systematically manage flood protection. The FCC monitors and collects hydrological data (rainfall and water level), data on the condition of operation facilities, on flood damage and water quality, using an online system. This helps city staff remotely monitor water gates and pumps of the main canals and the river of the city, so they can act quickly and efficiently in case of floods (OECD, 2015). The FCC has room for improvement (such as adding more elaborate analytical capacity, such as the 3Di tool), but could be used as a starting point for smart resilient infrastructure in the City of Bandung. A complementary initiative the City of Bandung could take to monitor river and canal management is to assess the conditions of waterway infrastructure, such as gates. In Santa Clara County, California, district field staff was sent to the field to catalogue the condition of such infrastructure, with the help of GIS tablets. Digitising information made it more easily accessible to the city government.[13] Bandung also needs to assess the quality of river and canal water, which could become a major health hazard in floods. Sensors could be placed in strategic locations to send data to the Bandung Command Centre for on-screen visualisation.

A critical issue undermining green growth and urban resilience in Bandung is poor solid waste management. Uncollected and untreated solid waste can become a severe health hazard when a flood occurs and ICT opportunities could be explored to improve its management. A smartphone application could be created to report uncollected solid waste in the city, so that citizens could alert a special waste management unit of the City of Bandung. The Bandung Command Centre could easily collect such input from citizens, as it already does through Twitter. The city government would need to conduct public programmes to communicate the benefits of such application. In Maputo, Mozambique, a World Bank initiative uses crowdsourcing via mobile applications to gather input from the citizens and waste collectors about the location of garbage in the city. This has reduced dumping in inappropriate sites.[14] The Love Clean London initiative similarly allows citizens to report environmental problems such as poor waste storage, through texts, uploaded photographs and reports submitted through a free application. The reports can be rendered in graphic form on a map by the city government to show where clean-up is most needed (Department of Business, Innovation and Skills [BIS], 2013). The GPS devices that have already been installed on garbage trucks sending data to the Bandung Command Centre could be an opportunity to digitally map the location of garbage bins where trucks stop, and to study the efficiency of the collection process. A total of 202 garbage trucks in the city directly collect waste from households on an irregular basis (Tarigan et al., 2015). In the longer term, smart city tools could be more ambitious. In the City of Barcelona, garbage bins are equipped with sensors that send alerts to residents when they are full, to encourage them to minimise waste and recycle. In Groningen, the Netherlands, smart bins automatically send text messages to the city government when they are full. This reduces labour and petrol costs – and thus the environmental impact – by sending garbage trucks only to bins that need emptying (Department of Business, Innovation and Skills [BIS], 2013). Similar technologies could be used in temporary site stations.

ICT could also provide a better understanding of the performance of infrastructure. Tools could be developed to grasp the complexity of the impact of a natural disaster on urban infrastructure, and how to co-ordinate management of all types of infrastructure (transport, energy, water, etc.) when a disaster occurs. Rio de Janeiro's Operations Centre is one innovative initiative, developed in partnership with IBM. The Operations Centre, a citywide data system, gathers information on different types of urban infrastructure. It collates all data, input online, to identify trends and complex impacts of potential disasters, such as floods, fires and landslides (Box 3.4). This can help decision makers select the most appropriate action and identify which urban areas need support. The City of Bandung could consider developing such technology, and integrating it into the Bandung Command Centre. This could extend the disaster response capacities of the current centre, which are mostly limited to police and fire brigade action.

Box 3.4. **Rio de Janeiro's Operations Centre**

In 2012, the city government of Rio de Janeiro and IBM signed an agreement to build a public information management centre for the city. Other partners engaged in the construction of this Centre are Cisco, Cyrela, Facilities, Malwee, Oi and Samsung. The facility is built on the principle that only by considering and co-ordinating the man-made and natural systems of a city holistically can municipal leaders manage the complexities of a large, modern city.

The Rio Operations Centre in Cidade Nova gathers information from more than 30 government departments and public agencies in the municipality to improve city safety and responsiveness to incidents such as flash floods and landslides. Its mission is to consolidate data from various urban systems for real-time visualisation, monitoring and analysis, giving operations managers a comprehensive picture of what is happening in the city at any time. Representatives of the various departments in the operations centre can look at live videos of city streets and facilities or graphic representations of data feeds, and make group decisions. The system was initially designed to forecast floods and related emergencies, but it can be extended to any event occurring in the city, such as sports events or a traffic accident. The aim is for the centre to integrate more city departments and information. The administration has already been developing routine operational uses for the centre: garbage trucks co-ordinated by GPS can be repurposed for other tasks if necessary, enhancing the efficiency of resources management.

Similar projects have already been implemented in New York City and Gauteng in South Africa, but this is the first centre in the world that will integrate all the stages of a crisis management situation: from prediction, mitigation and preparedness, to the immediate response to events, and finally to capture feedback from the system to be used for future incidents. The system is especially vital for protecting lives in the city's poor mountainside communities, or *favelas*, where tens of thousands of people live in areas with a high risk of flooding and landslides.

Source: IBM (2010), "City Government and IBM Close Partnership to Make Rio de Janeiro a Smarter City", www-03.ibm.com/press/us/en/pressrelease/33303.wss (accessed 30 August 2016); Hamm, S. (2012), "Smarter Leadership: How Rio de Janeiro Created an Intelligent Operations Center", *Building a Smarter Planet* (blog), http://asmarterplanet.com/blog/2012/03/smarter-leadership-how-rio-de-janeiro-created-an-intelligent-operations-center.html; Department of Business, Innovation and Skills (BIS) (2013), "The Smart City Market: Opportunities for the UK", *Research Paper*, No.136.

Involving local communities and the private sector in building resilience

In addition to urban planning and infrastructure, the private sector and local communities have an important part to play in ensuring the city's resilience. The Internet can diffuse information on natural disasters and how to prepare for them. The Greater

London Authority's website sets out key actions businesses can take in the event of disaster, and pools knowledge on best practices for urban resilience worldwide. The City of Bandung should replicate such digital tools while diffusing information about resilience more comprehensively. The overall objective should be to engage the private sector and local communities before, during and after a disaster.

Additional information could be shared with businesses and citizens to increase their preparedness for disaster. Hazard maps could be sent out on social media accounts associated with the mayor or the Bandung Command Centre, which citizens already consult regularly. This could help raise public awareness of the areas most vulnerable to a flood or an earthquake. The City of New York has developed Flood Insurance Rate Maps (FIRMs) of vulnerable urban areas to inform homeowners and tenants who might need to purchase disaster insurance (City of New York, 2013).

In a disaster, ICT could help develop efficient early-warning systems and mobilise emergency services more quickly. Coupled with meteorological weather forecasting systems, advance warning times can be increased from a matter of minutes or hours to one or more days. Increased advance warning can potentially allow those affected to move their families, livestock and assets out of harm's way, and to protect property and other possessions that cannot be relocated in time. The Bandung Command Centre could connect information on water levels collected through sensors and warning systems that could automatically be activated. A digitised, georeferenced database of natural streams and man-made drainage channels could help identify where to install such sensors. The centre already informs police and fire brigades if a disaster occurs, but the local government should also include citizens as a critical resource to ensure resilience. Early-warning systems could be installed throughout the city and remotely controlled. Screens in shopping malls and other public areas (e.g. green public space) could broadcast information on what citizens should do during a flood or earthquake. Social networks such as Facebook and Twitter, and SMS to citizens' mobiles could be used. Austin's Flood Early Warning System (FEWS) in Texas, a good example of a successful smart warning system, combines flood maps, real-time data and predictive modelling to improve the efficiency of evacuation decisions and plans. It predicts which streets will be flooded up to six hours in advance and maps flooded areas and road closures. Before this system was set up, evacuation was generally carried out after the disaster occurred. In Rio de Janeiro, slum settlements are alerted by smart city tools, and the Operations Centre remotely controls sirens that show residents of the poorest urban areas where to shelter in heavy rainfall.

Smart city tools could also help mobilise the resources of the private sector and local communities in responding to a disaster. Organising domestic and international support effectively was one of the issues the Philippines faced in 2013 after cyclone Haiyan struck. During the 2011 Bangkok mega flood, volunteers' help was critical in mitigating the flood's impact (OECD, 2015). Smart city tools could help local government contact volunteer communities (including companies that can provide such basic needs as water and food) and co-ordinate support. Leaders of volunteer communities should be identified, so they can easily be contacted to organise civil society in any emergency. They could for instance be equipped with mobile device so that the local government or the Command Centre can reach them directly. In general, a database should be built so this potential support can be mobilised in case of disaster.

Smart city tools can also help local government and agencies coping with a disaster to obtain street-level information from citizens to identify priorities. If Bandung were to face a major earthquake, flood or volcanic eruption, it should develop a system to identify priority needs. Typically, this might be through the emergency switchboard (e.g. 911 in the United States), but these can be overwhelmed by the volume of calls in a disaster. During Hurricane Sandy, New York City's switchboard received 20 000 calls an hour, many of which were not emergencies. The resulting slow response times and lack of prioritisation made it difficult to support residents in life-threatening situations. The city is trying to educate citizens about what qualifies as a 911 call, but is also developing a parallel 311 line able to analyse text and data received through SMS, calls and social media posts, for less urgent reports. This should become an effective reporting mechanism to help the Bandung City rank its priorities and act accordingly. The Bandung Command Centre could become a central unit collecting and organising such data. It is already collects citizen input on Twitter, but the staff in charge of the Command Centre must be ready to receive more input in case of disaster.

In the vulnerable areas, smart city tools can help predict medical needs in advance. In the United States, Direct Relief developed a database of areas most likely to need such support as Hurricane Sandy approached New York. It crossed-cut information between GIS-based vulnerability maps (assessed not only in terms of physical exposure but also social and economic vulnerabilities) with the location of buildings citizens were likely to choose as places to ask for help (including pharmacies). This helped the city plan for medical support by area, and prepared to dispatch aid effectively when disaster hit.

3.5. Making the smart city inclusive

One of the key challenges of the smart city is to make sure all the residents can benefit and contribute to the smart city services/opportunities developed by the local government and ICT companies. In a developing country like Indonesia, the Internet and smart devices such as smartphones are not ubiquitous, which can significantly undermine the efficiency of smart city services and in the poorest urban areas. A "digital divide" may prevent some citizens from accessing information online (e.g. on disaster risk management) and from participating in the city's life through an online platform of discussion. The smart city vision of Bandung aims to improve education, health care, security, community outreach, Internet literacy and citizen engagement. However, it is not clear what role digital technologies will play in this, especially for the more than 120 000 slum dwellers and the population living below the poverty line (around 8% of the total population, or around 200 000 inhabitants).

The City of Bandung should thus ensure the current smart city vision develops specific ICT strategies to make green growth inclusive. Targeted action in low-income communities and education and training programmes on ICT for the urban poor could reap high rewards. The local government could couple these initiatives with the slum revitalisation programme undertaken with the Ministry of Housing since 2014, which has included the provision of basic infrastructure and services.

Promoting smart green growth in low-income communities

The smart city strategy of Bandung promotes citizen engagement. The Command Centre has been developed as a privileged interface of communication between the local government and the people living in the city. It is directly accessible by citizens from social media, in particular Twitter, which can directly transmit via their phones or computers any concern they raise or problems they witness in the city, on a range of topics (environment, traffic etc.). For instance, they can report a road that needs repair by posting a photo of the problem on the City of Bandung's account. The Command Centre collects this feedback and digitally maps it on a screen visible to the local government. This system allows city staff to evaluate the problems citizens are encountering in each of the eight districts, and identify which problems have been most frequently pointed out, by area. This is a remarkable initiative, but many residents may not be able to contribute because they do not have access to ICT, such as smartphones. The City of Bandung should thus seek ways of involving low-income communities in this process, since they are more likely to face problems of access to public services, failing infrastructure and damage from natural disasters.

One solution for local government could be to rely on NGOs with a strong network in the urban slums, identify community leaders and give them the opportunity to contribute to the feedback system of the Command Centre, by installing a community computer connected to the Internet. In Dar es Salaam, Tanzania, local students were given access, trained to use smart technologies, such as OpenStreetMap, and tablet computers. Students used these technologies to map the slums in the city for the first time, providing a visual map of the slums and their needs in terms of people and infrastructure.[15] A similar strategy could be pursued in Bandung, which has no accurate map of urban slums, and could be combined with current projects to create a database on poor areas led by the Agency of National Unity and Community Empowerment (*Badan Kesatuan bangsa dan Pemberdayaan Masyarakat*). Smart city tools can also be used to tackle informality, by registering online slum residents and informal economic activities in municipal databases (which should be digitised).

Smart city tools can also allow the urban poor to access critical services. In Nairobi, Kenya, the M-Pesa mobile money service has given slum dwellers a virtual place to keep their cash, safe from slum fires and helping them to save money and time on travelling to banks. This has also resulted in initiatives such as a link-up with water-pump provider Grundfos Lifelink to provide communities with water paid for through M-Pesa, and NGOs making social payments to slum residents.[16] For Bandung's urban poor, such a project could have some impact. The local government should also find innovative ways to make access to the Internet more easily available in slums, as an expansion of current projects to multiply the number of Wi-Fi hotspots in the city. This would help support such objectives as online registration and e-learning. In New York City, a local government project aims to replace unused and obsolete payphones with Wi-Fi hotspots.

Online access can also be an opportunity to shed light on the issues faced in the poor urban areas and encourage participation of diverse stakeholders in improving living conditions. In India, an entrepreneur created an online collective platform where businesses, institutions, academics and residents could participate in a contest to build a house for USD 300. The idea was to use the platform to imagine new urban solutions, using open data and open innovation to better serve citizens. The experiment proved successful, and a house was built in a slum area.[17]

Ensuring access to smart services for all

One of the conditions for making smart city strategies inclusive is to ensure that digital technologies can be used by everyone. This will require not only access to such technologies, but a population that knows how to use them and is aware of their benefits. In the City of Bandung, digital technologies have great potential for success, since 60%

of the population is below 40 (City of Bandung, 2015a). The following ICT educational policies have already been initiated at the instigation of the mayor:

- One of the city's flagship educational policies is the "Bandung Digital Valley", a set of teaching programmes developing the use of IT and their development by local start-up companies. This involves a close partnership with alumni students of local universities and Indonesian companies.
- Digital classes for junior high and elementary schools (with a smart board and tablets in class) have been set up. Online submission and selection procedures were introduced in junior and high schools.
- Vocational high schools focused on ICT were created to develop an ICT workforce in the city.
- 108 schools have been connected by fibre optics to enhance Internet connections there.

More emphasis could be placed on scaling up ICT educational programmes and training, especially for the urban poor. The City of Bandung should create specific programmes for these communities, in collaboration with local academic institutions and NGOs. Bandung has more than 80 colleges, universities and higher educational establishments (City of Bandung, 2015a), and active NGOs such as YPBB (*Yayasan Pengembangan Biosains dan Bioteknologi*). E-learning should occupy a central role in educational methods for low-income communities, to compensate for the lack of skilled teachers in these areas and allowing residents to follow courses independently. In Stellenbosch, South Africa, electronic hubs with downloadable educational resources have been installed.[18] Such programmes not only encourage education but help develop ICT-friendly programmes for low-income communities. Bandung could replicate such initiatives in the poor areas of the city, while promoting them in awareness-raising programmes. Scholarship programmes focused on ICT education could also be created to encourage children from low-income households to benefit from and contribute to the smart city opportunities.

ICT can help increase performance in the education system. Bandung's *Sistem Informasi Manajemen Pendidikan* (SIMDIK) programme is a digital management system for educational establishments that support students' enrolment, financial operations and academic curricula. The national government's *Data Pokok Pendidikan* (DAPODIK) programme (Basic Education Data) has been applied in several cities: it aims to collect data on education in Indonesia and centralise it in online databases, to help policy makers formulate and target educational programmes. Such a programme could be expanded to create databases on ICT literacy of citizens by province, city and district.

To raise awareness of smart city tools among the urban poor, and help city government identify obstacles to their diffusion in poor areas, representatives of poor communities should be involved in developing Bandung City's smart city vision. These should be invited to the specific advisory group, among the six created by the mayor (see Chapter 4) focusing on the smart city. This would create a communication channel between the local government and the urban poor and help design projects to address poverty and access to basic urban services.

Main policy recommendations

- **Develop a clearer and more comprehensive smart city framework** for current and future projects in each critical policy sector, and their **benefits for urban green growth.**
- Create a roadmap for the progressive development of **smart devices that produce and collect urban data and knowledge on green growth.** Sensors for energy consumption and measuring water levels are most urgent.
- **Identify sources of congestion and the efficiency of the *angkot* system** through GPS and mobile phone data, improving parking management through an **automatic guidance system** and price adjustment.
- Develop **smart energy management systems** in new buildings, and smart electricity meters, supported by a national reform introducing real-time dynamic pricing of electricity.
- Enhance resilient urban planning through **GIS vulnerability mapping and flood simulation software.**
- Develop the **capacities of the Command Centre to manage infrastructure in times of disaster** by collecting real-time data on their condition.
- Create a **smart early-warning system** and ICT mechanisms to reach out to the private sector and local communities and provide assistance in case of disaster.
- Create mechanisms (scholarships, e-learning) to help the urban poor benefit from current **ICT educational programmes,** and use local residents and NGOs with strong networks in slums to provide data through digital tools such as GIS.

Notes

1. See: Smart Cities Council (2014), "Smart waste revolution to drive $42 billion in revenues over next decade", http://smartcitiescouncil.com/article/smart-waste-revolution-drive-42-billion-revenues-over-next-decade (accessed 2 April 2016).
2. See: Data Smart City Solutions (2013), "Streamlining the London Tube with Data", http://datasmart.ash.harvard.edu/news/article/oyster-cards-clarify-tube-congestion-202 (accessed 8 October 2015).
3. See: Data Smart City Solutions (2015), "Monitoring Air Quality and the Impacts of Pollution", http://datasmart.ash.harvard.edu/news/article/monitoring-air-quality-and-the-impacts-of-pollution-679 (accessed 8 October 2015).
4. See: NYC Open Data (n.d.), NYC Open Data website, https://nycopendata.socrata.com/.
5. See: OECD (2016), *Observatory of Public Sector Innovation*, www.oecd.org/governance/observatory-public-sector-innovation/ (accessed 31 August 2016).
6. The current bicycle-sharing programme works like a bicycle rental system, except that the bicycles can be returned to other stations in the city.
7. See: The Guardian (2014), "Cities in motion: how we mapped the matatus of Nairobi", www.theguardian.com/cities/2014/feb/19/cities-motion-how-we-mapped-matatus-nairobi (accessed 09 October 2015).
8. See: BlaBlaCar (n.d), BlaBlaCar UK website, www.blablacar.co.uk/ (accessed 31 August 2016).
9. See: Schneider Electric (n.d.), "La smart city : la ville devient intelligente", www.schneider-electric.fr/sites/france/fr/solutions-ts/enjeux-de-l-energie/Smart-City.page (accessed 31 August 2016).
10. See: The Guardian (2013), "Smart cities: adapting the concept for the global south", www.theguardian.com/global-development-professionals-network/2013/nov/21/smart-cities-relevant-developing-world (accessed 6 October 2015).
11. See local disaster preparedness hazard map for Kumamoto City: www.ntt-west.co.jp/shs/en/town/kumamoto/pdf/en_kumamoto.pdf.
12. The 3Di Water Management software was developed by Deltares, the Delft University of Technology and Nelen & Schuurmans, in the Netherlands.
13. See: Data Smart City Solutions (2016), "A Catalog of Civic Data Use Cases: How can data and analytics be used to enhance city operations?", http://datasmart.ash.harvard.edu/news/article/how-can-data-and-analytics-be-used-to-enhance-city-operations-723 (accessed 31 August 2016).

14. See: Sci Dev Net (2014), "Developing world gets city smart", www.scidev.net/global/cities/feature/developing-world-city-smart.html (accessed 31 August 2016).

15. See: The Guardian (2013), "Smart cities: adapting the concept for the global south", www.theguardian.com/global-development-professionals-network/2013/nov/21/smart-cities-relevant-developing-world (accessed 6 October 2015).

16. See: Sci Dev Net (2014), "Developing world gets city smart", www.scidev.net/global/cities/feature/developing-world-city-smart.html (accessed 31 August 2016).

17. For more information on the 300 dollar house see: www.300house.com/ (accessed 6 October 2015).

18. See: The Guardian (2013), "Smart cities: adapting the concept for the global south", www.theguardian.com/global-development-professionals-network/2013/nov/21/smart-cities-relevant-developing-world (accessed 6 October 2015).

Bibliography

BlaBlaCar (n.d), BlaBlaCar UK website, www.blablacar.co.uk/ (accessed 31 August 2016).

C40 Cities and Siemens (2013), "Singapore Climate Close-up", City Climate Leadership Awards.

City of Bandung (2015a), "Innovating Bandung", presentation at the third OECD Knowledge Sharing Workshop on Urban Green Growth in Dynamic Asia, 6 May 2015, Bandung, Indonesia.

City of Bandung (2015b), *Building a Collaborative Society*, Bandung, Indonesia.

City of Bandung (2013), *ICT Master Plan 2013-2018*, Bandung, Indonesia.

City of New York (2013), "Flood Hazard Mapping Status Report for Property Owners", New York City.

Data Smart City Solutions (2016), "A Catalog of Civic Data Use Cases: How can data and analytics be used to enhance city operations?", http://datasmart.ash.harvard.edu/news/article/how-can-data-and-analytics-be-used-to-enhance-city-operations-723 (accessed 31 August 2016).

Data Smart City Solutions (2015), "Monitoring Air Quality and the Impacts of Pollution", http://datasmart.ash.harvard.edu/news/article/monitoring-air-quality-and-the-impacts-of-pollution-679 (accessed 8 October 2015).

Data Smart City Solutions (2013), "Streamlining the London Tube with Data", http://datasmart.ash.harvard.edu/news/article/oyster-cards-clarify-tube-congestion-202 (accessed 8 October 2015).

Department of Business, Innovation and Skills (BIS) (2013), "The Smart City Market: Opportunities for the UK", *Research Paper*, No.136, London.

Hamm, S. (2012), "Smarter Leadership: How Rio de Janeiro Created an Intelligent Operations Center", *Building a Smarter Planet* (blog), http://asmarterplanet.com/blog/2012/03/smarter-leadership-how-rio-de-janeiro-created-an-intelligent-operations-center.html.

IBM (2010), "City Government and IBM Close Partnership to Make Rio de Janeiro a Smarter City", www-03.ibm.com/press/us/en/pressrelease/33303.wss (accessed 30 August 2016).

Kitchin, R. (2013), "The real-time city? Big data and smart urbanism", *Geojournal*, Vol. 79, pp. 1-14.

Le Monde (2015), "A Lyon, Hikari, le premier îlot urbain à énergie positive", www.lemonde.fr/planete/article/2015/09/17/a-lyon-hikari-le-premier-ilot-mixte_intelligent-a-energie-positive_4761665_3244.html (accessed 02 October 2015).

NYC Open Data (n.d.), *NYC Open Data website*, https://nycopendata.socrata.com/ (accessed 5 January 2016).

OECD (2016), *Observatory of Public Sector Innovation*, www.oecd.org/governance/observatory-public-sector-innovation/ (accessed 31 August 2016).

OECD (2015), *Green Growth in Bangkok*, Thailand, OECD Publishing, Paris, http://dx.doi.org/10.1787/9789264237087-en.

OECD (2013), *Disaster Risk Financing in APEC Economies; Practices and Challenges* OECD Publishing, Paris. https://www.oecd.org/daf/fin/insurance/OECD_APEC_DisasterRiskFinancing.pdf. (accessed 12 October, 2016)

Public Utilities Board of Singapore (2013), "Tapping into intelligent technology for floodcasting, New modelling software in development aims to forecast flood events", www.3di.nu/wp/wp-content/uploads/2014/03/Tapping-into-intelligent-technology-for-flood-casting.pdf.

Schneider Electric (n.d.), "La smart city : la ville devient intelligente", www.schneider-electric.fr/sites/france/fr/solutions-ts/enjeux-de-l-energie/Smart-City.page (accessed 31 August 2016).

Sci Dev Net (2014), "Developing world gets city smart", www.scidev.net/global/cities/feature/developing-world-city-smart.html (accessed 31 August 2016).

SF*park* (n.d.), SF*park* website http://sfpark.org/about-the-project/ (accessed 30 August 2016).

Smart Cities Council (2014), "Smart waste revolution to drive $42 billion in revenues over next decade", http://smartcitiescouncil.com/article/smart-waste-revolution-drive-42-billion-revenues-over-next-decade (accessed 2 April 2016).

Tarigan, A.K.M. et al. (2015), "City profile: Bandung City, Indonesia", *Cities*, Vol. 50, pp. 100-110.

The Guardian (2014), "Cities in motion: how we mapped the matatus of Nairobi", www.theguardian.com/cities/2014/feb/19/cities-motion-how-we-mapped-matatus-nairobi (accessed 09 October 2015).

The Guardian (2013), "Smart cities: adapting the concept for the global south", www.theguardian.com/global-development-professionals-network/2013/nov/21/smart-cities-relevant-developing-world (accessed 6 October 2015).

Washburn, D. et al. (2010), "Helping CIOs understand 'Smart City' initiatives: Defining the Smart City, its drivers, and the role of the CIO", Forrester Research, Inc., Cambridge, Massachusetts, http://public.dhe.ibm.com/partnerworld/pub/smb/smarterplanet/forr_help_cios_und_smart_city_initiatives.pdf.

Woods, E. (2014), "Results in for San Francisco's Parking Experiment", *Navigant Research Blog,* www.navigantresearch.com/blog/results-in-for-san-franciscos-parking-experiment (accessed 30 August 2016).

Chapter 4

Governance for green growth in Bandung

Chapter 4 examines governance challenges faced by all levels of government, the private sector, civil society and other stakeholders in the Bandung Metropolitan Area (BMA) to implement strategies and policies and encourage urban green growth. This chapter is structured into the four sections:

1) co-ordination challenges between governmental bodies

2) financing urban green growth

3) international co-operation for urban green growth

4) engaging and collaborating with local stakeholders.

Key findings

- **Co-ordination across levels of government** is a critical obstacle to urban green growth in Indonesia. While vertical alignment of strategies can enhance national guidelines on green growth to be translated at lower levels of government, national policy frameworks recognising the role of cities are missing in the solid waste management, energy and smart city sectors. The national government could work with provincial and local governments to improve local capacity for national policies.
- **Horizontal co-ordination** in the BMA is also an obstacle to green growth. Decentralisation reforms since the late 1990s have fragmented development processes at the local level, which in the BMA has translated into uncoordinated management of transport, solid waste and floods. Establishing a **BMA co-ordinating body** (which is currently in progress) would be a significant step in addressing these issues, but the national government's participation and authority is also critical. At a larger scale, the transport projects linking Jakarta and Bandung call for more analysis of the development dynamics linking both cities and potential needs for regional green growth strategies.
- **Financing** is a critical implementation lever for urban green growth. The budget of the City of Bandung is USD 652 per inhabitant in 2016, and has significantly increased over the past six years, thanks to rising amounts of local own revenue. The budget nevertheless remains low compared to investment needs for urban green growth. Tax revenue needs to be increased throughout Indonesia, but also locally, through **fiscal mechanisms that can simultaneously promote green growth**, such as charges on the construction of impermeable surfaces.
- **Private investment** should also be strongly encouraged. FDI inflows in Indonesia have been lower than in many other countries of Southeast Asia due to cumbersome restrictions, but the country has been a pioneer in the region in fostering **green investment banking**, by creating sustainability ratings in markets, for instance. Green investment accounted for USD 1.1 billion in 2013 and has mostly focused on mini-hydropower and geothermal projects. The local government's strategy of relying on public-private partnerships (PPPs) must also be supported by the national government in all steps of PPP project development.
- **International co-operation** could be another key source of finance for green growth in Bandung. Between 2002 and 2014, Indonesia received around USD 80 billion in official development finance, making it the top recipient in the whole Southeast Asian region. However, international public finance has made almost no contribution to Bandung's green growth. It is thus urgent to reconsider Bandung's involvement in application processes and access to official development finance. Bandung could also continue its efforts to create partnerships with international organisations, focusing on the development of green growth indicators and building flood resilience.
- The City of Bandung enjoys the advantages of a young population (60% of the population is below 40). The local government should take advantage of this by **involving further local communities** in their efforts to achieve green growth. A first need is to better identify and organise the support of what is referred to as the 5 000 "communities", groups of interests/hobbies that are not clearly defined and mobilised. Solid waste management also presents opportunities. **Raising awareness** is important, as citizens do not always fall in line with certain initiatives: for instance, the smart card for transport may be difficult to introduce successfully, since traditional habits of bargaining, paying cash, etc. persist.

Key findings *(continued)*

- Collaboration among a wide range of stakeholder, in particular with the education sector is a critical asset of Bandung. Bandung should also try to exploit the formidable opportunities offered by the city's 78 higher education establishments, as well as the relatively high proportion of the population with high educational attainment, by systematising collaboration with these entities. Existing innovation capacities, such as the Institute for Innovation and Entrepreneurship Development, should also be supported by the municipality.

4.1. Enhancing co-ordination for green growth between government bodies

Filling in policy framework gaps between the national, provincial and local governments

The government hierarchy in Indonesia has created a relationship of dependence between the national government, the provincial governments and the local governments (cities, regencies and districts). Plans and policies designed in the BMA are influenced to large extent by policies and regulations issued by higher levels of government, in particular the national government. This affects not only general development objectives but also sectoral policies in opportunity areas for green growth (e.g. transport, energy). The main components of Indonesia's **National Development Plans** (RPJPN 2005-2025 and RPJMN, 2015-2019) are translated at lower levels of government into the West Java Province Development Plans and into each of the five municipalities of BMA (e.g. Bandung Development Plans) (Table 4.1). This is a powerful instrument of policy harmonisation in Indonesia, and a means of boosting cities' economic and environmental performance. One of the eight missions of the RPJPN 2005-2025 is the realisation of "a green and sustainable Indonesia", acknowledging that "the long-term sustainability of development will face the challenges of climate change and global warming, which affect activities and livelihoods". The RPJMN 2015-2019 aims to create and to increase green cities development as a part of climate and disaster security, improve governance in natural resources, reduce greenhouse gas (GHG) emissions, and increase community resilience to the impact of climate change.

National Development Plans have a binding character, so lower levels of government must adopt their own development plans under national guidelines. This, however, is not the case for every national plan, which creates obstacles to the implementation of some national strategies with potentially high impact for urban green growth, in particular the national green growth initiatives (Table 4.1). ***Delivering Green Growth in Indonesia*** outlines the national agenda for inclusive and sustainable development in the next 35 years, to 2050. Launched in 2015, it aims to bring about change by influencing existing policy documents through the promotion of green policy alternatives. Nonetheless, in the absence of legal basis and binding targets, risks that it may not be implemented at all levels of government are great. Neither West Java Province nor the five municipalities of BMA have adopted a similar green growth agenda. The same applies to the National Action Plan for Climate Change Adaptation, and the National Energy Master Plan (RUEN). West Java Province in particular appears to have relatively weak development planning. No transport master plan is in place, while even Bandung City has developed its own Sustainable

Mobility Plan (Table 4.1). However, the role of the provincial government may play a larger part after the rearrangement of tasks and functions as regulated by the revised Law No. 23/2014 on local governance (decentralisation law).

Conversely, the innovative vision of a smart city developed by Bandung City faces the challenge of policy gaps at higher levels of government. The smart city strategy developed in the **2015 ICT Master Plan**, has no counterpart at the national and provincial level. The smart city is one of the five pillars of the **National Urban Development Strategy and Policy (KSPPN)**, but is loosely defined as "the capability of the city to utilise human resources, social capital and information and communication technology to support more competitive and sustainable cities in the future". The lack of a specific, detailed strategy makes it difficult to attract funds to support smart cities in Indonesia, and infrastructure-based smart city initiatives (e.g. air pollution monitoring systems, sensors in rivers, operations centres) are costly. Many smart city projects depend on the quality of national infrastructure systems: without good broadband connections, Wi-Fi technology and reliable electricity networks, mobile applications and smart meters cannot be optimised. Many smart city initiatives depend on national government regulation: and, as explained in Chapter 3, smart electricity meters can only be introduced through a national reform that replaces the current metering based on installed capacity of supply networks with real-time dynamic pricing of energy consumption. Similar issues emerge in the solid waste sector. The lack of local perspective for solid waste management makes it difficult for local governments to establish clear strategies and financial resources to tackle solid waste issues. It also affects the West Java Province, which does not have the budget to build the new sanitary landfill. The national government participates financially in the construction of landfills in Indonesia on an ad hoc basis; no systematic mechanism exists to provide funds for such projects.

Policy gaps between the national, provincial and local governments must be bridged to harmonise policies, regulations and to ensure funds for implementation. Clear and binding targets and roadmaps set up and enacted at all levels of government could maximise the chances of implementation. The recent decentralisation reforms provide opportunities to allocate more relevant responsibilities to sub-national governments, but policies must be vertically aligned. The following gaps are particular priorities:

- **National green growth and climate change:** related plans should be binding and clearly state their objectives and targets. Similar plans should be developed at the provincial and local levels and integrate strategies in other sectors (transport, energy, solid waste, water, smart city) which aim to enhance cities' economic and environmental performance. The Ministry of National Development Planning (Bappenas), the Ministry of Environment and Forestry or the Ministry of Finance could be the lead institution behind national green growth plans and capacity-building mechanisms at the local level, through a dedicated green growth agency.
- **Energy**: although energy networks are managed by the State Electricity Company Perusahaan Listrik Negara (PLN), cities have a critical role to play in reaching the national targets of RUEN and of the National Action Plan for Greenhouse Gas Emissions Reductions (RAN-GRK), by supporting energy efficiency in buildings and city-based renewable energy (RE) generation. RUEN and RAN-GRK do not sufficiently delineate the role cities could play in this regard. This creates a lack of incentives for local governments: the City of Bandung does not have a department responsible for energy issues. Recognising cities' role in translating

national objectives to the local level would help meet national targets. It should also be connected to smart city objectives.

- **Solid waste:** as noted earlier, a national legal framework would help secure proper funding. The provincial Solid Waste Management Unit that manages the provincial landfill Sarimukti and the upcoming Legok Nangka landfill could obtain clear responsibilities and financial resources with provincial co-ordination. Such a legal framework would help clarify responsibilities vertically but also between line ministries, since solid waste policy development is divided among the Ministry of Public Works and Housing (DPWH), the Ministry of Environment and Forestry and Bappenas (Chaerul, Fahruroji and Fujiwara, 2014).
- **Smart city**: Bappenas should develop a separate national smart city plan supporting the National Urban Development Strategy and Policy (KSPPN), co-ordinating with other national agencies and ministries (e.g. the State Electricity Company, PNL, and the Ministry of Finance) to align regulations and financing mechanisms for local smart city initiatives. This plan should clearly identify connections between development objectives and plans, including green growth, and smart city strategies. This will also be a good way of setting up smart city projects systematically in all Indonesian cities, rather than leaving it to ad hoc initiatives. The Ministry of Communications and Information Technology in 2016 launched a pilot smart city project for 15 cities. This links up with the government's effort to build a digital economy (Vincentia, 2016).

Table 4.1. **Major plans and policy guidelines at the national level and in Bandung**

Sector	Indonesia	West Java Province	Bandung City
General development	National Long Term Development Plan (RPJPN 2005-2025)	West Java Regional Long Term Development Plan 2005-2025 (RPJPD 2005-2025)	Bandung Long Term Development Plan 2005-2025 (RPJPD 2005-2025)
	National Medium Term Development Plan (RPJMN, 2015-2019)	West Java Regional Medium Term Development Plan 2013-2018 (RPJMD 2013-2018)	Bandung Development Plans 2014-2018 (RPJMD 2014-2018)
	National Urban Development Strategy and Policy (KSPPN)	n.a.	Local Urban Development Strategy and Policy (KSPPD) (not yet enacted)
Green growth	Delivering Green Growth in Indonesia (2015) and Green Growth Programme (2013)	n.a.	n.a.
Climate change (mitigation and adaptation)	National Action Plan to reduce Greenhouse Gas Emissions (2011)	West Java Action Plan for Reducing Greenhouse Emissions (RADGRK)	Bandung Low Carbon Society Bandung City's Climate Change Action Plan
	National Action Plan for Climate Change Adaptation (2012)	n.a.	Urban Climate Resilience Strategy (not yet formulated)
Land use	National Spatial Plan (*Rencana Tata Ruang Wilayah Nasional*)	West Java Provincial Spatial Plan Bandung Metropolitan Area Spatial Plan	Bandung City Spatial Plan
Energy	National Energy Master Plan (RUEN)	Provincial Energy Master Plan (*Rencana Umum Energi Daerah*/RUED)	n.a.
Environment	Environmental Law 32/2009 on Environmental Protection and Management	Environmental Management and Protection Plan (RPPLH) (not yet enacted)	Environmental Management and Protection Plan (RPPLH) (not yet enacted)
Transport	Sustainable Urban Transport Programme (NAMASUTRI)	n.a.	Bandung City Transport Master Plan Bandung Urban Mobility Project

Table 4.1. **Major plans and policy guidelines at the national level and in Bandung** *(continued)*

Solid waste	Solid Waste Management Act 18/2008 Presidential Decree on Domestic Solid Waste Management and Solid Waste (2012) Presidential Decree 18/2016 on Waste-Based Power Plants	West Java Solid Waste Management Master Plan	Bandung City Solid Waste Management Master Plan
Water supply and sanitation	National Policy on Water Supply and Environmental Health Presidential Decree 185/2014 on the Acceleration Drinking Water and Sanitation Provision	n.a.	Bandung City Sanitation Strategy Bandung City Water Supply Master Plan
Smart city	National Urban Development Strategy and Policy (KSPPN) (smart city is one pillar)	n.a.	ICT Master Plan (2015)

Source: Elaboration based on Government of Indonesia and GGGI (2013), *Green Growth Programme; Prioritising Investments: Delivering Green Growth.*

Enhancing co-ordination mechanisms between all levels of government

The existence of national and local plans will not be enough to tackle the implementation questions local governments in the BMA face. Local measures to design and implement the range of plans required for urban green growth could be better aligned. The decentralisation process started under the Decentralisation Act 22/1999 and continued under Act 32/2004 and Act No. 23/2014 on local governance, transferred to local governments the authority and financial resources for delivering such basic services as road and wastewater infrastructure. The central government's share in infrastructure investment was reduced from around 80% to about 35% (World Bank, 2013). This has been complicated by a lack of co-ordination between key stakeholders. Local governments in Indonesia do not always have the capacity to design and implement their assigned infrastructure projects and to manage natural resources (OECD, 2016a). Decentralisation has not necessarily benefited electricity and water infrastructure quality and local economic governance (Patunru and Rahman, 2014).[1] In addition, provincial powers are limited: West Java Province, for instance, only has the power to co-ordinate cross-municipal matters, with no strong authority over local governments. The national government's lack of support for Surabaya's Mass Rapid Transit (MRT) project, initially resulted in delays and risks of failure. The national government and municipalities in the BMA must try to avoid a similar outcome, especially in the City of Bandung, as it develops so many urban projects where the involvement of the national government will be critical. Local governments should maintain constant contact with the appropriate national agencies and ministries to ensure that regulations will not block their initiatives. Meanwhile, the central government must build capacities at the local level, by increasing resources, training local government staff and improving e-government tools (Box 4.1) (OECD, 2013a). One area for attention is developing local capacities for PPPs (see section on financing urban green growth).

Flood resilience is a serious concern in the context of vertical policy alignment. Despite national legislation, Bandung is one of the few cities that have not created a disaster risk management department with a comprehensive approach. The Fire and Rescue Department is still responsible for this task, and is mainly focused on disaster response for historical reasons. Bandung should improve co-ordination with Indonesia's National Agency for Disaster Management (BNPB), which has had extensive technical and financial assistance from the donor community in the past decade, to put into practice data and analytic methods developed for a multi-hazard early-warning system (EWS) as one of the Command Centre's main functions (see Chapter 3).

The Green Growth Programme developed for Central Kalimantan with the Global Green Growth Institute (GGGI) has experimented with some novel strategies in national-regional co-ordination. One of its three main components is regional engagement "to support key provincial governments in prioritising and implementing green growth". It includes producing and collecting data on green growth, to be co-ordinated between different levels of government. However, it is not clear how this will be accomplished, and the role and responsibility of cities is not mentioned. In addition, GGGI and the national government are only collaborating in two Central Kalimantan districts, Pulang Pisau and Murung Raya, not in the BMA. This governance strategy should be expanded to the BMA and other major urban areas in Indonesia.

Box 4.1. **Bridging the capacity gaps: Examples from OECD countries**

Capacity gaps arise when a local government lacks the human, knowledge-related and/or infrastructural resources to carry out development projects. OECD examples of capacity building include involving specialised non-profit organisations and improving the use of e-government tools. In **Greece**, as a response to the sovereign debt crisis, a special non-profit organisation was set up to assist small municipalities (of under 10 000 residents), that did not have the skills to prepare the four-year action plans required to access EU structural funds. In the **United States** in 2009, at the height of the financial crisis, distressed areas and small towns were less able to apply for relevant programmes and secure funding, given the rigorous reporting requirements of the Recovery Act, because they did not have the trained manpower for intensive contracting and monitoring. The federal government website supplied e-government tools as a result, to help recipients of recovery funds meet their quarterly reporting requirements by submitting their project updates online. Using this technology considerably enhanced the accountability, speed and transparency of the Recovery Act.

Chicago offers another interesting capacity-building initiative between national and local governments. The Chicago Metropolitan Agency for Planning (CMAP) does not have formal authority over land use and zoning, which fall under municipal jurisdiction. The metropolitan master plan GO TO 2040 is funded at the local level under a technical assistance programme, the US Department of Housing and Urban Development's Sustainable Communities Regional Planning Grant Program. The CMAP initiated the Local Technical Assistance (LTA) Program in 2010. The programme provides assistance to communities across the Chicago metropolitan region to undertake planning projects that advance the principles of GO TO 2040. The CMAP has initiated 160 local projects with local governments and non-profit and intergovernmental organisations to address local issues at the intersection of transport, land use and housing, including the natural environment, economic growth and community development. The CMAP announced 25 new LTA projects in October 2014. This fourth wave of projects emphasises implementation of past plans, such as updates of zoning and regulations, the creation of capital improvement plans and analysis of municipal review procedures.

Source: OECD (2015a), *Governing the City*, http://dx.doi.org/10.1787/9789264226500-en.

Institutionalising and perpetuating the new strategies of Bandung City

Co-ordination challenges affecting strategies for green growth (transport, solid, water, smart city, etc.) must also be tackled within local governments. Mayor Ridwan Kamil's initiatives, such as the creation of a new public-private partnership (PPP) team, the creation of eight advisory groups including citizens (see section on community engagement), the construction of small Command Centres in every district of Bandung City to decentralise smart city action, and the push for innovative projects (creative city, smart city) show the mayor's resolve to create new governance synergies.

Internal governance can be further improved. The flagship smart city project, the **Bandung Command Centre** (compare Chapter 3), is managed by the Information and Communication Agency but there is not enough involvement of line departments such as Bappeda, the Provincial Development Planning Agency (*Badang Perencana Pembangunang Daerah*), and those in charge of transport and environment issues to enhance the Centre's capacity to manage the city. These departments need to share information more regularly with the Command Centre and to develop joint strategies, and not simply initiate their own projects. Some departments have developed their own applications but have not shared them with the Centre. The Police Department, for instance, does not use the Centre's video analytics to detect illegal parking because it has its own system, and the Traffic Department has a similar issue. All departments in charge of the development plans listed in Table 4.1 must identify potential benefits of smart city tools for their own objectives and use it in their daily operations (and vice versa, as shown in Chapter 3). The ICT Master Plan helps provide more consistency for the smart city vision but needs to be integrated into other strategies. Including smart city strategies in all other plans will help perpetuate the smart city vision in the long term, rather than leaving it to sectoral, ad hoc initiatives dependent on the political agenda.

To encourage such integration of strategies in each local plan, some institutional innovations may be necessary. Bappeda could develop and lead cross-department task forces on smart city and green growth as a co-ordinating body for the whole local administration. These task forces could receive advice directly from a corresponding advisory group (i.e. green growth, smart city) constituted of private professionals, researchers and citizens. The smart city advisory body set up by the mayor could become the advisory body for the smart city taskforce. The environment advisory group to be created in the near future could be expanded to green growth and become a task force (see section 4.4).

Co-ordinating action for green growth in the Bandung Metropolitan Area

Urbanisation and economic development tend to be concentrated in the City of Bandung but are also in evidence in the wider BMA, which includes four other local governments: Bandung Regency (*Kabupaten Bandung*), West Bandung Regency (*Kabupaten Bandung Barat*), Sumedang Regency and Cimahi City (*Kota Cimahi*) (see Figure 1.1). Many people who work in the City of Bandung commute from one of these surrounding areas (see Chapter 1). Critical urban systems are shared between these administrative territories. Development and green growth strategies should thus be co-ordinated across local governments for full impact.

The establishment of a BMA co-ordinating body is under discussion and pending approval by presidential decree in 2016. Such a metropolitan body would be the first of its kind outside Jakarta in Indonesia.[2] This body, chaired by the governor of West Java

Province, with Bandung City's mayor as a vice chair, would aim to co-ordinate policies through BMA-wide master plans, and to facilitate private investment in the region. Such an executive structure could be helpful because the West Java Province is always involved in any project mobilising at least two municipalities, as in the case of such ongoing projects as the Light Rapid Transit (LRT) (see Chapter 2). It could also present an opportunity for the provincial government to co-ordinate cross-municipal issues in the BMA.

Co-ordination between BMA local governments has been a challenge. As noted, decentralisation reforms in Indonesia have empowered cities without creating incentives for horizontal collaboration, discouraging local governments from pooling resources with their neighbours.[3] Many local government officials are not aware of the need for co-ordination that decentralisation reforms have created and of their potential benefits (Firman, 2009). The parochial attitude of many local governments has hampered services that require cross-border co-operation, including solid waste management and water supply, in many regions (Firman, 2009). This has exacerbated the already limited provision of urban services, since the BMA's local governments are working at cross purposes. The new metropolitan co-ordinating body will need to address the following critical horizontal co-ordination issues that affect green growth in the BMA:

- **Traffic congestion**: as the BMA's population has grown, traffic volumes have risen from 10% to 15% annually (Bandung City, 2014), increasing average weekday travel times from 30 to 65 minutes, and over an hour on weekends. The minibus is the central mode of public transit, accounting in 2009 for about 31% of all motorised trips. Until recently, transport infrastructure in the BMA favoured the development of roads. The lack of land-use and transport co-ordination has reinforced inefficient mobility patterns between origins and destinations (Tarigan et al., 2015). No BMA-wide strategy exists to improve transport systems, including mass transit, to reduce increasing congestion and externalities of air pollution, GHG emissions (transport accounts for 60% of CO_2 emissions in Bandung City) and potential losses in productivity.

- **Solid waste management**: the City of Bandung does not have the appropriate space in sanitary landfills for collected solid waste. The waste generated already exceeds current collection and treatment capacities. BMA's five municipal areas rely on the same landfill site, which is under great stress and has been repeatedly scheduled to close, most recently in 2015 (IGES and City of Kawasaki, 2015). Negotiations on using vacant land in surrounding areas have been unsuccessful (Tarigan et al., 2015) and further co-operation is needed. Some current green projects, such as the introduction of biodigesters in Bandung City, will receive waste from surrounding municipalities and require co-operation on the conveyance system.

- **Flood risk management**: rapid land-conversion for real estate development in the BMA has decreased its ecological function and water absorptive capacities, increasing the risk of floods (Hudalah and Winarso, 2010). A metropolitan action plan for flood management could help, for example by creating buffer zones.

- **Water supply:** the BMA's five municipalities use the same ground water aquifer, which is under heavy pressure from high consumption from residential, commercial and industrial activities. To ensure a sustainable supply for households and economic activities, local government units must agree on a water supply and sanitation plan and harmonise water extraction rules throughout the BMA. The 2009 study on a drainage master plan recommended metropolitan-wide watershed management, such as building of dams and water ponds, which has not so far been implemented.

A key solution would be to set up **Medium- and Long-Term Development Plans for the five municipalities** and their 8.5 million residents. A green growth development plan should also be developed as a pillar strategy for the development of the BMA, and for national green growth initiatives (see Table 4.1). An alternative would be to systematically promote the green growth agenda in the main development plans. This would have to be carried out collaboratively and might initially prove more challenging, although it could yield higher returns in the long run, in managing natural resources and the transport sector, since each municipality would help the metropolitan area as a whole, rather than focusing on its own affairs. A single metropolitan development plan would facilitate more effective services, guarantee investors better returns, improve environmental amenities and enhance the quality of life (Box 4.2).

Box 4.2. **The benefits of metropolitan thinking**

The benefits of metropolitan planning include stronger economic development and environmental sustainability gains, as well as enhanced urban resilience.

Well-functioning cities require adequate governance structures. The density of opportunity for contact and exchange that makes cities so dynamic and productive also means that the actions of households and firms, and the interaction of public policies typically have greater spill-over effects than in less dense places. Governance structures should take the functional realities of metropolitan areas into account. Administrative boundaries are often based on centuries-old borders that do not correspond to patterns of human settlement and economic activity. Getting administrative structures right typically allows for better outcomes in most dimensions that make cities function well. These include transport and land-use planning, and co-ordinating both processes. Land-use regulations need to find the right balance between protecting existing neighbourhoods and green spaces and allowing new construction. The quality of public transport usually increases when services are integrated.

Source: OECD (2015b), *The Metropolitan Century: Understanding Urbanisation and its Consequences*, http://dx.doi.org/10.1787/9789264228733-en.

The new co-ordinating body should be given extended powers to help co-ordinate BMA-wide strategies. Comprehensive metropolitan development plans should involve each local government, and require each to develop its own plan along the guidelines established by the metropolitan plan. A critical structural deficit of the future BMA co-ordinating body is the lack of provision for the national government to guide its action. The input of the national government will be crucial for translating national policy guidelines at the provincial and local levels, so that the new metropolitan body can become a platform where local governments can communicate on national policy gaps (e.g. smart city) and regulations that are obstacles to urban green growth. This would create a mechanism for the national government to offer technical assistance to the provincial and local governments (see Box 4.1).

In the medium term, metro-wide authorities to manage critical urban systems should be created for more coherent infrastructure development in the BMA. Bangkok, where sectoral authorities manage the transport, water and electricity systems outside the city, can provide inspiration. The Metropolitan Transport Authority is now implementing a vast action plan for ten new subway lines extending to the provinces in the Bangkok Metropolitan Region (OECD, 2015c). BMA could also study the ***Area Metropolitana Barcelona*** **(AMA)** (Box 4.3) and ***Metro Vancouver***, two successful examples of metropolitan governance initiatives that have developed a systematic governance structure. In Malaysia, the ***Iskandar Regional Development Authority*** also provides a model, although implementation issues have yet to be resolved (OECD, 2016b).

Box 4.3. **Intermunicipal co-operation in Barcelona**

In 1975, Spain's central government created a Metropolitan Corporation of Barcelona (*Corporación Metropolitana de Barcelona*, CMB), covering 27 municipalities. It was dissolved in 1987, when political tensions escalated between the city of Barcelona and the autonomous community of Catalonia, after Barcelona was chosen in 1986 to host the 1992 Olympics. Three sectoral intermunicipal authorities were instead created in 1987:

- a planning authority (*Mancomunitat de Municipis de l'Àrea Metropolitana de Barcelona*, MMAMB), covering 31 municipalities (3.1 million people)
- a transport authority (*Entitat Metropolitana del Transport*, EMT), covering 18 municipalities (2.9 million people)
- an environmental authority (*Entitat del Medi Ambient*, EMA), covering 33 municipalities (3.2 million people) in charge of the water network and waste treatment.

Before and after the Olympics, a process of strategic planning began with a focus on the core city and gradually expanded to the metropolitan scale. Barcelona published its first strategic plan in 1990, a second in 1994 and the third in 1999, with the three sectoral intermunicipal authorities. These involved the regional government, all the municipalities, universities, the private sector, the port and civic organisations. The Association for the Strategic Plan of Barcelona (*Pla Estratègico Metropolità de Barcelona*, PEMB), a non-profit organisation created in 2000 with 300 members of the political, business and social communities, launched the first Metropolitan Strategic Plan in 2003, covering 36 municipalities. A new plan, *Barcelona Visió 2020*, was published in 2010 as a continuation of the 2003 plan. Finally, a metropolitan authority was set up in 2011 by Law 31/2010 of the Parliament of Catalonia. The *Àrea Metropolitana de Barcelona* (AMB) includes the three sectoral intermunicipal authorities (the MAAMB, EMT and EMA). Its Metropolitan Council is composed of the mayors of all 36 municipalities covered under the strategic plan, including the city of Barcelona. The AMB is in charge of planning, transport, water, waste treatment, social cohesion and economic development. In 2013, its budget was around EUR 600 million, composed mainly of subsidies and transfers (56%), fees and user charges (24%), and own taxes (17%). A specific authority in charge of public transport (*Autoritat del Transport Metropolità*, ATM), runs an integrated public transport network with a single unified fare system.

Source: OECD (2015a), *Governing the City*, http://dx.doi.org/10.1787/9789264226500-en.

Planning green growth strategies in the wider Jakarta-Bandung metropolitan region

A more ambitious initiative the national government and sub-national governments could undertake would be to consider development and green growth strategies not only in the BMA but also in the wider Jakarta-Bandung Metropolitan Region (JBMR). Bandung is only 150 kilometres south-east of the capital city and has been more closely linked with it since the Cipularang Toll Road, opened in 2005, reduced commuting time between the cities from 4 to 4.5 hours to 2 to 2.5 hours (Dorodjatoen, 2009). This has led not only to population flows but attracted investment along the corridor, in industrial and housing real estate, where land is cheaper. The Regency of Pruwakarta, located between Jakarta and Bandung, is undergoing rapid changes. The corridor is now a 150-kilometre urban belt with a mixture of urban and rural activities. Both cities can benefit, but negative impacts have included social segregation and uncontrolled land conversion and resource consumption (Firman, 2008). The construction of the new high-speed rail line between Jakarta and Bandung, reducing the commute between the two cities to a half-hour, (see Chapter 2), will further change the region's economic, environmental and social dynamics.

The links between the two urban centres have been acknowledged. The construction of the toll road, the high-speed train and a growing number of bus lines attests to some willingness to develop transport infrastructure between the cities. In the Java Economic Corridor, the Jakarta-Bandung relationship is critical and should be given specific attention. The national government should also address comprehensive perspectives integrating environmental issues. A priority for such regional strategies is to develop information on the Jakarta-Bandung Metropolitan Region, including data on the flows of capital and commodities between both cities, housing development along the corridor (Dorodjatoen, 2009) and on transport performance, emissions, consumption of natural resources, etc. Without tackling green growth at the regional scale, infrastructure may be locked into unsustainable long-term schemes, and should be an urgent consideration for the national government and BMA local governments.

4.2. Financing green growth in Bandung

Boosting public finance for urban green growth

Enhancing local governments' financial capacities in the BMA

The City of Bandung's budget in 2016 was USD 1.6 billion, after a dramatic increase. In 2010, its nominal budget was only USD 620 million, just over one-third of the amount in 2016 (Figure 4.1). The real budget also increased sharply, from around USD 600 billion in 2010 to around USD 1 billion in 2014.[4] The total budget is still low compared to the registered population. The City of Bandung in 2016 only had a budget of USD 653 per inhabitant, compared to a budget of USD 1 070 per inhabitant in the City of Bangkok in 2012 (Figure 4.2).[5] Low local budgets are common in Indonesia, forcing local governments to look for alternative funding opportunities (PPPs, grants, etc.).

Figure 4.1. **Evolution of the budget of the City of Bandung (2010-16)**

USD million

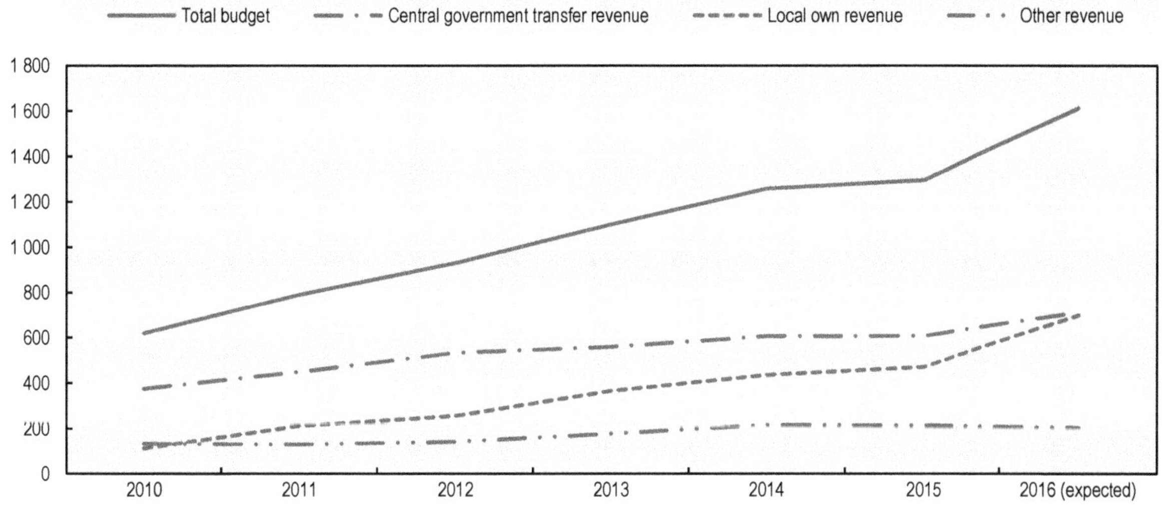

Note: Other revenue includes: tax-sharing revenues with the provincial government; adjustment and special autonomy fund, and grant revenues from provincial and other governments.

Source: Bandung City (2016), "Answers to the OECD case study questionnaire", internal document, unpublished.

Figure 4.2. **Budget per inhabitant in the cities of Bandung and Bangkok**

USD, PPP

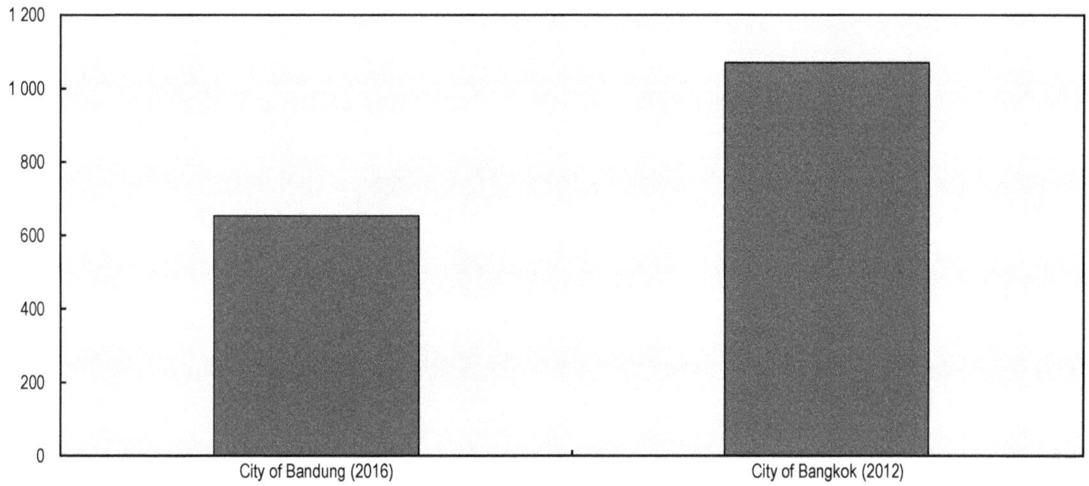

Source: OECD (2015c), *Green Growth in Bangkok*, http://dx.doi.org/10.1787/9789264237087-en. Bandung City (2016), *"Answers to the OECD case study questionnaire"*, internal document, unpublished.

The City of Bandung's budget can be broken down into three categories: locally raised revenue accounts for 43.3% of the total budget, transfers from the national government account for 44.1% and other revenues account for 12.6% (Figure 4.3). Locally raised revenue has risen sharply in recent years. In 2010, it only accounted for 16.7%, while the share of transfer revenues accounted for 78.2% (Figure 4.1). This is mainly due to the Decentralisation Act 22/1999, updated later as Act No. 32/2004 and more recently Act No. 28/2009 on Local Taxes and Charges and Act No. 23/2014 on local governance, which included fiscal decentralisation and granted local governments the right to manage local finance. Property taxes and land acquisition fees have been delegated to local governments. Bandung City performs much better than most Indonesian cities: from 2008 to 2013, own-source revenues increased from 9% to 13% on average in Indonesian municipalities (Patunru and Rahman, 2014). The proportion of total tax revenue collected by local governments in Indonesia remains low, at around 10% in 2013 (compared to Japan, for example, where local governments collect almost 25% of total revenue), although this share has been steadily increasing since the decentralisation reforms. It is now almost similar to the OECD average in unitary countries, calculated at 12% in 2012 (Table 4.2).[6]

Table 4.2. **Attribution of tax revenues to subsectors of general government as a percentage of total tax revenue**

	Central government			State or regional government			Local government			Social security funds		
	2000	2010	2013	2000	2010	2013	2000	2010	2013	2000	2010	2013
Federal countries												
Malaysia	94.7	94.3	95.2	..	..	..	3.4	4.0	3.3	1.9	1.7	1.5
OECD	56.5	53.8	54.5	15.3	16.3	16.5	6.9	7.9	7.6	21.1	21.8	21.3
Unitary countries												
Indonesia	96.8	92.8	90.4	..	..	..	3.2	7.2	9.6	..	..	..
Philippines	81.5	82.2	82.2	..	..	..	5.3	5.2	5.2	13.2	12.7	12.7
Japan	38.7	33.0	33.7	..	..	..	26.1	25.9	24.7	35.2	41.1	41.6
Korea	68.2	60.4	58.2	..	..	..	15.1	16.7	15.5	16.7	22.8	26.3
OECD	66.5	63.4	62.9	..	..	..	11.0	11.9	12.0	22.3	24.4	24.8

Source: OECD (2015d), "Tax Revenue Trends 1990-2013", in *Revenue Statistics in Asian Countries 2015: Trends in Indonesia, Malaysia and the Philippines*, http://dx.doi.org/10.1787/9789264234277-3-en.

Figure 4.3. **Revenue of the City of Bandung by source**

2016

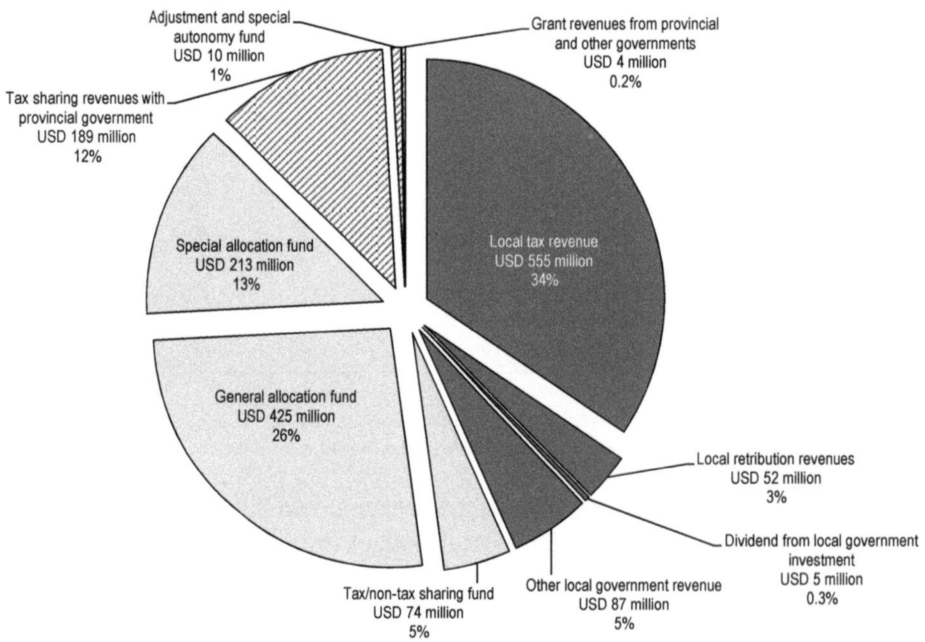

Note: Dark-blue items refer to own revenue of the City of Bandung. Light-grey items refer to transfer revenue from the central government, and hashed items refer to other sources of revenue.

Source: Bandung City (2016), *"Answers to the OECD case study questionnaire"*, internal document, unpublished.

Despite the recent positive changes in the City of Bandung's budget capacity, room remains to increase the local budget streams to promote urban green growth. This would help to raise tax revenues in the country, which in 2013 only represented 13% of Indonesia's GDP. This share is around 34% on average in OECD countries (OECD, 2015d). Both the local and the national governments have a role to play, helping to boost investment. At the local level, the local governments in the BMA should work to increase the amount of locally raised revenue. Revenues from tariffs and fees remain very low, while this accounts for 15.2% of sub-national government revenue in OECD countries (OECD, 2015e). Raising more revenues from these two sources would help finance urban green growth, and could be an opportunity to shape behaviour through fiscal policy instruments and to make green infrastructure systems financially sustainable. Taxes on new impermeable surfaces could be a tool to guide development more sustainably, discouraging developers from building in sensitive areas or to recover some of the cost of constructing flood-resilient infrastructure. Many cities and states including Maryland and Illinois in the United States of America are good examples of areas using the taxes on impermeable surfaces. A more systematic use of wastewater treatment, public transport and water supply tariffs and charges could help to raise more revenue while increasing the sustainability of green utility systems. Parking taxes and charges offer one such instance. The City of Bandung is considering increasing parking fees to discourage car use. This could be combined with West Java Province's current policy of reserving some parking slots for energy-efficient cars identified with a blue sticker. These could be subject to lower parking charges, through a control system at the entrance of parking areas, and in future, through smart cards that would recognise the blue stickers.

Increasing national government financial support for local governments

The national government plays a critical role in local finance in Indonesia. It still controls the main strategic sources of revenue, such as income and value-added taxes, while the local governments can only manage secondary streams of revenue, such as advertisement and restaurant taxes (Ritonga et al., 2012). In 2015, regencies and cities accounted for 30% of government expenditures (all levels of government included) but for only 4% of government revenues. The central government accounted for 57% of government expenditures and 89% of government revenues (OECD, 2016a). The Ministry of Finance is transferring part of the national budget to all local governments. The **General Allocation Fund (DAU)** and the **Special Allocation Fund (DAK)** accounted for 51% and 5%, respectively, of regency and city revenues in 2015 (OECD, 2016a); transfers also dramatically increased, from USD 9.1 billion in 2001 to USD 43.7 billion in 2011 (Ritonga et al., 2012). In Bandung City, 44% of total revenue in 2016 is expected to come in the form of transfers from the national government. A common problem with such automatic transfers is the way they are calculated. The General Allocation Fund is partly allocated based on the registered population in the local governments and does not take into account unregistered population, which is high in the City of Bandung. This reduces the funds for developing infrastructure that can ensure all residents' well-being. Grants, which are project-specific and include grants for education programmes, are another stream of revenue from the national government. Local governments have little autonomy in spending such grants (OECD, 2010).

The central government could use these (general or special) allocation funds more effectively for green growth. The Special Allocation Fund (DAK) is supposed to deliver earmarked funding to subnational governments, but in practice, the allocation remains quite general, as it is with the General Allocation Fund (OECD, 2016a). Increasing the volume of DAK and targeting green growth objectives would only be effective if the national government adopts a clearer national green growth strategy that clearly specifies local governments' role in line with national strategies. This would encourage local governments to spend more on green growth. Most of the City of Bandung's expenditures in 2014 were on employee salaries (49.5%).[7] Environmental projects accounted for only 3% of direct expenditure and it is difficult to know how much other direct expenditure, such as public works, contributed to green growth. Additional low-carbon infrastructure financing mechanisms could also be created at the national level. In Sweden, a national programme (KLIMP) provides local governments of all sizes financial support to manage GHG emissions and adapt to climate change. Local governments can apply for national subsidies for local investment to reduce emissions and improve energy efficiency and independence. Funded municipal activities include removing disincentives for individuals to reduce emissions, such as eliminating free parking, and subsidising the cost of retrofitting filling stations for pumps that supply renewable biofuels (Corfee-Morlot et al., 2009). The local governments in the BMA could support metropolitan-wide forms of financial management if they are developed in the future. Specific financial channels in key areas for green growth could be added to ensure that the appropriate policies are carried out.

Finally, the central government can play an important role in facilitating Bandung's access to large loans from public banks, especially given that Bandung's financial capacities have substantially increased in the past few years. The recent merger by the Ministry of Finance of the state-owned financial firms PT *Sarana Multi-Infrastruktur* (PT-SMI) and *Perusahaan Investasi Pemerintah* (PIP), to become the Indonesia Development Bank in 2017, with a capital of IDR 24.4 trillion, is an opportunity for Bandung City and local governments in the BMA to borrow from public banks. In addition to the increased capital, the IDB will be able to finance projects for 25 years (rather than the current 5 to 10 years).[8]

Efforts to attract private investment should be stepped up

Private investment in the BMA is key in maximising financial opportunities for green growth. The public administration will raise financial capacities at different government levels, but private sector participation will be critical in meeting the high cost of infrastructure. This would include foreign direct investment (FDI), specific green investment banking and PPP.

FDI regulations should be aligned with green growth

FDI, an important source of private external finance, has been significantly lower in Indonesia than in many other countries in Southeast Asia. It accounted for only 0.88% of GDP in the period 1981-2013, as compared with the average share in the region of 2.81% of GDP. More recently, Indonesia is relatively under-performing (Figure 4.4). FDI inflows have been lower than might be expected from Indonesia's size and population (Lipsey and Sjöholm, 2011). Manufacturing is by far the greatest sector in terms of FDI inflows, with 55.3% of total FDI in 2013, followed by service (22.1%), mining (16.8%) and crops and plantation (5.6%) (UNEP, 2015).

Figure 4.4. **Foreign direct investment, net inflows (% of GDP)**

1981-2013

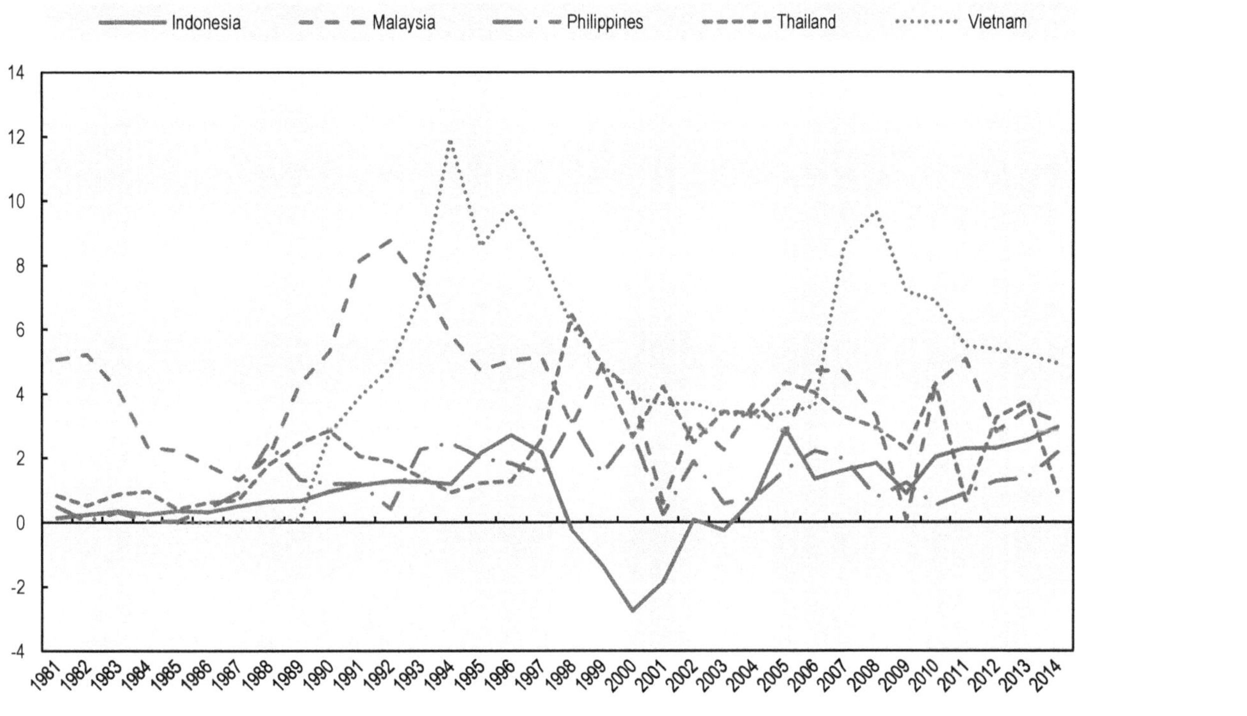

Source: World Bank (2015), *World Development Indicators*, http://data.worldbank.org/indicator/BX.KLT.DINV.WD.GD.ZS (accessed 2 April 2016).

Indonesia's difficulties in attracting FDI can partly be explained by disincentives such as limited infrastructure, and complicated and time-consuming investment procedures (Salim, 2014). One major constraint for foreign investors is that the **Foreign Investment Law** requires foreign investment to be approved by the Indonesia Investment Co-ordinating Board (*Badan Kordinasi Penanaman Modal*, BKPM) and that the share of foreign ownership is restricted in transport services, energy and mineral resources, agriculture, forestry, maritime and fisheries, finance and banking, and education (UNEP, 2015). These include sectors for green investment and may limit opportunities for green growth projects in Bandung and elsewhere. The government might consider loosening such restrictions. **Sustainability standards** to guide foreign investors and the decisions of the Board should also be created to ensure that FDI contributes to green growth.

National efforts to encourage green finance should be continued and developed at the local level

Green finance is not yet robust in Indonesia, but recent reforms may increase its contribution to development in future. Only 1.4% of total lending by 29 major banks in Indonesia was considered to be "green" in 2013, according to a Bank Indonesia survey (UNEP, 2015).[9] This accounted for about USD 1 billion. The 2014 Asia Sustainability Investment Review estimated that sustainable investments in Indonesia's capital markets totalled USD 1.14 billion at the end of 2013 (UNEP, 2015). This is low in comparison to total banking activities, but not negligible. The main sectors benefiting from green financing in 2012 were mini-hydropower (26.1% of green financing), geothermal (25.7%), environmentally efficient machinery (19.6%) and sustainable agriculture (19.5%) (Figure 4.5).

Figure 4.5. **Distribution of green financing by project in Indonesia**

2012

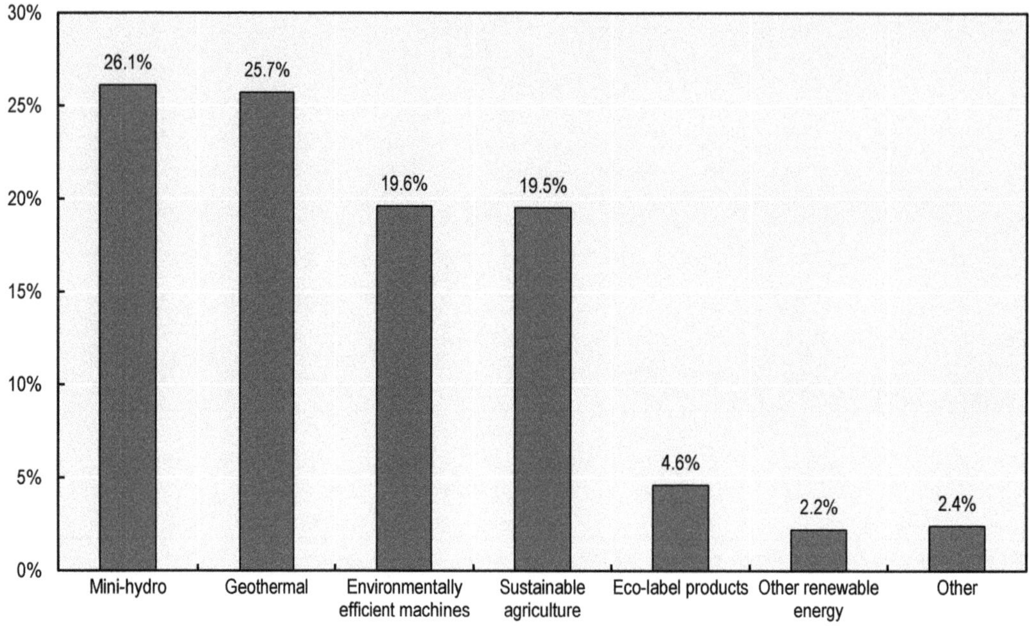

Source: UNEP (2015), "Towards a Sustainable Financing System in Indonesia", in partnership with IFC and AsRIA.

The government of Indonesia has made remarkable efforts to design innovations in financial markets to encourage green lending and investment, which can be expected to increase significantly in the coming years. One of the innovative flagship policies was the creation of the SRI-KEHATI Index and the SRI-KEHATI-ETF, sustainability ratings for the stock market. The Ministry of Finance is also considering green weighting for capital requirements, which could significantly encourage green finance (UNEP, 2015). Another promising policy is the development of the Roadmap for Sustainable Finance in Indonesia by the Ministry of Finance, which may include a binding regulatory framework for green finance, including the compulsory environmental and social management systems and reporting in both capital and stock markets (UNEP, 2015). The Ministry of Finance should include a regulatory framework, as many banks still do not consider developing green lending capacities a priority (UNEP, 2015) and all financing institutions should be left on an equal footing, so as not to leave individual initiatives suffering from competition with other institutions.

The Financial Services Authority (OJK) should also continue developing incentives for green investment, such as differentiated reserve requirements with lower required reserve rates for green assets and differentiated capital requirements for green lending (UNEP, 2015). OJK should also assess and encourage green financing in other areas of opportunities for green growth, in particular transport, water resilience and solid waste management, which do not feature in these surveys (Figure 4.7). Another area of opportunity for green finance is the Islamic Bank, which has great potential given Indonesia's large Muslim population and the bank's growing capital (OJK, 2015). Similar sustainability criteria could be incorporated in the bank's regulations to leverage investments in green infrastructure and green growth projects.

At the municipal level, the City of Bandung could encourage green bonds to attract institutional investors. The BMA does not at present issue municipal bonds, but could easily do so with the support of the national government and/or international financial institutions. The World Bank Group has supported municipalities to issue green bonds close to USD 12 billion since its inception in 2008, and its growth is accelerating rapidly. Green bonds could be set up jointly by local governments in the BMA and the national government. This instrument could help attract private investors and alleviate the actual or perceived financial risks associated with green investment. The city of Gothenburg (Sweden), with the support of the World Bank, has issued green bonds since 2013 to increase finance for climate change mitigation and adaptation projects and other environment-related activities (Climate Bonds Initiative, 2014.). In Bandung, this strategy could be explored in energy use and transport, where private investors are not yet effectively involved. Co-operation and co-ordinated action with the national government would be highly advantageous. The **Roadmap for Sustainable Finance in Indonesia** should include regulatory reforms allowing local governments to issue green bonds, so that local governments do not face legal obstacles in doing so.

Enhancing co-ordination with the national government to set up public-private partnerships

PPPs (*Kerjasama Pemerintah dan Swasta, KPS*) represent another opportunity to attract private finance to build green infrastructure. They were introduced in the 1990s to finance toll roads (AFD, 2014). By the turn of the 2010 decade, the government of Indonesia had made PPP a strategic instrument for rail construction and power generation. Complex issues such as defining the PPP policy and legal framework, identifying a project pipeline, setting up PPP expertise units and developing concepts to guide projects have been undertaken at the national level (OECD, 2012). The number of PPPs in 2010-12 was highest in the West Java Province, mainly in the form of concessions. In 2010 and 2011, 17 PPP infrastructure projects were registered in this province, against 13 in 2012. By contrast, DKI Jakarta – which has the second-highest number in terms of PPP development – developed only 11 PPP infrastructure projects in 2010 and 2011, and 2 in 2012 (Figure 4.6). Most of the existing PPP projects have been undertaken by the national government, although Bappenas has been promoting PPP to sub-national authorities (OECD, 2012). Only two cities in Indonesia have in fact successfully implemented PPPs: Tangerang (a water supply project) and Makassar (project on sewerage). In Bandung, the mayor has erected PPP projects as a new approach to financing urban development. A list of 91 projects, requiring total capital of around USD 6 billion, has been prepared by the current local administration. This strategy aims to overcome the lack of local government budget funds. The Bandung Light Rail Transit/LRT and the Integrated Gedebage Multipurpose Terminal (Railway) are two PPPs under development.

Figure 4.6. **Number of PPP infrastructure projects in Indonesia, by province**

2010-12

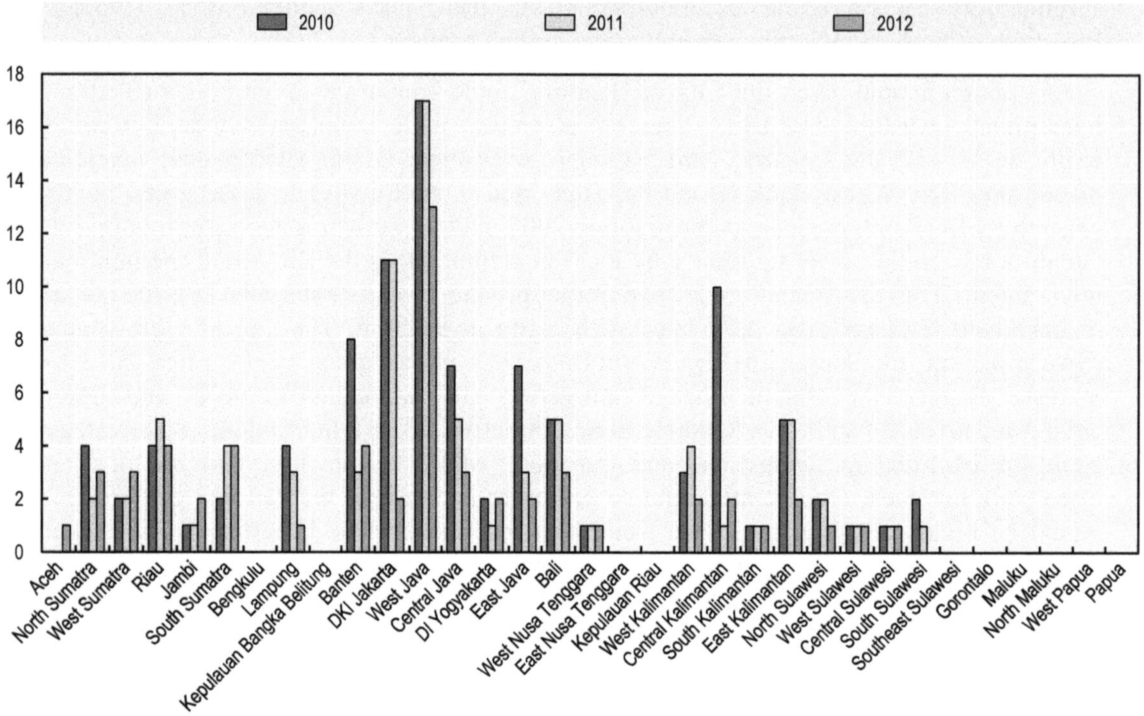

Source: OECD (2013b), *"The number of PPP infrastructure projects in Indonesia by province"*, in *Southeast Asian Economic Outlook 2013: With Perspectives on China and India*, http://dx.doi.org/10.1787/888932774205.

Effective PPPs can deliver value for money, but require complex procurement, administrative and legal procedures. Local governments including Bandung City and other municipalities of the BMA critically lack the capacity to implement PPPs effectively. Problems associated with attempts to lead PPPs by local governments were illustrated in Surabaya City. It took the local government several years to complete a feasibility study and to make the proposal commercially viable, even with the support of a consultant agency.[10] Assessing the value for money of a PPP project – compared to a traditional public procurement scenario – may be difficult, as it results from a combination of factors such as risk transfer, output-base specifications, performance measurement and incentives, competition in and for the market, private sector management expertise and the benefits for end users and society as a whole (OECD, 2012). The lack of observed impact and non-regulated tariffs, which imply low cost-recovery for utility infrastructure – and a poor return for private investors – are two major obstacles.

PPP process has also been complicated by a lack of co-ordination between government contracting agencies (GCAs) and the two main ministries involved in PPP procedures: MoF and Bappenas. GCAs, including subnational authorities, develop projects in isolation, and because the proposals may fall short of MoF requirements and fail to qualify for government guarantee and fiscal support, they are often abandoned or delayed. In 2015, the PPP unit was established under MoF, to tackle the lack of co-ordination at the national level between MoF and Bappenas, both of which have responsibilities in this regard.[11] While it is too early to assess the effectiveness of this national PPP unit, it could substantially improve co-ordination between the national ministries and subnational GCAs.

The national PPP unit could do more than co-ordination. It could help increase local capacities and improve local procedures for PPPs. Local governments need support from the inception of the PPP projects (i.e. the planning phase) through to the feasibility study, tender preparation, bidding and contract signing (OECD, 2012), complying with specific Presidential Regulations.[12] The support should go further to cover project implementation and operation. Furthermore, the national PPP unit could finance local feasibility studies and bidding processes undertaken by sub-national authorities. Currently no such assistance is given to sub-national authorities by the national ministries.

4.3. International co-operation for green growth in Bandung

Official development assistance to Indonesia could help Bandung

Bandung receives almost no official development finance

International co-operation plays a critical role in Indonesia's development. This includes official development finance, in particular Official Development Assistance (ODA) and non-concessional other official flows (OOF), such as the Clean Technology Fund (CTF). From 2002 to 2014, Indonesia received around USD 80 billion in official development finance,[13] more than any other country in Southeast Asia. It received about two and a half times the amount committed to the Philippines in the period, and more than eight times the amount received by Thailand (Figure 4.7).

Figure 4.7. **Total official development finance committed to selected ASEAN countries (USD billion)**

Constant 2013 prices, 2002-14

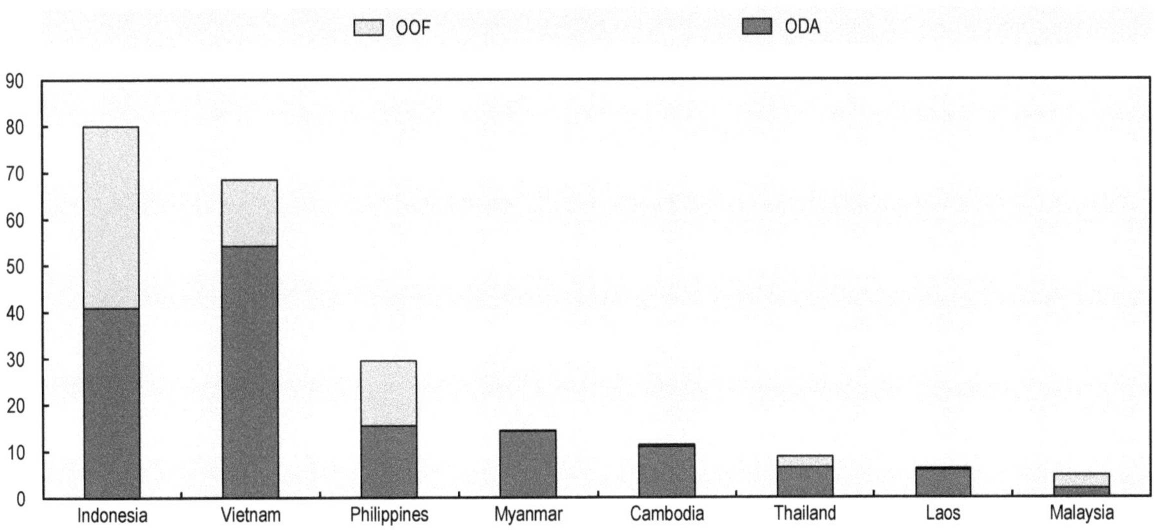

Note: This figure includes both bilateral and multilateral ODA. OOF stands for other official flows. ODA means Official development assistance.

Source: OECD (2016c), "Aid activities targeting Global Environmental Objectives", *DAC Creditor Reporting System* (database), https://stats.oecd.org/Index.aspx?DataSetCode=RIOMARKERS (accessed 23 November 2015).

Of official development finance committed to Indonesia, only 17.2% (USD 13.8 billion) benefits (urban) green growth, involving 3 388 projects which target the environment, climate change mitigation, climate change adaption, biodiversity and desertification (i.e. the objectives set by the Rio Conventions).[14] Of these, 162 projects totalling USD 3.4 billion (i.e. 25% of total environment-related official development finance) were committed to Indonesian cities, only USD 10 million of which was allocated to the city of Bandung (i.e. slightly less than 0.1% of all environment-related funds committed to Indonesia) (Figure 4.8).[15] The government of Korea is the largest contributor (around USD 8 million) through a project on water supply and a project on flood management. International public finance has made almost no contribution to Bandung's green growth. By contrast, Bangkok received USD 2.3 billion for environment-related projects in the period (OECD, 2015c), and the city of Hai Phong USD 500 million (OECD, 2016d), despite its much smaller population. Current projects include a study for the reorganisation of Bandung central railway station, financed by AFD and led by a joint venture between Systra and Arep consulting firms. The study aims to improve the station's accessibility and to explore the potential for an intermodal development around it. AFD also aims to finance a low-carbon initiative.

Official development finance for Indonesia, by comparison with other countries of Southeast Asia, involves a high number of projects for geothermal energy, gas pipelines and hydro-electric power plants. These accounted for nearly USD 1.6 billion between 2002 and 2014 (i.e. 12.3% of total official development finance). Indonesia has rich natural resources and high potential for RE production and climate change mitigation. Such activities, however, cannot be categorised as "urban" or "rural", as they benefit both. Many official development activities cannot be categorised in Indonesia, as shown in Figure 4.8.[16]

Figure 4.8. **Number of official development activities and funding for urban and rural areas in Indonesia for environmental purposes (including Rio Conventions) (2002-14)**

USD billion, constant 2013 prices

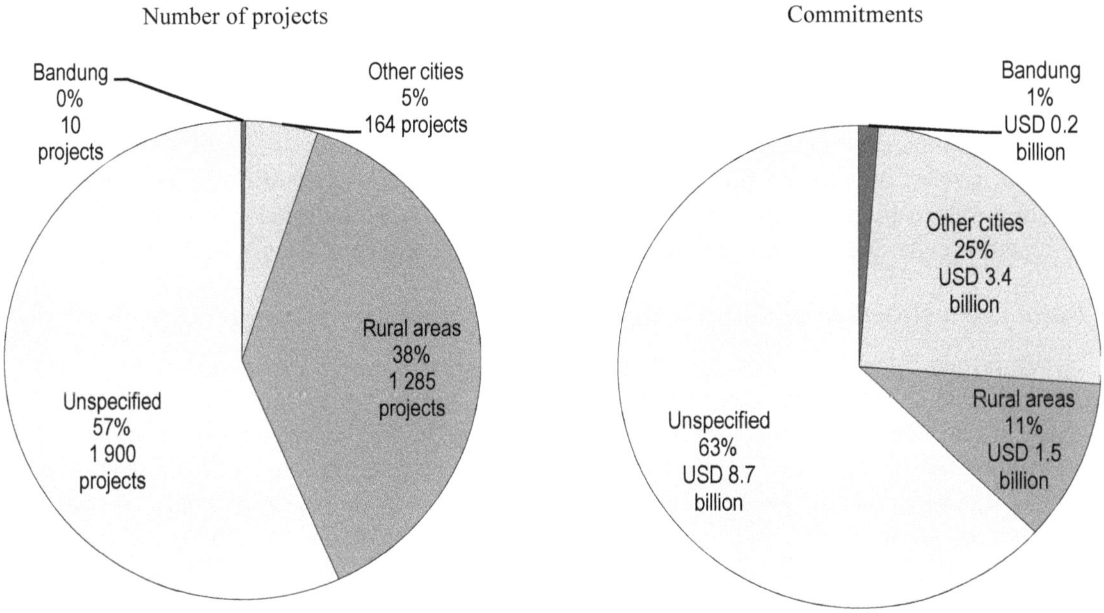

Source: OECD (2016c), "Aid activities targeting Global Environmental Objectives", *DAC Creditor Reporting System* (database), https://stats.oecd.org/Index.aspx?DataSetCode=RIOMARKERS (accessed 23 November 2015).

Developing national-local channels and direct local access to official development finance

These trends shed light on the need to improve Bandung's access to official development finance for urban green growth. The major obstacle is the inability of local government units (LGUs) to contract direct loans from foreign donors. To obtain additional funding, local governments are allowed to borrow from the central government, other local governments, domestic banks or financial institutions, and from the public through municipal bonds (Law 33/2004). LGUs can receive donor support, but only with a two-step loan (or Sub-Loan Agreement, SLA), which is complicated because it needs central government approval.

Involving the local government in application processes or project discussions early on could be an efficient strategy for ensuring that official development finance activities target cities' needs, and Bandung's in particular. This will require co-operation with the national government, which decides how to apply to grants and which proposals to approve. Local authorities and the national government together need to propose concrete, well-designed projects and programmes to international funds and donor organisations, to optimise Bandung's chances of getting financial and technical support for green growth.

Allowing LGUs – especially in a city like Bandung whose financial health is robust – to contract loans directly should be considered by the central government. One potential option for Bandung would be to set up a **local investment fund for urban development**. It could be an opportunity to attract official development finance in the city but also to give the local government a larger role in co-ordinating international finance for green growth. Such mechanisms have been set up in Ho Chi Minh City and a few other cities in Viet Nam, such as Can Tho and Da Nang. The French Development Agency has been the main international donor providing support to these local investment funds, and has channelled funds for projects in the health, education, housing, urban development and environment sectors.[17] For some projects, such local investment funds will need to collaborate with the national government. Regional railway development (over which the national government has authority) largely falls under the authority of the state, but it has a strong local dimension. In solid waste and flood resilience, the local government is less dependent on the national government, and local investment funds could be convenient.

Bandung's efforts to mobilise international partners for urban green growth

Bandung should also develop partnerships with international organisations for urban green growth. The importance of such partnerships is already well-recognised by the local government. The **Bandung Creative City Forum (BCCF)** is an important source of international promotion and networking, focusing on creative thinking, arts and design by youth. In 2013, it held a workshop with international experts on how youth can boost sustainable urban mobility.[18] The City of Bandung has been particularly active in reaching out to international partners to develop smart city projects. IBM has been a privileged partner in developing the Command Centre. International co-operation will be important in scaling up smart city tools and diffusing digital technologies in an emerging market. Systematic collaboration with international partners and target sectors can help encourage green growth, in such sectors as energy, solid waste and water management. The number of projects with potential for green growth involving international partners is relatively low, although it is likely to grow thanks to the current efforts of the administration (Table 4.3). In the smart city sector, global utility companies such as Cisco and Siemens could help support the city's efforts to address urgent green growth issues, such as water, energy, solid waste management and transport, where smart city tools are developing quickly. They could also be instrumental in increasing the quality of IT and engineering curricula in local universities, and diffuse formal and informal IT skills to the local population, to make the smart city vision more inclusive.

Table 4.3. **Urban green growth projects in Bandung involving international partners**

Name of partner	Description of the project
IBM	Development of the Bandung Command Centre
Alliander	Development of smart city tools
AFD	Construction of a Light rail transit (in partnership with the central government)
IGES	Development of a co-benefit action plan for the transport sector Feasibility Study for Realising Low-Carbon Society (with Kawasaki City)
Kawasaki City	Memorandum of Understanding (MoU) between Kawasaki City and Bandung City (concluded in February 2016 at the International Eco-tech Fair held in Kawasaki) Feasibility Study for Realising a Low Carbon Society (with IGES)
ICLEI	Study on Bandung's resilience

At the national level, the Global Green Growth Institute (GGGI) has partnered with the government of Indonesia to develop a Green Growth Programme incorporating green growth into existing planning and investment schemes. One of the programme's components is to encourage the collection of green growth indicators at different levels of government (Government of Indonesia and GGGI, 2013). The programme does not specify how this will be implemented. Partnerships between GGGI and the City of Bandung could be created (or with another international organisation to support GGGI's initiative), to develop local capacity to produce and collect green growth indicators and track progress in the city.

Numerous potentially useful initiatives could benefit Bandung, and the local government should pursue its effort to reach out to the international community. In terms of flood resilience, the **USAID-ADB-DFID-Rockefeller Foundation Trust Fund** is now part of the foundation's Urban Climate Change Resilience Partnership, which is designed to leverage financing, including an additional USD 1 billion in public and private investment, to scale up climate change resilience for 25 cities in Asia. Another initiative of **C40 Cities** could be of interest for the solid waste management issues Bandung has been facing: C40 Cities recently launched an initiative for city officials in different countries to communicate on waste-management issues using the WhatsApp mobile chat application. Most of the local government staff in the BMA already use this application, rather than e-mail, to communicate and to organise work groups, and could promote sharing of best practices in the solid waste management sector. Through C40 Cities, city administrators could be connected with officials and experts from other Asian and non-Asian cities, to discuss solutions for current problems in BMA. If successful, C40 Cities should expand this mechanism to other sectors related to green growth (e.g. transport, water and energy).

4.4. Engaging and collaborating with local stakeholders

Giving shape and impact to Indonesia and Bandung's community culture

Bandung and Indonesia benefit from a strong community culture. Many aspects of life are managed within local communities, which tend to be informal and loosely self-regulated. Local governments have increasingly acknowledged the potential of community involvement. The city of Surabaya offers a celebrated example of successful community mobilisation for urban green growth. The city is a pioneer in community-based solid waste management and is now one of the cleanest in Indonesia, thanks to an ambitious programme that since 2010, has involved residents in municipal efforts to collect and sort out solid waste. In Bandung, local government has recognised the benefit of local community participation in governance. Its mayor has tried to build a collaborative society where community-based development is seen as a process of internal decentralisation to manage the city more effectively (Bandung City, 2015). The following community engagement initiatives are particularly remarkable:

- The mayor has created eight **advisory groups** on eight different topics (smart city, public policy, law, creative economy, environment, green building, cultural heritage, arts), mainly constituted by citizens of Bandung City. This is an innovative approach to encourage public participation and raise public awareness on critical issues.

- Bandung has some community-based solid waste management systems. The city plans to set up biodigesters – waste decomposition machines – in addition to existing waste composting facilities, as residents are aware of the need for organic waste services. The organic fertilizer from biodigesters has been used for urban farming and stocks for citizens. Informal waste pickers also play an important role in the solid waste collection process (Tarigan et al., 2015). In April 2015, the City called for volunteers to help clean up Asia Afrika Street in preparation for the 60th Asia-Africa Conference commemoration. Thousands of residents participated in the collection process, demonstrating the potential for the community to be mobilised by local government. The **Pick Up the Trash Movement** launched by the municipality in June 2014 encourages garbage collection three days a week (Bandung City, 2015), and the **Clean Cikapundung River programme** launched in 2010 encourages community participation in clearing solid waste from river banks and reintroducing fingerlings to restore river ecosystems.

- The City of Bandung recently set up an innovative system of "**biopores**" to build the city's resilience to flash floods. These are community-based or household-based holes dug in the ground to absorb water in heavy rain, reducing run-off and flood risk. Organic waste can be added to the hole to make compost (see Chapter 2). The city already has 350 biopores and intends to install 120 in each of the 9 561 neighbourhood units, or *Rukun Tetangga* (RT) of the city (Tarigan et al., 2015).

- An **urban farming** programme has been started in every district, at the mayor's initiative, to increase food security and encourage community participation in the city's sustainability. Increasing the amounts of green/agricultural spaces in the city can also have positive benefits on flood resilience, by increasing the urban environment's absorption capacity. Meanwhile, the **Bandung Agri-Market**, held every month, promotes locally grown food.

- Festivals are another example of community-building. At the Angklung and Culinary Night festivals, residents and the municipality celebrate their local identity (Bandung City, 2015).

Efforts to mobilise local communities should be continued. The Board of National Unity and Community Empowerment (*Badan Kesatuan bangsa dan Pemberdayaan Masyarakat*) could be the lead agency, working closely with other departments that can have an impact on urban green growth. Identifying and organising such communities would be a first step. City administrators often speak of the importance of local communities, but it is not clear what they are referring to. In its vision to build a collaborative society, the City of Bandung mentions the city's 5 000 communities, without specifying what they are (people often vaguely refer to them as loose groups of people united by family ties, urban areas and social activities or interests). The municipality should draw up lists of the main communities, and identify those that could support green growth objectives by geographical location or area of opportunity.

One new institutional initiative is the **Forum on Waste Management**, for practitioners, NGOs, academics and government staff. Thanks to recent support from the local government, this has become a large platform for knowledge exchange and even policy input for the local Waste Management Master Plan. The City of Bandung could increase its governance capacity by expanding this mechanism to other critical urban sectors, in particular transport and disaster risk management, and integrate relevant communities in the discussions. Also, it should make more efforts to reach out to NGOs working with the urban poor – as these organisations do not work much in co-operation with the local government – to give voice to the low-income communities and promote social inclusion. It will also be important to make sure local communities are involved in the **Innovation Programme for Regional Development and Empowerment Bandung City** (*Program Inovasi Pembangunan dan Pemberdayaan Kewilayahan Kota Bandung*, PIPPK), whose goal is to allow district-based institutions to make project proposals for their development (Bandung City, 2015). This could be supported by smart city tools, and the main and decentralised Command Centres could serve as databases for community practices and proposals for green growth (see Chapter 3).

Surabaya offers a useful model for solid waste management. Communities have been more formally organised around community leaders, who are contact points for the municipality, and who help to steer community efforts towards solid waste management goals. To some extent, the contribution of informal waste pickers can be formalised. Their role in recovering waste has not been well recognised in Bandung (Damanhari, Wahyu and Tri Padmi, 2009), although the Environmental Management Agency of Bandung City is considering strategies for collaborating with them. Around 800 scavengers, mostly volunteers organised by local communities and universities, support the waste collection system, bringing waste to the 151 transfer stations scattered throughout the BMA. No benefit mechanism is in place, offering no incentive to ensure large-scale community support in the long term. The City of Bandung could consider developing initiatives like the **Zero-Baht Shop** in Bangkok, which encourages informal activities by giving scavengers direct incentives like food and social benefits (Box 4.4). This would not only support waste collection but inclusive development.

Box 4.4. **Zero-Baht shop: Community-based recycling in Thailand**

A "Zero-Baht shop" is a cash-free barter system that allows the trade of recycled materials in communities for necessities, goods and services.

The system works as follows: i) community members collect recyclables; ii) they separate the collected recyclables by type and bring them to a "Zero-Baht shop"; iii) the recyclables are weighed; iv) the community members receive an invoice from a member of the shop's staff; v) they bring the invoice to the shop and exchange it for goods and services of the same value, or deposit it into a "bank" as savings; vi) the collected recyclables are sold to junk collectors; vii) the income is used to create a welfare fund and provide services to community members.

Through the system, low-income community members are officially registered as formal garbage collectors and separated from informal waste pickers. They are also able to receive some social support (such as medical care, support for funeral services, etc.) as community members. Overall, the system helps to formalise the informal sector, to promote recycling and alleviate poverty.

In 2006, the Thailand Institute of Packaging and Recycling Management for Sustainable Environment (TIPMSE) established, with the Federation of Thai Industries (FTI), the concept and continued expansion of the network of Zero-Baht shops. They can send a consultant to communities and organisations interested in the establishment of Zero-Baht shops. As of 2013, 12 Zero-Baht shops were in operation in Thailand. The TIPMSE also organised the "Zero-Baht Shop Mobile," as a showcase of the project to communities, educational institutes and governmental agencies.

Source: TIPMSE (2014), presentation at the Bangkok Knowledge Sharing Workshop on Urban Green Growth in Dynamic Asia, 6-7 August, Bangkok.

Raising public awareness to shift behaviours to support local green growth initiatives

Raising public awareness of urban green growth and how the city plans to achieve it is another critical strategy at the community level. Creating a segregated lane for a Bus Rapid Transit (BRT) may face opposition from the residents, because they might see this as a further cause of traffic congestion. Communicating about the benefits of public transport for the city in the short and long term, will help make sure they participate with the municipality in the shift towards green growth. In Bangkok, the lack of public awareness of the benefits of the BRT was a major reason for the failure of the programme (OECD, 2015c). Raising awareness of the *angkot* associations will help require higher service quality and efficiency and to encourage sustainable consumption patterns to promote Bandung's smart city vision. Introducing a smart card system for transport (including parking) and other services will require public awareness campaigns, as people still prefer to rely on traditional habits (e.g. bargaining, payment in cash etc.). For energy savings, the City of Bandung could study the example of the Bangkok Metropolitan Administration, which partnered with businesses in 2012 to teach students in 16 schools of the city how to reduce energy consumption, and which also created youth camps on the subject in 2008-09. Raising awareness within private companies could be an efficient way to promote energy savings (and other environmental objectives) not only at the office but also at home. This was exemplified in a study undertaken in Japan after the Great Tohoku Earthquake of March 2011.

The City of Bandung could leverage the mayor's current awareness programme to promote green growth. Under this initiative, each day of the week was given a specific topic (in order of the days of the week: free travel on public buses for school children, non-smoking, Sundanese, English, bicycle) and every citizen is encouraged to promote the topic of the day in his/her behaviour. For instance, everyone should try to speak English as much as possible on Thursdays. City administrators are the first persons to show the example. On Fridays, the use of bicycles is promoted, the mayor himself being famous for commuting to work by bicycle. This day could be expanded into a broader topic of "green" day or "eco" day, to raise public awareness on a broader range of environmental topics such as climate change, energy and water consumption, solid waste collection and treatment, urban farming, etc.

Collaborating with universities, research institutes and the private sector for innovation

The education sector is a critical asset of Bandung. In 2014, Bandung City had 78 higher education establishments, including colleges and universities, enhancing its potential to become a world-class knowledge-based city. Many are among the best in Indonesia and attract talented people from across the country (Tarigan et al., 2015). A high proportion of the city's population has attained higher education levels, as compared to general trends in West Java Province (see Chapter 1).

This also offers an opportunity for the city to enlist co-operation on green growth objectives. Universities and research institutes can support the local government in producing, collecting and analysing data, given the lack of relevant data, which makes it difficult to evaluate the situation and track progress. Data on GHG emissions, electricity consumption and water consumption are not adequate (Table 4.4). Some data are also only available at the scale of the City of Bandung or the West Java Province, rather than at the scale of the Bandung Metropolitan Area. The definition of the functional urban area is also unclear. The City of Bandung should thus identify the most appropriate institutions in each opportunity policy area to outsource data research and analysis. Metro Vancouver, for example, has created an overall Memoranda of Understanding (MoU) with several local universities and research institutes to improve existing knowledge on the dynamics of the metropolitan area (Box 4.5). One useful initiative that the City of Bandung could consider would be an open data portal, similar to the Open Data NYC website.[19] Since there are still some restrictions in the access to data, this could help other institutions with the data production and analysis work (see Chapter 3). In future, ambitious research projects such as the City Science MIT MediaLab could be developed to undertake advanced urban analytics.[20]

Table 4.4. **Data on green growth not available in Bandung**

Category	Indicator	Scale
Population	Population census from the 1990s	Jakarta Bandung Metro Region
	Projection of population in 2020, 2030, 2040 and 2050	Jakarta Bandung Metro Region BMA (including breakdown of districts)
	Current unregistered population	BMA (including breakdown of districts)
Economic	Informal employment	BMA (including breakdown of districts)
Environment	Frequent and dispersed PM_{10} and $PM_{2.5}$ concentration measurement	BMA (including breakdown of districts)
	Health issues deriving from air pollution	BMA (including breakdown of districts)
	Evolution of total greenhouse gas emissions (including breakdown by source)	BMA (including breakdown of districts)
	Vulnerability Assessment Map	BMA
Transport	Public transport modal split (in total trips and in commuting)	BMA (including breakdown of districts)
	Commuting patterns	BMA (including breakdown of districts)
	Congestion	BMA (including breakdown of districts)
Land	Evolution of population density by smallest administrative units possible	BMA
	Location of slums	BMA
Energy	Final energy consumption by sector	BMA (including breakdown of districts)
	Energy intensity by sector	BMA (including breakdown of districts)
	Renewable energy potential	West Java Province BMA (including breakdown of districts)
	Actual renewable energy generation	West Java Province BMA (including breakdown of districts)
	Generation cost for renewable energy	Indonesia
Water	Share of ground water use of total water supply	BMA (including breakdown of districts)
	Non-revenue water	BMA (all districts except City of Bandung, as data is available there)
	River and canal pollution	BMA
	Share of population treating black water	BMA (including breakdown of districts)
Solid waste	Hazardous solid waste generation	BMA (including breakdown of districts)
	Methane emissions from landfills	BMA

Box 4.5. **Metro Vancouver's MOU with the University of British Columbia**

Metro Vancouver and UBC have a strong history of working together on a variety of projects within Metro Vancouver's areas of service. Researchers and students from the university's key faculties and research centres have been brought together with staff from Metro Vancouver's line departments. Collaboration has also focused on operational issues involving UBC's main campus operations and Metro Vancouver's departments. A compendium of joint initiatives put together by Metro Vancouver staff identified over 80 past and current joint projects between Metro Vancouver and UBC. Building on the success of this relationship, in late 2014, senior staff from UBC and Metro Vancouver met to discuss the goals and needs of their organisations, and the range of opportunities for collaboration. These discussions led to the concept of a Strategic Collaboration Memorandum, allowing staff from both organisations to work on a model to explore opportunities for future partnerships.

The Strategic Collaboration MOU is a non-binding document that expresses the shared commitment of Metro Vancouver and UBC "to the principles of sustainability and to the belief that the long-term liveability, prosperity and sustainability of the region – indeed the entire planet – require approaches to problem-solving that are characterised by innovation, creativity, entrepreneurship and collaboration". The MOU is a framework document within which the parties will identify and pursue joint initiatives. The scope of the MOU focuses the parties' efforts on developing initiatives under three areas of collaboration:

- **Research, learning and innovation**: under the MOU, the parties would endeavour to identify new opportunities to share knowledge and research findings, jointly undertake research to further individual and shared goals, and collaborate in the development of approaches designed to address important regional and global sustainability challenges. The parties would also regularly hold discussion forums and workshops for staff and researchers from the two organisations. Information on best practices, innovations, technologies and approaches would be shared at these events, as would ideas for new initiatives and ongoing collaboration. Finally, the parties would seek ways to better engage UBC students in specific projects identified by Metro Vancouver.

- **Operations**: their respective servicing responsibilities and activities involve Metro Vancouver and UBC in a range of operational issues, some best addressed collaboratively. Collaboration on these issues has been largely reactive and inconsistent, but through the MOU, the parties would endeavour to identify issues pro-actively on which joint approaches for action can be considered.

- **Regional prosperity**: the MOU would bring the parties together as part of multi-party initiatives, to address a range of topics related to prosperity. These might focus on reducing regional greenhouse gas emissions, adapting to climate change, aligning growth in the region with viable transport strategies and investment, and promoting conditions for a competitive metropolitan economy.

The MOU is managed by a Joint Steering Committee co-chaired by a senior staff member from each organisation. One of the key roles of the Steering Committee is to monitor and co-ordinate the initiatives pursued under the MOU. The Steering Committee also ensures that the regular discussion forums and workshops important to the exchange of ideas and development of collaboration opportunities are held as envisioned under the MOU. The proposed MOU with UBC may serve as a template for similar framework documents with other institutions, and can be viewed as the first in a series of strategic collaboration initiatives. Metro Vancouver staff has had preliminary discussions on the topic with representatives of Simon Fraser University, for instance.

Source: Metro Vancouver (2015), "Greater Vancouver Regional District Inter-government and Finance Committee", held 26 November 2015.

Finally, Bandung should support the private sector for innovation, through the great potential localised in the city. The Teknopolis project developed by the local government will consist of collaboration between academics, investors, communities and government bodies, particularly around biotechnology, nanotechnology and information technologies (City of Bandung, 2015b). This should have high impact in the medium to long term in developing Bandung as a smart city with modern ICT. Telkom Indonesia, IBM and ITB have already collaborated with the local government on smart city projects. These should focus on the needs identified in Chapter 3 as priority research areas with the smart city framework.

One important local initiative is the **Institute for Innovation and Entrepreneurship Development**, an incubator of around 30 start-ups working in various sectors. One is waste management – an urgent green growth issue in Bandung – and the Institute is exploring options to treat the waste using flies. However, it lacks financial support and relies on voluntary involvement. The City of Bandung could provide financial support for this initiative, because it can help solve problems of technical capacity and bureaucracy in the local administration. It could also communicate systematically on the problems city administrators face in managing the city, to guide innovation priorities. Greater Lyon (France) encourages innovative start-ups and companies in collaborative spaces and services, including Lyon Urban Data and TUBÀ. Projects include developing tools for measuring household gas consumption and a mobile application for estimating the arrival of trains, buses and tramways in the Greater Lyon area.[21] Local governments in the BMA could replicate such initiatives to increase the role of the private sector in encouraging urban green growth.

Main policy recommendations

- Develop a **national framework for solid waste and energy management in Indonesian cities**, and a **national smart city plan** and implementation strategy.
- Develop **capacity-building** mechanisms between the national, provincial and local government to implement national green growth-related strategies, managed by a dedicated national agency for green growth under Bappenas.
- Expand the eight advisory groups created by the City of Bandung to include professionals and researchers, and link them to **specific task forces (in particular smart city, green growth) headed by Bappeda** and co-ordinating policies for all local departments.
- Provide sufficient power and resources to the future BMA co-ordinating body and create a **comprehensive development plan for the metropolitan area**. Ensure the involvement of the national government in its operations.
- Develop **data production, collection and analysis mechanisms for the Jakarta-Bandung region** to understand linkages and needs for regional green growth strategies.
- Create **mechanisms for national funding support** for metropolitan-wide green growth-related projects.
- Create **sustainability standards for FDI** and loosen current restrictions.
- Develop **national incentives for green investment in the transport, solid waste and flood resilience sectors**, and develop capacity to issue green bonds at the local level.
- Develop initiatives at the national PPP unit to **help increase local capacities for PPPs**, so that local governments are supported from the planning phase through to project implementation and operation. Consider financial support for local feasibility studies and bidding processes undertaken by sub-national authorities.
- Involve the BMA in official development finance processes and consider direct access through **local development funds**.
- **List and formally engage and organise local communities** in supporting local green growth-related projects, such as providing social benefits to waste scavengers.
- **Raise awareness of the benefits of green growth**, transforming the Bicycle Day into a Green Day or Eco-Day.
- Enhance collaborating with local university and research institutes **supporting data production and analysis on urban green growth**, and scale up existing innovation initiatives. Prioritise assisting private sector initiatives to support innovation in green growth.

Notes

1. Infrastructure development remains unequal across Indonesian provinces. OECD's *Economic Survey of Indonesia* (2016a, forthcoming) provides detailed information and comparison across provinces.

2. The Jabodetabekpunjur (JMA) Development Co-operation Board (*Badan Kerjasama Pembangunan Jabodetabekpunjur*), including DKI Jakarta and the regencies of Bogor, Tangerang and Bekasi, was established in 1975.

3. One of the consequences of the decentralisation reforms was the blossoming of local government units. Between 1999 and 2015, the number of provinces increased from 26 to 34, the number of regencies/cities increased by 55%, districts by 77% and villages by 20% to over 83 000 (OECD, 2016a).

4. The real budget for 2015 and 2016 could not bc calculated because the Consumer Price Index is only available until 2014.

5. Figures given in this sentence were calculated using the purchasing power parity (PPP) conversion factor for Indonesia and Thailand.

6 However, the figure for OECD unitary countries includes social security contributions in the total tax revenue, while such funds do not exist in Indonesia. The figure for Indonesia is therefore biased upward.

7. Indonesia, personnel accounted for 47% of all regency/city expenditure, up from 31% in 2009. This is mainly financed by the General Allocation Fund: half is used to cover wages and salaries in regencies and cities (OECD, 2016a).

8. See: Deal Street Asia (2015), "Indonesia: SMI to double infrastructure funding to $1.6b in 2016", www.dealstreetasia.com/stories/indonesia-smi-to-double-infrastructure-funding-to-1-6b-in-2016-23137/ (accessed 20 June 2016)

9. "Green" lending was defined in this survey as lending contributing to renewables, sustainable agriculture, green industry and eco-tourism.

10. Eventually, the PPP project was discontinued, due to a change in the national political agenda.

11 The 2012 OECD report OECD Reviews of Regulatory Reform: Indonesia 2012: Strengthening Co-ordination and Connecting Markets recommended the creation of the PPP unit (OECD, 2012).

12. Presidential Regulations 67/2005, 13/2010 and 56/2011.

13. All the figures related to ODA given in this chapter are expressed in 2013 constant prices.

14. Bilateral ODA activities targeting environmental objectives can be identified in a dataset accessible through the OECD statistical website and from the CRS database. This dataset contains commitment data on aid in support of environment sustainability and aid targeting the objectives of the Rio Conventions (biodiversity, climate change mitigation, climate change adaptation and desertification). Multilateral ODA activities targeting environmental objectives can be identified in the CRS database accessible through the OECD statistical website. The main approach to identifying projects committed to urban areas was based on a word search of their

purpose name (e.g. "urban development and management"). For all other projects whose purpose name did not make it possible to determine whether the project was urban, the "urban" character was identified by examining each project description. Similarly, the main element used to identify projects committed to rural areas was their purpose name ("rural development"). A second step, if the purpose name was not conclusive, was to look at the titles and a short description of the projects. Agricultural, fishery and forestry projects were classified as rural. The remaining rural projects were identified based on their long description. Unspecified projects refer to all other projects, with no detailed description, no details on the geographical scope or inconclusive geographical scope.

15. Hai Phong also benefited from projects financed by the International Development Association (IDA) of the World Bank, at USD 440 million. These projects, however, also benefited the cities of Ho Chi Minh City, Can Tho and Nam Ding, without specifying how much of this was spent for Hai Phong. It was therefore excluded from the calculations and included in the category "Other cities" in Figures 2 and 3.

16. This problem is also encountered in other countries of the region, but the size (in terms of finance) of such hard-to-categorise activities is particularly large in Indonesia.

17. See: Agence Française de Développement (AFD) (2015), "Projets d'appui aux Fonds urbains", www.afd.fr/home/pays/asie/geo-asie/afd-vietnam/cac-du-an-cua-afd-tai-viet-nam/phat-trien-o-thi/projets-d-appui-aux-fonds-urbains (accessed 18 September 2015).

18. http://creativeeconomy.bandung.go.id/networking/collaborations/ (accessed 8 March 2016).

19. See: NYC Open Data (n.d.), *NYC Open Data website*, https://nycopendata.socrata.com/ (accessed 5 January 2016).

20. http://cities.media.mit.edu/research/urban-analysis (accessed 5 January 2016).

21. See: Grand Lyon économie (n.d.), "Grand Lyon, Smart city", www.economie.grandlyon.com/smart-city-services-entreprises-lyon-france.348.0.html (accessed 5 January 2016); Greater Lyon business (n.d.), *Business Services*, www.business.greaterlyon.com/ (accessed 5 January 2016). TUBĀ (n.d.), *TUBĀ website*, www.tuba-lyon.com/ (accessed 5 January 2016).

Bibliography

AFD (2014), "Finding Urban Transport Solutions: The Challenges of Financing and Integration of Networks", seminar held in Bandung on 23 June 2014.

Agence Française de Développement (AFD) (2015), "Projets d'appui aux Fonds urbains", www.afd.fr/home/pays/asie/geo-asie/afd-vietnam/cac-du-an-cua-afd-tai-viet-nam/phat-trien-o-thi/projets-d-appui-aux-fonds-urbains (accessed 18 September 2015).

Bandung City (2016), "Answers to the OECD case study questionnaire", internal document, unpublished.

Bandung City (2015), "Smart bdg City", a presentation by Mayor of Bandung at the fourth OECD Knowledge Sharing Workshop, May 2015, Bandung, Indonesia.

Bandung City (2014), Low Carbon City Planning in Bandung, www.iges.or.jp/isap/2014/PDF/pl11/pl11_07_ayu%20sukenjah.pdf (accessed 15 February, 2016).

Chaerul, M., A.R. Fahruroji and T. Fujiwara (2014), "Recycling of plastic packaging waste in Bandung City, Indonesia", in *Cycles Waste Management*, Vol. 16(3), pp. 509-518.

City of Bandung (2015a), *Building a Collaborative Society*, Bandung.

City of Bandung (2015b), *Bandung Teknopolis: Conceptual Master Plan*, Bandung.

Climate Bonds Initiative (2014.), "World Bank goes retail with 3 small green bonds for $5m, EUR10m & $30m - all with complex coupon structures. Last one was 3x oversubscribed", https://www.climatebonds.net.

Corfee-Morlot, J. et al. (2009), "Cities and climate change: Harnessing the potential for local action", *Competitive Cities and Climate Change*, OECD Publishing, Paris, www1.oecd.org/gov/regional-policy/50594939.pdf.

Damanhari, E., I. M. Wahyu and R. R. Tri Padmi (2009), "Evaluation of municipal solid waste flow in the Bandung metropolitan area, Indonesia", in *Cycles Waste Management*, Vol. 11(3), pp. 270-276.

Deal Street Asia (2015), "Indonesia: SMI to double infrastructure funding to $1.6b in 2016", www.dealstreetasia.com/stories/indonesia-smi-to-double-infrastructure-funding-to-1-6b-in-2016-23137/ (accessed 20 June 2016).

Dorodjatoen (2009), "The emergence of the Jakarta-Bandung Mega Urban Region and its future challenges", in *Jurnal Perencanaan Wilayah dan Kota*, Vol. 20(1), April 2009, pp.15-33.

Firman, T. (2009), "Decentralisation Reform and Local Government Proliferation in Indonesia: Towards a Fragmentation of Regional Development", in *Review of Urban and Regional Development Studies*, Vol. 21(2/3), pp. 143-157.

Firman, T. (2008), "The Continuity and Change in Mega-Urbanisation in Indonesia: A Survey of Jakarta-Bandung Region (JBR) development", in *Habitat International*, Vol. 33, pp. 327-339.

Government of Indonesia and GGGI (2013), *Green Growth Programme; Prioritising Investments: Delivering Green Growth*, Jakarta.

Grand Lyon économie (n.d.), "Grand Lyon, Smart city", www.economie.grandlyon.com/smart-city-services-entreprises-lyon-france.348.0.html (accessed 5 January 2016).

Greater Lyon business (n.d.), *Business Services*, www.business.greaterlyon.com/ (accessed 5 January 2016).

Hudalah, D. and H. Winarso (2010), "Planning by opportunity: An analysis of peri-urban environmental conflicts in Indonesia", in *Environment and Planning A*, Vol. 42(9), pp. 2 254-2 269.

IGES and City of Kawasaki (2015), *Feasibility Study on FY2014 Large-Scale JCM Project for Realizing Low-Carbon Development in Asia – Developing a Low-Carbon Society Under Collaboration between Bandung City and Kawasaki City,* www.env.go.jp/earth/coop/lowcarbon-asia/english/project/data/EN_IDN_2014_03.pdf.

Lipsey, R.E. and F. Sjöholm (2011), "Foreign Direct Investment and Growth in East Asia: Lessons for Indonesia", in *Bulletin of Indonesian Economic Studies*, Vol. 47(1), pp. 35-63.

Metro Vancouver (2015), "Greater Vancouver Regional District Inter-government and Finance Committee", held on 26 November 2015.

NYC Open Data (n.d.), NYC Open Data website, https://nycopendata.socrata.com/ (accessed 5 January 2016).

OECD (2016a), *Economic Survey of Indonesia*, OECD Publishing, Paris, forthcoming.

OECD (2016b), *Green Growth in Iskandar Malaysia*, OECD Publishing, Paris, forthcoming.

OECD (2016c), "Aid activities targeting Global Environmental Objectives", *DAC Creditor Reporting System* (database), https://stats.oecd.org/Index.aspx?DataSetCode=RIOMARKERS (accessed 23 November 2015).

OECD (2016d), *Green Growth in Hai Phong*, OECD Publishing, Paris, forthcoming.

OECD (2015a), *Governing the City*, OECD Publishing, Paris, http://dx.doi.org/10.1787/9789264226500-en.

OECD (2015b), *The Metropolitan Century: Understanding Urbanisation and its Consequences*, OECD Publishing, Paris, http://dx.doi.org/10.1787/9789264228733-en.

OECD (2015c), *Green Growth in Bangkok*, OECD Publishing, Paris, http://dx.doi.org/10.1787/9789264237087-en.

OECD (2015d), "Tax Revenue Trends 1990-2013", in *Revenue Statistics in Asian Countries 2015: Trends in Indonesia, Malaysia and the Philippines*, OECD Publishing, Paris, http://dx.doi.org/10.1787/9789264234277-3-en.

OECD (2015e), *Subnational Governments in OECD Countries: Key data* (brochure), www.oecd.org/gov/regional-policy/Subnational-governments-in-OECD-Countries-Key-Data-2015.pdf.

OECD (2013a), *Structural Policy Country Note, Indonesia*, OECD, Paris. https://www.oecd.org/dev/asia-pacific/Indonesia.pdf (accessed 13 October, 2016)

OECD (2013b), "The number of PPP infrastructure projects in Indonesia by province", in *Southeast Asian Economic Outlook 2013: With Perspectives on China and India*, http://dx.doi.org/10.1787/888932774205.

OECD (2012), *OECD Reviews of Regulatory Reform: Indonesia 2012: Strengthening Co-ordination and Connecting Markets*, OECD Publishing, Paris, http://dx.doi.org/10.1787/9789264173637-en.

OECD (2010), *OECD Economic Surveys: Indonesia 2010*, OECD Publishing, Paris, http://dx.doi.org/10.1787/eco_surveys-idn-2010-en.

OJK (2015), *Islamic Banking Statistics*. http://www.bi.go.id/en/statistik/perbankan/syariah/Documents/SPS%20Juni%202015.pdf (accessed 13 October, 2016).

Patunru, A.A. and E.A. Rahman (2014), "Local Governance and Development Outcomes", in Hal Hill (Ed), *Regional Dynamics in a Decentralized Indonesia*, Singapore: ISEAS, pp. 156-85.

Ritonga, I. T., Clark, C., & Wickremasinghe, G. (2012), "Assessing financial condition of local government in Indonesia: an exploration", in *Public and Municipal Finance*, *1*(2).Salim, Z. (2014), "Indonesia's Ways to Sustainable Economic Growth and Development", in R. Looney (ed.), *Handbook of Emerging Economies*, Routledge, Oxford and New York, pp. 265-286.

Tarigan, A.K.M. et al. (2015), "Bandung City, Indonesia", in *Cities*, Volume 50, pp. 100-110.

TIPMSE (2014), Presentation at the Bangkok Knowledge Sharing Workshop on Urban Green Growth in Dynamic Asia, 6-7 August, Bangkok.

TUBĀ (n.d.), *TUBĀ website*, www.tuba-lyon.com/ (accessed 5 January 2016).

UNEP (2015), "Towards a Sustainable Financing System in Indonesia", in partnership with IFC and Association for Sustainable and Responsible Investment in Asia (AsRIA), Geneva.

Vincentia (2016), "Indonesia sets up 15 smart cities as pilot to create digital economy", *Deal Street Asia*, https://goo.gl/anxPwZ (accessed 12 October, 2016).

World Bank (2015), *World Development Indicators*, http://data.worldbank.org/indicator/BX.KLT.DINV.WD.GD.ZS (accessed 2 April 2016).

World Bank (2013), Indonesia Economic Quarterly FY13, May, Washington, D.C.

World Bank (2011), "Geothermal Clean Energy Investment Project", Washington, DC, in Friedrich Ebert Stiftung, *Green Growth Strategies in Asia: Drivers and Political Entry Points*.

ORGANISATION FOR ECONOMIC CO-OPERATION AND DEVELOPMENT

The OECD is a unique forum where governments work together to address the economic, social and environmental challenges of globalisation. The OECD is also at the forefront of efforts to understand and to help governments respond to new developments and concerns, such as corporate governance, the information economy and the challenges of an ageing population. The Organisation provides a setting where governments can compare policy experiences, seek answers to common problems, identify good practice and work to co-ordinate domestic and international policies.

The OECD member countries are: Australia, Austria, Belgium, Canada, Chile, the Czech Republic, Denmark, Estonia, Finland, France, Germany, Greece, Hungary, Iceland, Ireland, Israel, Italy, Japan, Korea, Latvia, Luxembourg, Mexico, the Netherlands, New Zealand, Norway, Poland, Portugal, the Slovak Republic, Slovenia, Spain, Sweden, Switzerland, Turkey, the United Kingdom and the United States. The European Union takes part in the work of the OECD.

OECD Publishing disseminates widely the results of the Organisation's statistics gathering and research on economic, social and environmental issues, as well as the conventions, guidelines and standards agreed by its members.

OECD PUBLISHING, 2, rue André-Pascal, 75775 PARIS CEDEX 16
(04 2016 11 1 P) ISBN 978-92-64-26213-3 – 2016

www.ingramcontent.com/pod-product-compliance
Ingram Content Group UK Ltd.
Pitfield, Milton Keynes, MK11 3LW, UK
UKHW051504290926
15471UKWH00008B/1410

9 789264 262133